April 2020

TRESPASSERS ON THE ROOF OF THE WORLD

Peter Hopkirk has travelled widely over many years in the regions where his six books are set—Central Asia, the Caucasus, China, India and Pakistan, Iran, and Eastern Turkey. Before turning full-time author, he was an ITN reporter and newscaster for two years, the New York correspondent of the *Daily Express*, then worked for nearly twenty years on *The Times*; five as its chief reporter, and latterly as a Middle and Far East specialist. Back in the 1950s he edited the West African news-magazine *Drum*, sister-paper to its legendary South African namesake. Before entering Fleet Street he served as a subaltern in the King's African Rifles—in the same battalion as lance-corporal Idi Amin, later to emerge as the Ugandan tyrant. No stranger to misadventure, Hopkirk has twice been held in secret police cells—in Cuba and the Middle East—and also been hijacked by Arab terrorists. His works have been translated into fourteen languages. In 1999 he was awarded the Sir Percy Sykes Memorial Medal for his writing and travels by the Royal Society for Asian Affairs.

TRESPASSERS ON THE ROOF OF THE WORLD

The Race for Lhasa

PETER HOPKIRK

OXFORD
UNIVERSITY PRESS

OXFORD
UNIVERSITY PRESS

Great Clarendon Street, Oxford OX2 6DP

Oxford University Press is a department of the University of Oxford.
It furthers the University's objective of excellence in research, scholarship,
and education by publishing worldwide in

Oxford New York

Athens Auckland Bangkok Bogotá Buenos Aires Cape Town
Chennai Dar es Salaam Delhi Florence Hong Kong Istanbul Karachi
Kolkata Kuala Lumpur Madrid Melbourne Mexico City Mumbai Nairobi
Paris São Paulo Shanghai Singapore Taipei Tokyo Toronto Warsaw

with associated companies in Berlin Ibadan

Oxford is a registered trade mark of Oxford University Press
in the UK and in certain other countries

Published in the United States
by Oxford University Press Inc., New York

© Peter Hopkirk 1982

First published in 1982 by John Murray (Publishers) Ltd
First issued as an Oxford University Press paperback 1983
Reissued in 2001

British Library Cataloguing in Publication Data
Data available

Library of Congress Cataloging in Publication Data
Data available
ISBN 0-19-280205-4

1 3 5 7 9 10 8 6 4 2

Printed in Great Britain by
Cox & Wyman Ltd, Reading, Berkshire

Contents

Illustrations

MAPS *between pp* 14 *and* 15

Tibet and surrounding areas

Greater Tibet showing Sir Charles Bell's boundary line

The Chumbi Valley

SOURCES OF ILLUSTRATIONS

Nos. 1, 2, 4, 5, 9, 10 and 11 from *Tibet, the Mysterious* by Sir Thomas Holdich, published by Alston Rivers, London; No. 3 by courtesy of the Royal Geographical Society; No. 6 from *Three Years in Tibet* by Ekai Kawaguchi, published by Theosophical Publishing Society, 1909; No. 7 from *With the Tibetans in Tent and Temple* by Dr Susie Rijnhart, published by Oliphant, Anderson and Ferrier, 1901; No. 8 from *Two Lady Missionaries in Tibet* by Isabel Robson, published by S. W. Partridge, London; No. 12 from *India and Tibet* by Sir Francis Younghusband, published by John Murray, 1910; No. 13 from *Peking to Lhasa* compiled by Sir Francis Younghusband, published by Constable, 1925; No. 14 from *My Journey to Lhasa* by Alexandra David-Neel, published by William Heinemann, 1927; No. 15 from *In the Forbidden Land* by H. S. Landor, published by William Heinemann, 1898; No. 16 from *Francis Younghusband* by George Seaver, published by John Murray, 1952; Nos. 17 and 18 by courtesy of the National Army Museum.

Acknowledgements

In piecing together this narrative my greatest debt must be to those remarkable men and women – all long dead and little remembered – who took part in the race to reach Lhasa. Their adventures and misadventures, as related at the time, provide much of the book's drama. I owe a similar debt to those other travellers whose trespasses into Tibet also form part of the story. Without their first-hand accounts of what befell them in this wild and remote Asian backwater this book could not have been written. All these sources, today long forgotten and out of print, are acknowledged in my bibliography.

For my knowledge of the political and diplomatic history of the period I owe much to Professor Alastair Lamb's works, particularly to his *Britain and Chinese Central Asia*, a book which no one writing on modern Tibet can afford to ignore. Like him I have spent illuminating hours combing the so-called political and secret files, and I am grateful to the staff of the India Office Library and the Public Records Office for their help. For my understanding of more recent events in Tibet, I found Hugh Richardson's *Tibet and its History* invaluable, its author having personally witnessed many of them and participated in not a few.

The individual to whom I owe most, however, is my wife Kath whose thoroughness in all things has contributed so much to this book at every stage. Others to whom my gratitude is due for assistance include Dr Michael Aris of Wolfson College, Oxford, and Zara Fleming, formerly of the Victoria and Albert Museum, both Tibetan specialists. I am also indebted to Mrs Joan Mary Jehu of Fulham who, as a pre-war teenager, was the second Englishwoman ever to visit Lhasa (her mother being the first), and her memories of it were a valuable source of insight to me. My gratitude, too, is due to Janina Slater, once of Peking, now of *The Times*, who battled against the clock to produce the final typescript and who suggested a number of useful clarifications.

Finally I must thank my publisher and editor, John R. Murray, without whose constant encouragement this book would have remained no more than a synopsis scribbled on the back of an Income Tax demand.

P.H.

Prologue

This book tells the story – often bizarre, sometimes tragic, frequently hair-raising – of the prising open of Tibet by an inquisitive outside world. For no country has ever challenged man's imagination quite like this mysterious kingdom locked away in the heart of Central Asia. Inhabited by a people whose only wheel was the prayer-wheel, and ruled over by a God-king, Tibet has always been the stuff of travellers' dreams. In a world with few secrets left, here almost anything still seemed possible.

Although both Herodotus and Ptolemy had heard tales of a shadowy land beyond the Himalayas, it was not until the fourteenth century, when a Franciscan traveller named Friar Odoric claimed to have stumbled on it, that the first description of Tibet reached the West. Whether he really set foot there, or merely heard tales of it as he passed through Asia, is still disputed by historians. But his account of Lhasa, a lurid mixture of truth and fantasy, was to bring others in search of what some believed might be the legendary Christian kingdom of Prester John. Ever since, this inaccessible land has lured men and women to face almost any peril or hardship in their efforts to get there.

At first the Tibetans made no attempt to prevent travellers from the West from crossing their frontiers and even visiting Lhasa. For only a handful, mostly Jesuits and Franciscans, had managed to penetrate Tibet's massive natural defences or run the gauntlet of murderous tribes guarding its approaches. But then as Britain and Russia, the new great powers in Asia, began to expand their empires, edging ever closer to Tibet's ill-guarded frontiers, the Tibetans took fright, fearing for their way of life and religion, not to say their gold-fields. From that moment this strange (to everyone but the Tibetans) mediaeval kingdom became a forbidden land – closed, that is, to all except the Chinese. For the Manchu emperors had maintained an uneasy presence there since the beginning of the eighteenth century, and had come to regard it as part of their huge but rickety empire. A Chinese *amban*, or resident, was stationed in Lhasa, but his influence was gradually to decline with the fortunes of the Manchus.

But the closing of Tibet's frontiers was not to deter for a moment those foreigners who had set their hearts, and sometimes their reputations, on reaching Tibet and – if humanly possible – its holy capital. Armed with sextants and theodolites, modern rifles and gold, and often in disguise, these determined trespassers sought out the secrets of its lonely passes and played hide and seek with the Tibetan border guards. Very soon it was to become a race, with travellers from some nine different countries competing for the honour of being the first to reach Lhasa.

Drawing on a cast of remarkable men and women – secret agents and soldiers, explorers and missionaries, mystics and mountaineers – I have endeavoured to show how the world's last stronghold of romance and mystery was slowly forced to divulge its secrets. The motives which drew these men and women inexorably towards Lhasa were as varied as their characters. Some were Government men on shadowy missions whose reports are to be found today in files labelled 'political and secret' in the archives of the British Foreign Office. Some came to unravel the secrets of the Tibetan mysticism, or to solve geographical conundrums like the age-old riddle of the sources of India's sacred rivers. Others were intent on preaching the Gospel in the Buddhist holy city. All of them took their lives in their hands.

The narrative opens in the middle of the nineteenth century with the secret activities of those amazing British-trained Indian spies, the 'pundits'. Posing as holy men, and for little reward, they mapped huge areas of Tibet for their imperial masters. For those were the high days of what Kipling and others called The Great Game, the clandestine struggle between Britain and Russia for political ascendancy in Central Asia. It is here that we encounter the great Tsarist trespasser, Colonel Nikolai Prejevalsky, hell-bent on being first into Lhasa.

The tales which some travellers told on their return from Tibet were scarcely credible. Others never came back at all. Buried in a medicine chest somewhere beneath the Chang Tang, Tibet's desolate northern plateau, lie the remains of a little boy called Charlie. His father also perished there, only his mother surviving to tell the story. Another trespasser, the French explorer Dutreuil de Rhins, was attacked and tossed, mortally wounded, into a river. Others also had close shaves, but got back alive. The Victorian adventurer Henry Savage Landor, whose narrative sometimes stretches credulity to its limits, was seized and tortured by the Tibetans when he refused to turn back. But he got what he wanted from his misadventure – a best-selling book.

Armed as they were only with matchlocks and swords, the Tibetans could not hope to maintain their self-imposed isolation for ever. Eventually, in 1904, Lhasa capitulated before the force of British arms and the persuasive powers of Sir Francis Younghusband. But although the race for the capital was won, Tibet's mysteries were far from exhausted. Trespassers continued to don disguise and try their luck with the border guards. Mount Everest now became the goal of some, beginning with the secret journey in 1913 of Captain John Noel, who is still alive at the time of writing. Others were less fortunate. One trespasser, Maurice Wilson, was to leave his frozen body, together with his diary, on the slopes of Everest. His bizarre plan had been to crash-land his plane on the mountainside and then scramble to the top with a Union Jack, thus claiming it for Britain.

Others found themselves in Tibet by accident, like the US Air Force crew who parachuted into the Forbidden Land during World War II when they ran out of fuel while lost in a storm over Central Asia. Their story has now passed into Tibetan folklore. Then there was Heinrich Harrer, a pre-war Austrian mountaineer, who sought refuge in Lhasa after fleeing from a British prisoner of war camp in India. But it was not until the early 1980s, when the first western tourists began to fly into Lhasa, that the last veil of mystery was finally torn away from this extraordinary land.

This book is not a catalogue of every traveller who set out for Tibet from the 1860s onwards. However, I have included all those seriously intent on reaching Lhasa, as well as every trespasser of interest or importance. To avoid monotony, itineraries have had to be greatly compressed at times, while for the same reason I have given more space to some characters than to others. But these travellers had one thing in common. All were unwelcome to the Tibetans. Even today, the package tourist is really a trespasser, for it is not the Tibetans but the Chinese who have invited him there.

It is from the narratives of all these gatecrashers that I have pieced together, for the first time, the story of the forcible opening up of a land which only ever wanted to be left in peace. But before setting out in their footsteps across the towering Himalayan passes, we have first to turn to the map of Central Asia. For it is here that all the events in this long-forgotten story took place.

1. Tibet – The Forbidden Land

In the heart of Central Asia, buttressed by the highest mountains on earth, soars the immense natural fortress of Tibet. Its extraordinary altitude – nearly three miles up in the sky – caused Victorian travellers to christen it 'The Roof of the World'. Lhasa, its remote and mysterious capital, so long closed to foreigners, they named 'The Forbidden City'.

One celebrated explorer, Sven Hedin, described Tibet as 'the most stupendous upheaval to be found on the face of our planet', and a glance at a relief map will show this to be no exaggeration. Some of its passes teeter at over 20,000 feet, while two-thirds of this vast, storm-swept tableland lies at 15,000 feet or more. Lhasa, standing at 12,000 feet, is the world's highest capital, and those with raised blood-pressure are well advised to stay away. Travelling in Tibet presents other peculiar problems. Water boils there at a lower temperature than at normal altitudes. To plunge one's hand into boiling water is bearable – just. Cooking thus becomes a laborious business, and Tibet has never been famous for its cuisine.

How, in geological terms, did this dizzy land, towering above all its neighbours, come to be there? Some sixty million years ago, scientists believe, a massive but incredibly slow-motion collision took place between the Indian sub-continent, then a huge island, and the rest of Asia. This caused the entire ocean bed between them to heave violently upwards, giving birth to the Tibetan massif and the mountains encircling it. The discovery of marine fossils in Tibet, so far from any sea, seems to bear this out.

But whatever the cause of this monstrous upheaval, it has

given the Tibetans a stronghold possessing some of the finest natural defences anywhere. On three sides it is cut off from the rest of Asia by the highest mountains on earth. From the north it is protected by the Kun Lun, or Mountains of Darkness, and the Nan Shan which together form a forbidding bastion against invaders. Sealing off its western approaches are the mighty Karakoram and Ladakh ranges, while defending its southern flank is the great chain of the Himalayas. Occasional passes pierce these icy battlements like giant staircases, but they can easily be watched and defended against intruders, and most of them are closed by snow for much of the year.

As the Chinese showed in 1950, Tibet's eastern frontier is less well protected by mountains. But when most of the events in this book took place, large tracts of this area were controlled by hostile tribes and bandits, making an approach from the east extremely hazardous. It was here that Lhasa's frontiers with its powerful neighbour China were least clearly defined and often the subject of dispute. Today Tibet's frontiers with China are no longer an issue. For better or for worse, Tibet is part of China. However, as most of what follows occurred before the Chinese invasion, it is necessary to understand what Tibet consisted of at that time.

There are really two Tibets. Sir Charles Bell, the leading authority on the country between the wars, drew a distinction between 'political' Tibet, where the Dalai Lamas or their regents had ruled more or less continuously, and the far wider 'ethnographic' Tibet. This embraced not only 'political' Tibet but also those surrounding regions where people of Tibetan stock predominate. These include the Chinese province of Sikang, parts of Chinghai, Kansu, Szechuan and Yunnan, as well as Ladakh, way over to the west. In fact, until the tenth century, the warlike Tibetans were one of the great imperial powers of Asia, their armies campaigning as far afield as Samarkand, Kashgar and Turfan, and well into western China.

Because Tibet's wild and lawless eastern frontier with China had always (until the invasion of 1950) been ill-defined and often fought over, it tended to vary considerably in outline at different periods and on different maps. Here I have used those boundaries which would have been readily accepted by most, if not all, of the travellers in this book, albeit not by the Chinese. They are those used by Sir Charles Bell in the maps accompanying his four classic studies of Tibetan history, and embrace the large and desolate tract of desert and swamp around Koko Nor and Tsaidam whose actual sovereignty has always been somewhat vague. The Tibet of this narrative one might call Greater Tibet.

Within its long frontiers is to be found one of the cruellest environments on earth. Here, over thousands of years, there evolved a remarkable way of life. On this lofty tableland lived a community totally isolated from all outside influences. It was denied those amenities and everyday materials, such as wood, which most other societies take for granted. It had to survive one of the harshest climates known to man (one can suffer from frostbite and sunburn simultaneously in Tibet). Adjustment over thousands of years to high-altitude living means that Tibetans feel unwell – mountain sickness in reverse – if they descend to the plains of India or China. Conversely, Chinese aircrews flying up to Lhasa today are not allowed to stop overnight there lest it affect their health. It comes as no great surprise to learn that the Tibetans, among the most stoical people on earth, have a higher threshold of pain than more ordinary mortals.

Until the Chinese invasion, their spartan way of life had hardly changed since the Middle Ages. They had no electricity, no wireless, no clocks or watches, no sewing machines, no modern medicines, no cars or bicycles, nor even the simplest wheeled transport. Apart from a few individuals of noble family who had travelled outside Tibet, most Tibetans had no idea that such things even existed. Like Shangri La, the 'lost' valley of James Hilton's *Lost Horizon*, Tibet was a land where time stood still and people had not yet lost their innocence. It was this, perhaps above all else, which made it so alluring to trespassers from the West. Here, surely, lived Rousseau's Noble Savage.

Almost everything about the Tibetans was mysterious. For a start, how many of them were there living in self-imposed isolation in this vast mountain eyrie? Estimates have always differed wildly. One eighteenth-century Capuchin traveller put it (quite how is not clear) at more than thirty million. Even as recently as the 1930s estimates ranged from one to four million, the latter being the official Chinese estimate, as well as that of Bell. Counting Tibetan heads is not made easy by the fact that anything up to half of the population has always been nomadic. Until the Chinese invasion, no census had been held since 1795.

Today Tibet's population is put officially at around 1,800,000. In a region nearly the size of Western Europe, and today part of the world's most populous nation, this is a surprisingly small figure. It means that, on average, there are fewer than four people to the square mile. This is explained, however, by the extremely inhospitable conditions, a high infant mortality rate, polyandry, disease, and – interestingly – widespread celibacy in a society where one man in six used to live in a monastery.

The population is at its most sparse in the desolate Chang Tang, Tibet's vast northern plateau. This treeless wilderness, corrugated by barren valleys and mountain chains, is inhabited only by nomads. Continuously moving in search of what little pasture exists there, they live in characteristic black, yak-hair tents guarded by huge mastiffs ('as large as donkeys', reported Marco Polo, who had never seen them). Many were forced by poverty into banditry, robbing the caravans of merchants and pilgrims crossing the Chang Tang from Mongolia and Sinkiang.

The climate of the great northern plateau is extremely severe, temperatures plunging to as low as minus forty-four degrees centigrade. Frozen for some eight months in the year, much of this trackless region turns to swamp in summer when the snow and ice melt. Rarely does the altitude fall below 15,000 feet. One of the Chang Tang's most alarming characteristics is its explosive winds, sometimes so violent that they can knock a rider off his horse. Yet the atmosphere is so uncannily clear that a man can be seen some ten miles off. Innumerable lakes – the highest in the world – are another curiosity of this sterile moonscape. Some of them are fifty miles or more in length, but because of the sudden and violent squalls which sweep across them they are too dangerous to navigate. Most of them being brackish, moreover, they are of little use to the thirsty traveller. So forbidding is this region even to nomads that one western traveller journeyed across it for eighty-one days without seeing another soul.

Most of Tibet's population is concentrated in the four largest towns: Lhasa, Shigatse, Gyantse and Chamdo. The first three lie in the south, in the valley of the Tsangpo – Tibet's principal river – or its tributaries. Chamdo lies in eastern Tibet, on the ancient Tea Road between Lhasa and China. There are few other towns or villages of any size or consequence. Phari, one of the highest inhabited places on earth, lies on the main route south between Lhasa and India, as does Yatung, eight miles short of the Sikkimese frontier. Rudok and Gartok, little visited even today, are situated far away to the west, astride the old caravan trail to Ladakh.

Rising in the Tibetan uplands, and fed by its melting snows and glaciers, are some of Asia's mightiest waterways. These include the Yellow River, the Yangtze, the Mekong, the Salween, the Brahmaputra and the Indus. Because Tibet was closed to explorers, the exact sources and routes taken by these giant waterways before flowing down into China, Burma and India remained a mystery for years, and the subject of fierce controversy among geographers. As can be seen from the map, three of these rivers – the Yangtze, Mekong and Salween – converge in a series of gorges only fifty miles apart in the south-eastern corner of Tibet. These gorges are so deep in places, as they bore their way through the Himalayan massif, that a day's sunlight is gone within the hour. Equally eager, though for different reasons, to solve the riddle of Tibet's rivers were Hindu and Buddhist holy men who considered them sacred. If they could discover their sources they might then acquire religious merit by making pilgrimages there. But the ultimate mystery was the question of what became of the Tsangpo, greatest of Tibet's waterways, after it vanished into the Himalayas. Considerable ingenuity and courage were to be devoted to trying to solve this.

Such then is the harsh and inhospitable geography of Tibet, crucible of one of the world's strangest peoples. But from where, in a region of so many migrations, did the Tibetans originally come? Anthropologists are far from certain. However, the Tibetans themselves have no such doubts. Anticipating Darwin, Tibetan tradition maintains that they are the descendants of a monkey-saint and a she-demon who lived in a cave at a place which is still pointed out today. Fed on magic grain, the six children of this union gradually lost their simian characteristics and turned into men and women – the first Tibetans.

Their earliest kings, they believe, descended to earth on ropes suspended from the sky. When they died they simply returned the way they had come. All went well, it appears, until the death of the eighth in line of these semi-mythical rulers. Somehow, whether by accident or design, his 'sky-rope' was severed, so preventing him from returning to heaven. His earthly tomb, Tibetans say, still exists at Kongpo in southern Tibet. However, because excavation has never been allowed, no archaeological evidence exists to throw any light on Tibet's earliest history. Central Asian historians, therefore, have little else to go on other than Tibetan legends. Nor has the task of the anthropologist been made any easier by a shortage of human skulls, the raw material of their trade. For Tibetan funeral custom requires the corpse to be cut up, the bones – including the skull – to be crushed, and the remains to be fed to vultures and wild dogs. The reason for this was that the ground was too hard during much of the year for graves to be dug, while the scarcity of wood in this treeless land ruled out cremation.

It was not until the early 1950s, following the Chinese

invasion, that an anthropologist – Prince Peter of Greece and Denmark – was able to take detailed measurements of the heads and other bodily features of five thousand Tibetan refugees from all parts of the country as they passed through Kalimpong into India. Apart from its scientific importance, his work also produced moments of hilarity, for even in adversity the Tibetans have a rich sense of humour, as many travellers have noted. One man he examined assured him lewdly that he had measured everything that was of no importance and nothing that was. When he asked them whether they had hair on their bodies – an important detail in anthropology – they merely roared with laughter, for Tibetans, like the Japanese, have little body hair. On being shown the hair on the Prince's own chest, the Tibetans became greatly excited, saying that he must be a monkey. One man asked him quite seriously why he bothered to wear a shirt when he already had hair.

Prince Peter's work ended abruptly when pressure was brought to bear on the Indian Government by the Chinese who claimed that he was really there to select and train agents for sending back into Tibet. In fact, his findings did no more than confirm what historians had long believed – that the Tibetans appear to belong to the Mongoloid race. He noted that in those from the south, and thus nearer to India, the Mongoloid characteristics were somewhat diluted with Europoid traits. Similarly, Tibetans from the east and north-east, showed more pronounced Mongoloid features, due to their proximity to Mongolia and China.

The name Tibet, by which the country is known to all except the Tibetans, appears to have been borrowed by the West from the Arab geographers, who called it *Tubbat*, or from the Chinese who in ancient times knew it as *Tu-bat*. The precise meaning of the name has never been satisfactorily explained, although it is possibly a corruption of the Chinese word *To*, meaning high, and the Tibetan word *Bod*, the name they themselves use for their country. Historians are equally uncertain of the origin of the word *Bod*, although it is very likely derived from *Bon*, the devil-worshipping, shamanistic religion practised by Tibetans before the arrival of Buddhism. To add to the confusion, there are two further names for Tibet in current use. *Gangjong*, meaning 'Land of Snow', is sometimes used by the Tibetans themselves, while *Xizang* is the modern Chinese name for Tibet. The latter is derived from two characters, one meaning 'the West' and the other 'to hide' – in other words, 'Hidden in the West'.

Buddhism first reached Tibet in the middle of the seventh century, and was destined to bring about a remarkable change in the Tibetan people. Until their conversion to Buddhism, they had always been a warlike race with imperialist ambitions who represented a perpetual threat to their neighbours, particularly the Chinese. For a while they had even ruled Chang'an, China's ancient capital, and occupied virtually the whole of Kansu, much of Szechuan and northern Yunnan, as well as Upper Burma and Nepal. But following their gradual conversion to Buddhism, with its gentle message of submission, the once dreaded martial reputation of the Tibetans began to decline. Finally, around the tenth century, the last of their empire collapsed. The Tibetans withdrew behind their mountain ramparts and their centuries of isolation began.

The Buddhism which reached Tibet more than a thousand years after its founder's death was of the late and debased northern Indian school. This debasement was due to an infusion of Tantrism, an animistic creed which embraced magic, witchcraft and spells. In Tibet the new religion immediately found itself in violent conflict with the old Bon faith and its devotees. The latter practised an even more primitive kind of animism, indulging in human sacrifice, cannibalism, devil worship and sexual orgies. Although banned altogether at one time, Buddhism gradually prevailed. But the Bon faith nonetheless continued to be practised, never being completely ousted. In fact, Tibetan Buddhism was to borrow freely from the Bon pantheon as well as from other religions, including Nestorian Christianity, which by then had reached Central

Asia. In its final form, the Buddhism of Tibet – or Lamaism as it is sometimes called – would scarcely have been recognised by its saintly founder. One Catholic missionary who visited Tibet in the seventeenth century even claimed that it was simply a degenerate form of Christianity.

Lamaism is so named after its priestly upholders, the lamas, or 'superior ones'. In effect it came to mean rule by a religious hierarchy headed by the Dalai Lama. The first Tibetan Buddhist monastery is said to have been built around the year 775, the final total of such institutions eventually reaching some 2,700. One early traveller described the country as 'a huge monastery inhabited by a nation of monks'. For every Tibetan family was expected to provide one child for the church. It was a custom which their Chinese neighbours – and at times overlords – were to encourage, for more monks meant fewer soldiers. As a result every town and village had its own monastery, often perched strategically on hill-top or mountainside, from where a disciplinary eye was kept on the local populace.

The first Dalai Lama dates back to the fifteenth century, although the actual title was introduced, retrospectively, a century later. He was the leader of a sect called the Yellow Hats (so called because of their yellow garb) of Tibetan Buddhism which, with powerful Mongol support, gradually supplanted the rival Red Hat sect as the dominant power in Tibet. Until then the country had been ruled by a dynasty of kings supported by the Red Hats. Nominally the kings continued to rule, but gradually temporal as well as religious power passed to the Dalai Lamas. By the middle of the seventeenth century this transfer of power was complete, and Tibet was firmly controlled by the formidable fifth Dalai Lama from the Potala, the now world-famous palace which he built specially for himself and his successors or, more correctly, his reincarnations. The Great Fifth, as he is still known, also created an institution which some of his successors had cause to rue. This was the office of Panchen – or Tashi – Lama which he bestowed as a gesture of veneration upon his aged and revered teacher, the Abbot of

Tashilhunpo monastery, near Shigatse, Tibet's second largest town. Both the Dalai and Panchen Lamas, Tibetans believe, are reincarnations of different aspects of the Buddha himself, the Panchen being concerned exclusively with spiritual matters while the Dalai is additionally entrusted with the nation's sovereignty. So long as the Panchen Lamas confined themselves to spiritual affairs, leaving all temporal matters to the Dalai Lama, no problems arose, but this did not always prove to be the case.

Whenever a Dalai Lama died a search began for his reincarnation. The chosen male child had to possess certain mystic qualities which distinguished him from ordinary mortals. One was the ability to identify the possessions of his predecessor, or rather his previous self. Another requirement was that he should have large ears, upward-slanting eyes and eyebrows and that one of his hands should bear a mark like a conch-shell. The successful candidate, usually aged two or three, was then removed from his family to Lhasa to begin a long period of spiritual training for his future role. The Panchen Lamas were chosen in a similar way. Invariably the reincarnated leaders were 'discovered' in the households of lowly families rather than of noble ones. This, it has been said, was deliberate, to ensure that no single and powerful lay family could seize the title and make it hereditary.

Until he reached the age of eighteen, the young Dalai Lama's temporal responsibilities were carried out by a Regent. Some of these were clearly reluctant to relinquish their powers, for a suspiciously large number of young Dalai Lamas died before attaining the age of eighteen. During one period of a hundred and twenty years, five successive Dalai Lamas ruled for a total of only seven years. Nor were all the Dalai Lamas models of saintliness. The sixth, who was enthroned in 1697, showed little interest in his spiritual and secular responsibilities, preferring to indulge in sexual adventures, drunkenness and writing erotic poetry. He was nonetheless popular with his people who resisted an attempt to have him deposed.

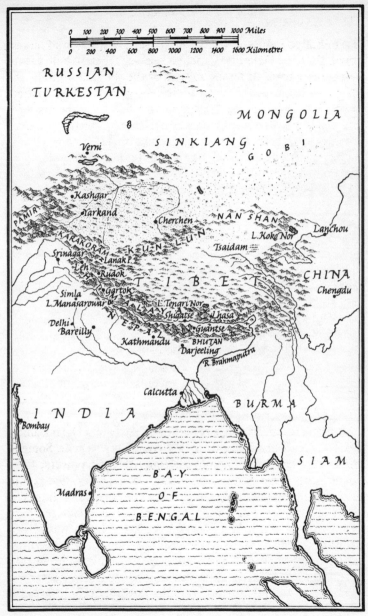

Tibet and surrounding areas

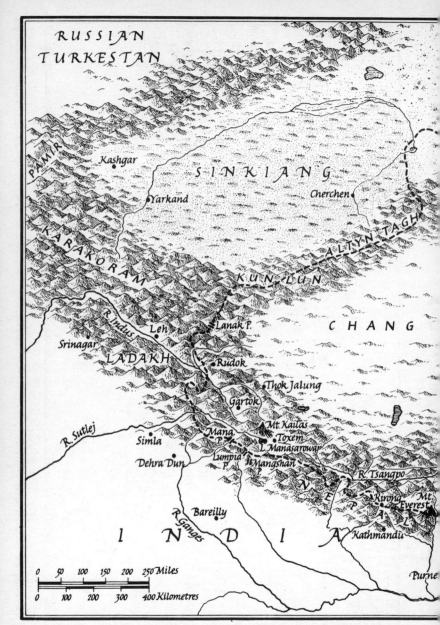

Greater Tibet showing Sir Charles Bell's boundary line

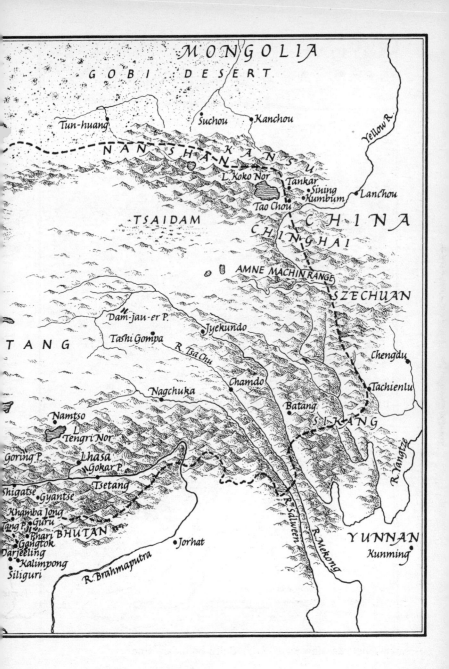

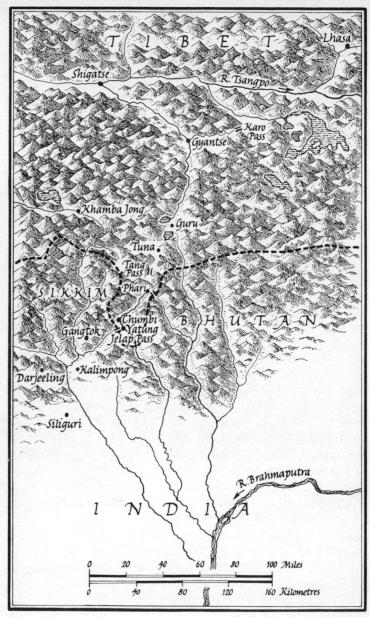

The Chumbi Valley

Religious belief and everyday life were inextricably entwined in this unique theocracy. Until the Chinese invasion, every Tibetan family worshipped daily at the household shrine. Whether rich or poor (and the rich were only modestly so by comparison with other countries), whether dwelling in palace, hovel or nomadic tent, each household set aside a corner in which were placed devotional objects. In addition to the numerous monasteries and nunneries scattered across the country, there were many thousands of *chortens* or *stupas*, erected as monuments to saints or as repositories for offerings and sacred relics. It is necesssary to use the past tense as almost all of these were destroyed by the Red Guards during the Cultural Revolution, if not before. Everywhere too there were strings of prayer flags, either hung from poles or draped over the rooftops. Each flutter of one of these flags, the Tibetans believe, sends the prayer written on it heavenwards.

Another ingenious idea, unique to Tibet, is the prayer-wheel, or *mani-chuskor*. This consists of a metal cylinder – ranging in height from a mere two inches to a colossal eight or nine feet – and containing a long scroll of paper bearing countless repetitions of the mystical, all-powerful Tibetan prayer: '*Om! Mani Padme Hum!*' Translated literally, this means 'Hail! Jewel in the Lotus!', although its actual meaning is obscure. Every time the cylinder is rotated, Tibetans believe, a stream of prayer ascends skywards. The most common type of prayer-wheel is the small, individually-owned and hand-rotated kind. Attached to a wooden handle, the cylinders of these are usually made from copper or silver and often finely decorated. A small metal weight on a short chain attached to the cylinder enables the user to whirl it at speed. Some of the largest prayer-wheels, to be found in monasteries or temples, are said to contain as many as a million printed repetitions of the mystical formula. Because of their weight, these giant wheels are usually rotated by means of a hand-turned crank, or by wind or water power, thus enabling hundreds of millions of invocations to be released heavenwards with the minimum of effort.

Another aid to prayer is the Tibetan rosary. Usually of bone (often human), coral or wood, these always consist of one hundred and eight beads, a sacred number. A bead is slipped each time a prayer is repeated, until a complete circuit has been made of the rosary. Also attached to the rosary are two or more secondary strings, each consisting of ten much smaller beads. These are used to register each completed circuit of the rosary. Thus very large numbers of prayers can be recorded. These rosaries, as well as the innocent seeming prayer-wheels, were adapted by the Raj spymasters to less reverent use, as will be seen.

Learned tomes have been written on the religion of the Tibetans to which those wishing to pursue the subject further can turn. For it is too complex to go into here and beyond the scope of this book. But there are certain beliefs and practices of interest to us because they illustrate Tibetan attitudes to life and death and the immense power of their faith. (If they seem repugnant to us, it should be pointed out that some western customs strike Tibetans as equally bizarre.)

One of the most horrifying of these was self-immurement. The length of time a hermit might spend in solitary confinement walled up in a pitch-dark cave could vary from a few months' retreat to a lifetime, in which case the ordeal ended only at death. Recourse to this slow form of suicide, it was believed, would enable the devotee to avoid endless cycles of rebirth, and so achieve Nirvana, or self extinction, in one lifetime. Many of those who attempted this feat understandably went mad. Their only human contact was the gloved hand which once a day, and in total silence, passed food through a tiny aperture in the wall. It needs no imagination to visualise the conditions inside a cave cell thus occupied for thirty or forty years. When the anchorite knew that death – and hopefully Nirvana – was close, he would drag himself into a corner and compose himself, Buddha-like, in cross-legged posture to await the end. When those outside noticed that he had failed to accept food for several days, death would be assumed. The wall was then knocked

down and the devotee's body reverently removed and ceremoniously burned instead of being cut up and fed to the
vultures.

Another harsh ritual was that of making a pilgrimage by the
slow and painful means of repeated prostrations of the body.
Pilgrims sometimes covered hundreds of miles in this way, each
time placing their feet on the spot where their foreheads had
previously touched the ground. Usually Lhasa, with its holy
places, was the pilgrim's goal, but it could be any sacred site.
Sven Hedin once came upon two young lamas engaged in such a
pilgrimage around Mount Kailas, regarded by Tibetans as the
centre of the universe. It had taken them nine days to reach this
spot from their village, and they calculated that it would take a
further twelve or so days to complete the circuit of the mountain. After that, one of the two – just twenty years old –
planned to wall himself up for the rest of his life. Other pilgrims sometimes carried heavy rocks with them to demonstrate
their devotion.

Tibet abounds in tales of supernaturally-endowed saints,
wizards with great destructive powers, and mystics who could
fly to the tops of Himalayan peaks, raise the dead and perform
other miracles. Many of these stories were no doubt invented by
the priestly hierarchy to impress their authority on simple
villagers, whose aims and faith they depended upon. But many
modern-minded Tibetans still half believe in these miracles.
Tibetan refugees tell of the *lung-pa*, or wind men, who after
years of extreme asceticism and preparation can free themselves
from the normal weight of their bodies and thereafter defy
gravity, flying hundreds of miles in a day. One well-known
European traveller actually claimed to have observed one of
these.

Magic plays a key role, too, in traditional medicine. Tibetan
doctors claim to be able to tell from a patient's pulse when
another member of his or her family, however far away, is ill,
and then to be able to diagnose and cure the malady. There are
four hundred and forty different forms of illness, it is claimed,

each of which can be cured by a special charm or spell, although herbal medicines are also used. Even more bizarre are some of the potions used by the lama doctors in the past. According to David Macdonald, a British official who perhaps came to know the Tibetans better than any other westerner, the most prized and expensive of all Tibetan medicines were the pills made from the mixed excreta of the Dalai and Panchen Lamas. Another outlandish belief was that drinking the urine of young boys would restore virility in elderly men.

Like almost everything else in this larger-than-life land, punishments, too, were extremely harsh. Mutilation – including the removal of the eyes – and amputations were widely used to punish serious crimes. Writing in 1929, Macdonald observes that eyes were rendered sightless either by thrusting red-hot irons into the sockets, or by pouring boiling oil or water over them. 'Sightless beggars', he recounts in *The Land of the Lama*, 'their eyes put out or blinded for murder, theft from monasteries or the houses of high officials, may be seen in the bazaars soliciting alms.'

The death penalty, although rarely carried out (for Buddhism forbids the taking of life), usually involved pushing the victim over a cliff, or tossing him, stitched up in a bag, into a river. Another punishment which could be ordered, though only by the Dalai Lama, was that of denying a man's soul the possibility of rebirth, thus condemning him to eternal limbo. This could be accompanied by a death sentence, in which case the victim's head was dried and placed in a special building near Lhasa – 'a sort of rogues' gallery', Macdonald calls it. If execution was not ordered, then the victim was shunned as an outcast for the remainder of his or her life – a fate almost more to be dreaded than death in such a society. As if all this were not enough, Tibetan sinners lived in perpetual fear of sixteen different kinds of hell, eight of them scorchingly hot and eight icy cold.

But despite the harshness and cruelty of Tibetan life – haunted not merely by demons and despotic lamas, but by earthquakes, smallpox, wolves and brigands – travellers throughout history have always found the Tibetans an exceptionally attractive people. Blessed with a robust humour, they showed themselves to be both hospitable and trustworthy. Generally speaking they were amazingly forbearing towards gate-crashers. But if they felt threatened, and were inflamed by the lamas, they could be fierce and implacable, even if their armaments and tactics were mediaeval. They could also be extraordinarily brave, even pathetically so, as British machine-gunners were to discover on the battlefield at Guru.

The tale which now follows begins in the middle of the nineteenth century, after Tibet had become a land closed to foreigners. Tsarist armies were advancing – menacingly the British believed – across Central Asia towards India. It was fears for the safety of the latter which stirred strategists in London and Calcutta to look with sudden new interest at the kingdoms and khanates lying in the path of the Russian advance. Until then, apart from Afghanistan, these had counted for little. But now they acquired a crucial significance. And none more than the Buddhist kingdom of Tibet, the largest and least known of them all.

2. The Unholy Spies
of Captain Montgomerie

As the heavily laden caravan wound its way through the snow-filled valleys and passes of southern Tibet towards Lhasa, a solitary Buddhist pilgrim, rosary in hand, could be observed toiling alongside the straining yaks. As he strode his companions could hear him repeating endlessly the sacred Tibetan mantra *'Om! Mane Padme Hum!'* Sometimes he would draw a prayer-wheel from the folds of his thick sheepskin coat and rotate it with a flick of the wrist for hour after hour, filling the thin Tibetan air with prayer. Conscious of their pious companion's need for privacy, the Ladakhi caravan men avoided questioning or talking to him at such times.

It was the winter of 1865. The leader of the caravan, bringing goods from Ladakh to Lhasa, had agreed to allow this good-natured pilgrim to accompany them on the final, three-month stage of their journey to the Tibetan capital. What they did not know, and never did discover, was that this was no Buddhist holy man. Had they suspected this, and troubled to count the beads of his rosary, they would have found that there were only one hundred of these, instead of the sacred one hundred and eight. Had they removed the top from his prayer-wheel while he slept they would have discovered, instead of the usual scroll bearing block-printed prayers, tiny pencilled figures and mysterious jottings in Urdu.

Once their suspicions had been aroused, they might have noticed that sometimes this holy man dropped behind the slow-moving caravan. Then he would remove surreptitiously from his sleeve, a small, curious-looking device made of metal and glass, through which he would peer hastily at some distant feature, afterwards scribbling a brief note which he would then conceal inside his prayer-wheel. At other times, after making quite sure he was not being observed, he would carefully remove from the top of his pilgrim's staff a thin glass object (which some of his companions might have recognised as a thermometer), and dip it fleetingly into a boiling kettle or cooking vessel. Again, he would note down the reading and hurriedly secrete this in his prayer-wheel.

Not merely was this traveller not a Buddhist, but neither was he a holy man. He was a Hindu – and worse, he was a British spy. Had his identity been discovered, he would undoubtedly have been killed on the spot. Not long afterwards he was to witness the public beheading of another traveller who had entered Lhasa without permission. But who was this man, and why was he prepared to take such terrible risks, and face appalling hardships, for his British masters?

At this period in the history of the Raj, ever since the Tibetans had closed their frontiers with India, knowledge of what was going on there was extremely meagre. To those British Indian officials entrusted with gathering political and other intelligence from their northern neighbour, it must have seemed at times rather like waiting for signals from outer space. What little intelligence frontier officials did manage to glean came from native traders who travelled regularly between India and Tibet. A certain amount more was passed on by the British Legation in Peking and by the handful of consuls and foreign missionaries living in western China. But for the latest movements of the advancing Tsarist armies in Central Asia, the intelligence chiefs in Calcutta and Whitehall were almost entirely dependent on the St Petersburg newspapers. To make matters worse, much of the information reaching them from these sources proved to be highly unreliable, especially that to do with Tibet, just three hundred miles north of Calcutta, then the capital of British India.

British official maps at this time show Tibet as one huge white blank, as though the whole area was obliterated by snow. At their headquarters in the hill station of Dehra Dun, the cartographers of the Survey of India preferred to ignore the positioning of towns and rivers shown on the old, Chinese-made pictorial maps of Tibet. Thus, in the 1860s, the locations of towns even as important as Lhasa and Shigatse, and – further afield in Chinese Turkestan – Yarkand and Kashgar, were known only to the nearest hundred miles or more. Much the same applied to roads and passes, mountains and rivers. But now, with the Russians advancing across the great empty spaces of Central Asia, suddenly there was a call for accurate maps of this vast political no-man's land to the north.

There was no easy solution, if there was one at all. To send through the passes young officers trained in map-making, however brave, willing and well disguised, would have been not only personally hazardous but politically so also. Already one celebrated traveller – William Moorcroft – had been murdered in the unpoliced approaches to Tibet. Others were to meet with a similar fate, including old Central Asian hands like Andrew Dalgleish, hacked to death by a giant Afghan on a lonely Karakoram pass, and George Hayward, about whose violent end Sir Henry Newbolt wrote the epic poem *He Fell Among Thieves*. Anyone brave – or foolish – enough to trespass in these badlands was regarded as fair game by the lawless tribes and brigands who lived there by rapine. And because there was little or no chance of those responsible ever being brought to justice, any such enterprise by adventurous Raj officials (and there was no shortage of volunteers) was expressly forbidden. Even if they had succeeded in evading the murderous tribesmen, there was very little likelihood of their being able to outwit the vigilant Tibetan border guards who waited at every pass or approach.

In a celebrated incident in 1849, the distinguished botanist Joseph Hooker and a friend had crossed briefly into Tibet from Sikkim on a plant-hunting expedition despite the tearful entreaties of the Tibetan guard commander (who, it is said, later paid for this lapse with his life) and also the protests of

Sikkimese officials. The following month they attempted to bluster their way across again, but were turned back by Tibetan troops. On returning to Sikkim they were arrested and Hooker's companion, a Raj official, mistreated by having bamboo cords twisted round his wrists and being made to march with his hands bound to the tail of a mule. The perpetrators were punished for this, but it was the very sort of incident that the British authorities wished to avoid, and Hooker and his companion, Dr Archibald Campbell, were lucky to escape a severe reprimand.

Year after year Tibet thus continued to remain a no-go area for map-makers, and therefore a blank on everyone's charts. Then, in 1862, a young Royal Engineers officer attached to the Survey of India hit upon a brilliant solution. Why not, he asked, send native explorers, hand-picked for their intelligence and resourcefulness, and trained in clandestine surveying techniques? The officer, Captain Thomas George Montgomerie, explained his idea thus:

'When I was in Ladakh I noticed the natives of India passed freely backwards and forwards between Ladakh and Yarkand in Chinese Turkestan, and it consequently occurred to me that it might be possible to make the exploration by that means. If a sharp enough man could be found, he would have no difficulty in carrying a few small instruments amongst his merchandise, and with their aid good service might be rendered to geography.'

Montgomerie's chiefs agreed to let him put his idea to the test, confident perhaps that a native could always be disowned if it came to it, and that reprisals would hardly be called for in the event of his death. Nonetheless, in view of their anxiety not to upset their Asiatic neighbours, especially Manchu China, it was a surprising decision. For Yarkand, in the heart of Chinese Central Asia, was chosen as the target for this sensitive mission.

Montgomerie's first recruit was Mohamed-i-Hameed, a young Muslim clerk already trained in simple survey work. In the summer of 1863 he set out from Ladakh, the last outpost of

British influence, and headed across the Karakoram passes towards Yarkand, an oasis town on the ancient Silk Road. Both he and Captain Montgomerie knew that he was taking his life in his hands, and that detection meant almost certain death. Every effort, therefore, had been made to reduce to an absolute minimum the risk of discovery. The surveying instruments he carried were of the smallest possible size, designed and made specially in the Survey of India workshops. These were still early days, and Montgomerie and his colleagues had not yet begun to adapt Buddhist prayer-wheels and rosaries to clandestine ends. Chinese Turkestan, although only a stone's throw from Tibet, was in any case a Muslim region.

Mohamed reached Yarkand safely, residing there for six months, all the time taking furtive observations with his secret instruments, and keeping his ears open for any news of Russian activities in the region. Then, towards the end of his stay, he was warned by a friend that Chinese officials had become suspicious of his activities and were making enquiries about him. The only thing to do was to leave discreetly but fast, and this he did, hastily returning across the Karakoram towards Ladakh, and safety. But he never got there.

At first it was surmised that he and a travelling companion had been murdered, possibly on Chinese orders, but subsequent investigations proved that both travellers had, in fact, died of illness, possibly precipitated by the hardships of their journey through the grim passes of the Karakoram. Fortunately, however, the young explorer's carefully kept notes were recovered, and eventually delivered to Montgomerie. These proved to contain valuable topographical intelligence enabling Montgomerie, among other things, to fix the precise position and altitude of Yarkand and other nearby towns and villages. They also contained a brief report of Russian activities in this remote corner of the Chinese empire. It must have been with considerable satisfaction, albeit tinged with sadness at the fate of his agent, that Montgomerie was able to report to his superiors on the success of his first secret mission.

It was now agreed that this ingenious idea should be extended into Tibet. In anticipation of this, two Tibetan-speaking hill-men of British nationality had already been chosen for the task by Montgomerie and his immediate superior, Colonel James Walker, with the help of Major Etwall Smyth, a government education officer working in the frontier region. The two men were Nain Singh, aged thirty-three, the headmaster of a village school at Milam, lying 11,000 feet up in the Himalayas, and Mani Singh, his slightly older cousin. Both were experienced mountain travellers, having some years earlier accompanied a German expedition whose members had found them intelligent and resourceful.

The two recruits were brought to Dehra Dun, where they were given two years' training in route survey and reconnaissance work. They were taught the use of sextant and compass, how to identify the stars and use them for fixing positions, and how to calculate altitudes by observing the boiling point of water. But that was no more than the Survey of India taught all its newly recruited native surveyors, or 'chain men' as they were known in the business. Nain and Mani Singh now entered what today would be called a spy-school, a world curiously familiar to readers of *Kim*, Kipling's story of a small boy caught up in the Great Game and eventually recruited into the Raj intelligence service. Here they were schooled in the ingenious techniques devised by Montgomerie and Walker for conducting clandestine surveys of territories which were hostile, politically sensitive, or belonged to other governments – or, in the case of Tibet, all three.

First they were trained by endless practice to take a pace which, whether they walked uphill, downhill or on the level, always remained the same – thirty-three inches in the case of Nain Singh. Next they learned how to keep an exact count of the number of such paces they took in a day, or between any two landmarks. This was done with the aid of a Buddhist rosary, which as we have noted normally comprises one hundred and eight beads. Eight of these were removed, leaving a mathematically convenient one hundred, but not a sufficient reduction to be noticeable. At every hundredth pace a bead was slipped. Each complete circuit of the rosary, therefore, represented ten thousand paces – five miles in the case of Nain Singh, who covered a mile in two thousand paces. Because the Buddhist rosary has attached to it two short secondary strings, each of ten smaller beads, these were used for recording every completed circuit of the rosary.

Nain and Mani Singh were trained in the use of cover stories and disguise, just as Kim was at Simla by the shadowy Lurgan Sahib. Their lives were to depend on just how convincingly they could play the part of holy man, Himalayan trader, or whatever the delicacy of the situation demanded. Their disguise would have to stand the test of months of travelling, in the closest intimacy with real traders and pilgrims. Like Kim, they also learned to forget their own names, and work under a number or a cryptonym. Thus Nain Singh became simply 'Number One', 'the Pundit' or 'the Chief Pundit'. His cousin was known in the Survey records as 'Pundit Number Two', 'the Second Pundit', or just 'G-M', which was arrived at by taking two of the letters of his name and reversing them. The word 'pundit', which suggests a man of certain learning, was to become the generic name by which they, and all subsequent recruits, were referred to. Their real names were not revealed until they were too old to make further secret journeys.

Not only was the Buddhist rosary ingeniously adapted to Montgomerie's purpose, but so were prayer-wheels. These were fitted with a secret catch which enabled the pundit to open the copper cylinder and insert or remove the scrolls of paper bearing his route notes and other intelligence. Later the workshops at Dehra Dun were to conceal compasses inside the wheels, so that a pundit could take bearings while pretending to be at prayer. Larger instruments like sextants were concealed in specially built false bottoms in the travelling chests which native travellers carried, while secret pockets were added to their clothing. Thermometers, for measuring altitude, were concealed in hollowed out staves, and mercury – necessary for setting an artificial horizon when taking sextant readings – was hidden in a sealed cowrie shell and poured into a pilgrim's bowl whenever needed.

For his novel *Kim*, which was written nearly forty years after Nain and Mani Singh graduated from the Dehra Dun spy school, Kipling borrowed at least two of his characters from Montgomerie's twilight world. The amiable Hurree Chunder Mookerjee – R.17 on the Great Game payroll – is known to have been modelled on Sarat Chandra Das, one of the later pundits, while Colonel Creighton, who recruited the youthful Kim and masterminded his education, can only have been Montgomerie himself.

Their training now complete, it was time for Montgomerie's two protégés to show their paces. The route which he and Colonel Walker worked out was aimed to carry them some twelve hundred miles through Tibet to Lhasa and back. The two men, it was hoped, would return with a route survey which would enable Montgomerie to fill in a number of embarrassing blanks on the map of Tibet. These included the precise location and altitude of Lhasa, the route that the great southern caravan trail took from Lhasa westwards towards Gartok, and the course of the mysterious Tsangpo river as it flowed from west to east across Tibet. It was also hoped that the explorers would return with useful political intelligence. Despite the fact that they had spent nearly two years being schooled for it, it was a daunting task for the two hillmen – all for some twenty rupees a month and the promise of a larger reward if they were successful.

The journey would take them many months, every minute of which they would have to be on their guard against Tibetan suspicions. Every yard of the way would have to be paced, latitudes and altitudes calculated and carefully recorded. In the event, despite all Montgomerie's painstaking preparations, the two were to get off to a bad start.

3. With Prayer-Wheel and Sextant to Lhasa

With Montgomerie's final words of advice still ringing in their ears, and filled no doubt with trepidation at what they had taken on, the two pundits set out for Tibet in January 1865. Although unaware of it as they said their goodbyes, only one of them was destined to cross into Tibet – and then not for another eight months. Already there had been one false start, for Montgomerie's original plan had been to infiltrate them across the border at a point only one hundred and fifty miles from Dehra Dun. But for reasons that he does not go into in his official report on the mission (he merely states that the two pundits 'did not find it practicable'), they returned to Dehra Dun.

Disappointed but undeterred, Montgomerie now dispatched them eastwards to try to slip in from Nepal, a country which had regular intercourse with its isolated northern neighbour. After calibrating their instruments at the small town of Bareilly, whose location was known exactly to the Survey authorities, they crossed successfully into Nepal, reaching Kathmandu on March 7. Here they made enquiries about the best route to the Tibetan capital. The most direct one, everyone agreed, was likely to be impassable so early in the year as the snows would not yet have melted. They settled, therefore, for another route via the Tibetan border post at Kirong. Two days before reaching the frontier they switched to a disguise which would be familiar to Tibetans by adopting the costume and character of Bisaharis, a people living in a valley of that name near Simla. For many years the Bisaharis had been coming and going freely through the passes between India and Tibet, so there was no reason for them to be given a second glance provided they looked the part. They let it be known that the reason for their journey to Lhasa was to worship at its shrines and to buy horses there.

Now, at the Nepalese-Tibetan frontier, came their first real test. It must have been an anxious moment as the customs men examined their baggage, including the two boxes with secret compartments containing the highly compromising surveying instruments. But Montgomerie's craftsmen had done their work well, and the sextants and other equipment remained undetected. After paying a poll tax Nain and Mani Singh were allowed to make their way across the no-man's-land towards the Tibetan frontier post. Here their baggage was searched once more. Again the secret compartments withstood careful scrutiny. But their cover story did not satisfy the officials who ruled that the matter must be referred to the local governor. Fortunately they were not brought before him, for they later discovered that, by chance, he had known Mani Singh when in a previous frontier posting not far from their home village, and would almost certainly have recognised him.

But to the pundits' dismay the governor refused to allow them into Tibet. He sent a message saying that he found their tale unconvincing. For a start it was the wrong time of year for Bisahari horse traders to be visiting Tibet, and secondly the route they had chosen was a most unusual one for men in their particular business. To add insult to injury they had already had to pay a Tibetan poll tax which was non-refundable. There was nothing more to be done but to return to Kathmandu. They were fortunate, however, not to have been arrested.

In the Nepalese capital they began to make fresh enquiries, eventually finding two small parties of merchants preparing to leave for Tibet, both willing to take them. It was now some four months since they had said farewell to Montgomerie, and they were still only in Nepal. To increase the chances of one of them getting through the two cousins now decided to separate, each joining a different party. But then the leader of the caravan which had agreed to let Mani Singh accompany it suddenly changed his mind. However, there could be no question of Mani switching to his cousin's caravan because this planned to enter Tibet at the spot from where they had just returned, and where the governor knew him. Nain, too, faced the danger of being recognised there by the officials who had just turned them back, but decided nonetheless to take a chance. But first he adopted a new disguise, as a Ladakhi, which involved wearing a pigtail.

His dispirited cousin meanwhile tried a more circuitous approach through a pass further west, but failed once again to cross into Tibet, finally returning to Dehra Dun. Although the pundit himself blamed his failure on poor health and the dangers of the road, a disappointed Montgomerie attributed it in his official report 'in great measure due to his own want of determination'.

Whether or not this was just, Nain – the younger of the two – was certainly not lacking in determination. He was to prove himself a man of astonishing resolution and resource, and was destined to become a legend among explorers everywhere, even before they were allowed to learn his real identity. From all accounts he also possessed remarkable charm and was a popular member of any caravan he joined, and welcome at any campfire. It was no doubt with the help of this charm that he managed to ingratiate himself with the leader of the Nepalese caravan which finally got him safely across the frontier at Kirong, some eight months after his departure from Dehra Dun. His new disguise completely fooled the frontier officials, and once again the false bottom of his travelling trunk survived scrutiny.

The Nepalese caravan now turned westwards towards Lake Manasarowar, the opposite direction to that in which he wished to go, so feigning illness, he let it proceed on its way. But not before he had watched three of his companions swept to their deaths when the yak-skin coracle ferrying them across the angry Tsangpo capsized. It was his first encounter with this mighty waterway which flows some nine-hundred miles eastwards across Tibet, eventually falling thousands of feet to the Indian plains where it becomes the sacred Brahmaputra.

Before long the pundit managed to attach himself to a Ladakhi caravan approaching from the west and bound for Lhasa. At one stage, however, the Ladakhi traders transferred their goods to coracles and shipped these and themselves for some eighty-five miles down river to Shigatse, Tibet's second largest town. But Nain Singh, of course, had to continue the journey on foot (on what pretext is not known) so that there would be no gap in the secret route survey he had been conducting ever since leaving Bareilly – without any of his fellow travellers suspecting for a moment what he was really up to with his rosary, muttered prayers and spinning prayer-wheel.

During a halt in Shigatse while he waited for the main body of the caravan to catch up, to his dismay he was invited to attend an audience with the Panchen Lama at the great monastery of Tashilhunpo. Posing, as he was, as a Buddhist pilgrim, there was no possible way of avoiding a meeting which might well prove to be his undoing. For if anyone was going to penetrate his disguise, then surely it would be at the court of this living Buddha. Nain Singh was aware, moreover, that like the Dalai Lama the Panchen Lama was supposed to be able to read the secrets of all men's hearts. To his great relief, Tibet's second holiest authority turned out to be a boy of eleven who appeared, the pundit later told Montgomerie, to be no different from any other child of that age, and certainly of no greater intelligence.

Eventually, exactly one year after leaving Dehra Dun, Nain Singh reached Lhasa having counted every single pace of the way as well as taking innumerable clandestine compass bearings and other observations. He was to remain in the holy city for three months, hiring two rooms in a caravanserai particularly suited for making secret stellar observations. Having been away for so long, however, the money with which Montgomerie had provided him was now running low, and the resourceful pundit managed to supplement this by teaching Nepalese traders living in the capital the Hindu method of keeping accounts. It also provided him with a useful cover, behind which he set about completing the tasks which Montgomerie had set him.

First and foremost, he had to establish the precise position and altitude of the capital since neither of these was accurately known. This involved taking some twenty separate observations, both solar and stellar, enabling him to determine its exact latitude (the pundits were not trained in the far more difficult skills required for calculating longitude). Nain Singh's observations showed that Lhasa was located at 29 degrees, 39 minutes and 17 seconds. (Today's Times Atlas shows him to be less than two minutes out, putting it at 29 degrees 41 minutes). Altitude calculations based on boiling point thermometer readings showed the Tibetan capital to stand at 11,700 feet above sea level. This compares very favourably with the 12,000 feet generally given as Lhasa's altitude today, the discrepancy possibly being due to the readings being taken at different spots.

In addition to collecting scientific data, Nain Singh busied himself gathering more general intelligence, including a very detailed description of the town and its surroundings, its climate, agriculture, water supply, way of life, government and religious customs. These observations represented an important updating of what was known at that time. All the while, Nain Singh was having to live a cloak and dagger existence, hoping that no one would realise what he was really up to. His cover was, in fact, finally penetrated by two Muslim traders living in Lhasa who forced him to admit to them his true identity. But for reasons of their own they chose to keep their discovery to themselves, even helping the hard-pressed pundit with money.

Nain Singh was now beginning to get nervous, particularly after witnessing the public beheading, ordered by Peking, of a Chinese who had entered Lhasa without permission and was accused of stirring up trouble. He therefore made up his mind to leave at the earliest opportunity, and in the meantime moved his quarters and ventured out as little as possible. He had now completed all the tasks entrusted to him by Montgomerie – and more, for he had actually attended an audience with the Dalai Lama, then only a teenager, inside the Potala. Not many secret agents could claim to have penetrated, undetected, the sanctum of the Head of State, and sipped tea with him.

In a clandestine diary which he kept throughout his journey (only the compromising route survey details, it seems, were concealed in the cylinder of his prayer-wheel), Nain Singh describes being ushered into the throne room of the young God-King. The Dalai Lama, the twelfth, was seated on a throne some six feet high. On his right, on a lower throne, sat the Regent, for the Dalai Lama was then only thirteen and had not yet assumed his full sovereign powers. He was fated, moreover, to die mysteriously shortly after doing so. But although the Regent officially ran the country, Nain Singh reported that he was really under the thumb of the Chinese *amban*, Peking's representative in Lhasa. (This is disputed by Tibetan historians who claim – not entirely convincingly – that Manchu power in Tibet was by then minimal, that the *amban*'s functions were already reduced to attending official ceremonies, and that the small Chinese garrison was forced to earn its living by going from house to house performing lion and dragon dances.)

After drinking yak butter tea and an exchange of traditional white scarves and other gifts, the Dalai Lama placed his hand on the head of each of his visitors in turn before asking them three questions. But the pundit, with his guilty secret, need not have feared. If the God-King could read the secrets of all men's hearts, he showed no signs of having read Nain Singh's. His questions were merely about the health of each visitor's own ruler, the well-being of their country and their own health. With that the audience was over, the visitors being shown some of the rooms of the Potala, with their rich silks and golden sculptures, before departing.

In the middle of April, 1866, Nain Singh learned that the Ladakhi caravan he had accompanied to Lhasa was ready to return home, laden with quantities of Chinese tea purchased in Lhasa. The pundit, who had now been in the capital for more than three months, asked the caravan leader whether he might once again accompany them. To attempt the journey westwards by himself would have been too perilous for, as Nain Singh noted in his diary, the country was infested with brigands, all armed to the teeth. Safety for travellers lay only in numbers. Nain Singh was popular with the caravan men, and the Ladakhi readily agreed.

The five-hundred-mile march took over two months and followed the ancient Jong-lam, the great trade route which stretches across Tibet from east to west. For much of the way it forms the most elevated highway in the world, with an average altitude of 15,000 feet. Only at one point does it drop as low as 11,000 feet. During their journey the caravan was frequently passed by official messengers, riding hell for leather, carrying important mail. Nain Singh was told that these hardy men rode continuously, day and night, until they reached their destination, only halting to snatch a meal, change horses or ford a river. To ensure that they never removed their clothes, a seal was attached to the fastening of their overcoat which no one but the official to whom the messenger was being sent might break. The pundit had already witnessed the arrival of one of these express messengers at Lhasa after an eight-hundred-mile ride across Tibet from Gartok. The skin on his face was badly cracked, his eyes sunken and bloodshot, and his body raw from lice bites.

Once again, without any of his companions suspecting him, Nain Singh was able to pace every yard of the way and take the necessary secret observations for his route survey. Because the Jong-lam and the Tsangpo travel much of the way close together, he was thus able to map accurately the routes of both of these great arteries, the latter as far as its source near Lake Manasarowar. There, on June 17, 1866, he bade farewell to his Ladakhi friends who were continuing westwards. He now struck southwards, his mission completed, and headed for the nearest pass leading out of Tibet and into British India. But without the protection of his armed companions he was totally at the mercy of brigands and the lawless tribesmen roaming this wild frontier region. At one point he was seized and briefly held captive, but managed to escape, finally descending into British India, and safety, after an absence of one and a half years.

It had been a remarkable feat, and as an intelligence gathering operation highly productive. Montgomerie, who debriefed Nain Singh at Dehra Dun and later assimilated all his mileages, bearings, altitudes and latitudes into a map of this crucially important region of Tibet, was eulogistic. He wrote to Sir Roderick Murchison, then President of the Royal Geographical Society: 'I wish I could present the Pundit to you in person. I am quite sure he would make a good impression anywhere and I can quite understand his being an immense favourite with the Ladakhis who conveyed him into the sacred city. Without their assistance he would have found it a very much more difficult matter than he did, though it was difficult enough in every way. The Pundit I think deserves all praise, his work has stood every test capitally . . .'

Turning to the geographical achievements of Nain Singh, whose real name or identity he did not disclose even to Sir Roderick, Montgomerie reported that his latitude readings seemed to be extremely accurate, and that the position of Lhasa had now been fixed to probably 'well within half a minute of the correct value'. Its longitude, which he himself calculated from the pundit's route survey, was probably accurate to within a quarter of a degree, he thought. 'Considering the great distance traversed,' Montgomerie added, 'the longitude could hardly be much closer.' Nain Singh's figure of 11,700 feet for the altitude of the Tibetan capital was, he thought, 'some two or three hundred feet probably in default', a canny judgement in the event.

Nain Singh's route survey, during which he had walked some twelve hundred miles and counted two-and-a-half million individual paces with the aid of his rosary, had disproved the previously held belief that existing maps of Tibet might be correct in some respects. The pundit's observations, Montgomerie told Murchison, proved that the old maps were 'not even tolerably correct in latitudes'. So far as he knew, no observations had ever been taken in Tibet by any of the Jesuit missionaries.

One of the 'old' maps to which Montgomerie refers dates from the early eighteenth century and has an interesting history. Impressed by Jesuit mapping methods after seeing one they had made of the Peking region, the Emperor Kang-hsi invited them to survey the whole of his empire, including Tibet. Work commenced in 1708, and to collect topographical data from Tibet the Jesuits trained two lamas in surveying techniques. The result was the picturesque map of 1717 which was published in Paris in 1735 in D'Anville's famous atlas. Because the rest of the Jesuits' survey of China had proved to be remarkably accurate, it had hitherto been assumed that this might to some extent be true of their map of Tibet, even if it was not good enough for military and strategic purposes. Now Nain Singh, working under infinitely more difficult conditions, had finally exposed the failings of the so-called 'Lama Survey'.

Reminding Murchison that Nain's ancestors had been Buddhists, Montgomerie observed: 'You can easily imagine his feelings when ushered into the great Lama's presence with his prayer-wheel stuffed with survey notes and an English compass in his sleeve.' But finding that his thoughts had not been read by the all-seeing one, the resourceful pundit had even managed to measure up the Potala itself for his masters back at Dehra Dun.

Montgomerie and his colleagues, having created a superspy, were not now going to let him rest on his laurels. Within six months of his return to India, Nain Singh was sent off on another secret mission. This time it was to explore the legendary Tibetan gold-fields of Thok Jalung.

4. Panning for Gold
on the Roof of the World

Since earliest times the peoples of the Indian sub-continent had believed Tibet to be a land fabulously rich in gold. For most of the great rivers descending from the Tibetan highlands brought down gold dust, and for centuries those living beside them had panned the silt for the gleaming metal. This belief that Tibet was an Asiatic El Dorado can be traced back in Europe to Herodotus, 'the father of history', and the first writer in the West to refer to this shadowy land north of India. Some four centuries before the birth of Christ, he had written of 'great ants' living in the desert there which dug up heaps of sand full of gold. In fact, in neighbouring Ladakh gold was known as 'ant gold' until comparatively recently in the belief that these insects, in disturbing the earth to construct their ant-hills, sometimes left the nuggets exposed.

The British appetite for Tibetan gold had first been whetted in 1775 when the Panchen Lama sent Warren Hastings a gift of some gold ingots and gold dust. With Nain Singh's return from Tibet it now received a fresh impetus. For among the intelligence he brought back were reports of gold-fields in various parts of the country. Moreover, he had seen with his own eyes the many richly-gilded Buddhas and other golden objects in the temples of Lhasa and Shigatse. But he also learned that the Tibetans were reluctant to exploit their gold-fields because of a curious conviction that the nuggets contained life and were the parents of gold dust. Interference with the former, they believed, would terminate the supply of the latter and thus impoverish their country. If a nugget was excavated in error, it was immediately reburied. A similar superstition existed about silver, and Nain Singh heard of a Chinese who, not long before, had had his hands amputated when the authorities discovered that he had excavated quantities of silver ore from a hill four miles south of the capital. But the pundit also heard that, provided they were far enough away from the capital and other religious centres, certain gold-fields were allowed to be, and indeed were, exploited.

Montgomerie was determined to discover the truth about these fabled gold-fields. The nearest active ones, it appeared, lay near a small town in western Tibet called Thok Jalung. Provided one could get past the Tibetan border guards, this desolate region was most easily approached from Ladakh, to the west, and an area about which Montgomerie knew more than most men. For nine years he had been in charge of the Survey of India's map-making operations in Kashmir, including the Ladakh region. Altogether this embraced an area of some seventy thousand square miles, obstructed by mountains and, during much of the survey work, teeming with mutinous soldiery. But Montgomerie, without the loss of any lives, had successfully completed this crucially important map by 1864, thereby winning for himself the Royal Geographical Society's coveted gold medal.

But he knew better than anyone how vigilantly the Tibetans watched their frontier with Ladakh. For they were highly suspicious of the activities of the British surveyors just beyond the passes. He consequently decided to slip his men – this time there would be three – into Tibet via the 18,570-foot Mana Pass, once again in the guise of Bisahari traders. He chose as leader the brilliant Nain Singh, with his cousin Mani and a third, newly-trained, pundit as his companions. They reached the Mana Pass in June 1867 to find that it was still blocked with snow. They also learned that each year the pass had to be officially opened by the Tibetans after they had satisfied themselves that nothing untoward – like war, plague or famine – was going on at the Indian end. The following month the Tibetans formally opened the pass and the three pundits set off, together with eight retainers they had hired during their wait. They were well armed and prepared to fight off, if necessary, the bands of brigands who terrorised this wild and unpoliced region. At the frontier their baggage was thoroughly searched, but the Tibetan customs officers failed to find their clandestine surveying instruments.

Tramping through the desolate mountains towards Gartok, they crossed the Sutlej River by an ancient chain suspension bridge some seventy-six feet long which, local legend claimed, had been built by Alexander the Great more than two thousand years before. Seven feet in width and hanging forty feet above the raging waters, its great iron chains were forged from links one foot long and shaped like the figure eight. Every year, to prevent them from rusting, the chains were thoroughly lubricated with yak butter. Finally, after crossing two very high passes of more than 19,000 feet and another of 17,650, the pundits reached a large nomadic camp. Here, at first, the headman challenged their story that they were Bisahari traders selling coral and hoping to buy Tibetan shawl wool for the Indian market. But, with the help of gifts, the persuasive and resourceful Nain Singh managed to half convince him that they were genuine Bisaharis and to allow them to proceed. However, as a security against their return, they were forced to leave the luckless Mani behind as a hostage.

Once clear of the camp, Nain Singh dispatched the third pundit on a route survey as far up the Indus River as he could get, while he himself struck eastwards towards the rich gold-fields said to exist around Thok Jalung. As he neared this remote region, counting his every pace as usual, Nain Singh could hear the eerie sound of many voices chanting in the distance. These, it transpired, were the miners and their families singing to keep their spirits up as well as to keep warm on the barren, wind-swept plain. Although it was still only August, the pundit told Montgomerie afterwards that he had never experienced such cold in all his travels.

Fortunately the canny Nain Singh had taken the trouble to

discover in advance the particular partiality of the mine boss, an official from Lhasa. Even so, while clearly pleased with the pundit's gift of the finest quality Indian tobacco, he was extremely suspicious of his visitor, advising him to complete what business he had to do in town as quickly as possible and then depart. There was, he told Nain Singh, an order banning all Bisaharis from the region. But by a stroke of luck the mine chief's wife discovered that Nain Singh was trading in coral, for which she had a passion, and persuaded her husband to buy her some for gold. After this he became less suspicious of the pundit and talked freely with him about life and work in the gold-fields which Nain Singh's discreet calculations showed to lie at 16,330 feet above sea level.

Because of the terrible winds which ravaged this grim upland, the ragged miners lived in yak-hair tents pitched in specially-dug holes seven or eight feet below ground level. Their excavations, spread over a mile or so, were carried out with long-handled spades to a depth of around twenty-five feet. A small stream which ran conveniently across the site was used for washing the gold from the excavated soil. The Thok Jalung gold-field appeared to Nain Singh to be extremely productive, and he spotted one nugget weighing at least two pounds. He also noticed a number of abandoned gold-fields in the vicinity, and learned that there were many more of these between Thok Jalung and Gartok, some eighty miles away.

Nain Singh was told that any Tibetan who wished to might dig at the Thok Jalung gold-fields on payment of a prospector's fee to the government. He learned too that in winter the number of diggers, rather surprisingly, rose sharply to nearly six thousand from a mere three hundred in summer. The reason for this was that in summer the soil sometimes collapsed on top of the miners, making the work very dangerous, while in winter, being frozen, it was safer. But despite the grim living and working conditions, Nain Singh found the Tibetan miners a cheerful community, ever singing as they dug, their families joining in the choruses from a distance. On this treeless plateau the only fuel they had for cooking and for warmth was the dried dung from their yaks, ponies and sheep. At night they slept in that strange Tibetan posture – on knees and elbows, with their heads tucked in, and every extra piece of clothing they possessed heaped over them. In this land of perpetual cold, this curious habit was intended presumably to keep the more vulnerable parts of their bodies away from the deep-frozen earth.

Nain Singh was only able to spend four days at this weird Central Asian Klondike, for the mine boss, despite the entreaties of his coral-loving wife, refused to let him stay longer. But in that short time the pundit managed to collect for Montgomerie an amazing amount of intelligence. The price paid to the diggers for the gold, he learned, was low – less than thirty Indian rupees an ounce. It was paid for in silver, and its principal market outside Tibet was China. In return the Chinese sold large quantities of tea, for which the Tibetans have a remarkable appetite. Nain Singh found that they greatly preferred Chinese brick tea to the Indian variety, even though the latter was considerably cheaper, having to be transported less far. The diggers told him that they found Indian tea too 'heating', whatever that meant, and considered it fit only for the very poor. This was hardly encouraging news for British tea growers in Darjeeling who had long harboured hopes of replacing China as the principal source of tea for a people who drank anything up to fifty or sixty cups a day – albeit mixed with yak butter. In fact there was another obstacle in the way of their capturing this trade. The powerful Tibetan monasteries held a virtual monopoly of all tea coming in from China, and neither they nor the Chinese would have let their joint control of this highly lucrative market go without a bitter fight.

On August 31, 1867, Nain Singh left the dreary camp site and headed westwards to rejoin his colleagues, carefully counting his paces as always. All this time Mani Singh had been held hostage against the party's return, but the new pundit, Kalian, had meanwhile been carrying out his route survey of the Indus headwaters. Although he knew he was very close to its source, he had been forced to abandon his survey because of bandits. The trouble began when two armed robbers attacked his servant. Hearing his cries, Kalian had rushed to his assistance. A giant of a man, he seized one of the attackers by his pigtail and swung him round by it. The two bandits at once began to pretend that it was all a joke, before hastily making off. Kalian, although so close to his goal, feared that in this bandit-infested region reinforcements might appear, and decided to return to the rendezvous.

Their secret mission was now almost over, and Mani Singh having rejoined his colleagues, the three pundits and their servants turned for home. However, they took different routes, for Montgomerie wanted as much ground as possible to be covered while they were still within Tibet's forbidden frontiers. Nain Singh himself returned via the town of Gartok, which they had deliberately bypassed on their outward journey. Here he was alarmed to discover that someone was spreading word that he was a British spy, causing him to leave town in haste. Eventually, however, all three men were reunited, and made their way together through the Himalayas to India and safety.

The achievements of the three men, when evaluated in Dehra Dun, proved to be considerable. Apart from the wealth of intelligence which Nain Singh had brought back about the Thok Jalung gold-fields and the Tibetan gold industry in general, they had carried out route surveys totalling eight hundred and fifty miles. These enabled Montgomerie and his cartographers to fill in many of the blanks in an area of some eighteen thousand square miles and also to join the map of this little-known region of Tibet to that of Kashmir. They had taken one hundred and ninety latitude observations at seventy-five different points and calculated some eighty altitudes. Because they had found it obscured by cloud, they had not been able to measure the altitude of Kailas, a mountain sacred to all Buddhists. But Montgomerie and Colonel Walker were well pleased with the three pundits, even if Mani Singh had still failed to achieve the brilliant showing of his younger cousin.

So successful were these clandestine explorations proving that Montgomerie, with the help and advice of Nain Singh, began to recruit and train other pundits, all of them literate hill tribesmen of exceptional intelligence, and often related to one another. But now Walker and Montgomerie did something positively mystifying. Although, as we have seen, absolute secrecy was obviously essential to the success of these illicit and politically sensitive infiltrations, in January 1868 Walker sent to the Royal Geographical Society for publication in their journal a detailed account of Nain Singh's first great journey. The actual document which he sent, and which lies today in the society's archives, was nothing less than Montgomerie's full official report of his man's clandestine trip. It is clear that this was done with Montgomerie's knowledge and approval, for Walker's letter is followed shortly by one from Montgomerie which nowhere asks for any part of his report on Nain Singh's mission to be censored or suppressed.

Thus, in the next issue of the *Journal of the Royal Geographical Society*, the secrets of the pundits were revealed to all and sundry, including their bogus prayer-wheels, doctored rosaries, concealed sextants, measured strides and their use of disguises and cover stories. In view of the ingenuity, time and patience devoted to the training of the pundits, as well as the inventive genius of the Dehra Dun workshops, this elementary yet massive breach of security is hard to understand. Not only were the pundits' own lives thus put at risk, but so too were all future operations. How then can it be explained? Other secret journeys, including Nain Singh's visit to the Thok Jalung gold-fields, were also soon to be publicised in this way. Although we are not privy to Montgomerie's reasoning, there are a number of arguments which can be put forward to justify this seemingly foolhardy policy.

For a start, the pundits' names or identities were never disclosed, but merely their code names of which they sometimes had more than one. Furthermore, hundreds if not thousands of pilgrims and traders came and went through the Himalayan passes every month, making the detection of the rare pundit less likely. Also the *Journal of the Royal Geographical Society* was not on public sale but distributed to Fellows only. However, the society's membership was international. Russian soldiers, explorers and geographers read the *Journal* avidly – at least one Tsarist traveller in Tibet was to be awarded the society's gold medal – just as their British confrères followed the Russians' professional literature. But although they were rivals in Central Asia, it was not in the Tsarists' own interests to tip off the Tibetans or Chinese about what the British were up to. For St Petersburg too was trying to penetrate this closed land and uncover its secrets. To the Russians the *Journal* was an invaluable source of intelligence on Tibet and Asia generally. So long as it continued to publish the details of these clandestine journeys along with maps derived from the pundits' endeavours St Petersburg remained happy.

The Chinese, on the other hand, would have every reason to try to prevent Montgomerie's agents from carrying out secret intelligence work in a country which they regarded as part of their empire. But it seems that they never found out about it. Although they had a Legation in London, it would appear that they did not read the *Journal*, or even know that it existed. However, it only needed one busybody to draw their attention to these highly irregular goings on for instructions to be sent to all Tibetan frontier posts to check prayer-wheels, rosaries – as well as travellers' chests for false compartments. To publish the results of the pundits' route surveys was one thing, but to reveal in detail exactly how it was done appears to be taking an unwarrantable risk with men's lives, not to say the missions themselves. In fairness to Montgomerie, it should be added that the pundits were not on the payroll of India's military intelligence service (which did not even exist at this time) but on that of the largely army-run Survey of India. But there is no other word for what they were doing than spying. They were sent, at considerable risk to their lives, to gather intelligence of any kind that was going, especially of roads and passes which would be of vital importance to the military in the event of hostilities. Had they been caught by the Tibetans or Chinese they would certainly have suffered the fate of all spies.

The 1870s were busy years for the pundits, now increased in numbers to almost a dozen. There is not space here to follow them all as they crossed and recrossed vast tracts of unknown Tibet, endlessly pacing and counting. But two remarkable journeys stand out. The first, which was to last four years, began in 1878. It was, ironically, the year of Montgomerie's death. Broken in health, he had died in England at the age of forty-seven, but not before he had seen his protégé Nain Singh win the Royal Geographical Society's gold medal for having 'added a greater amount of positive knowledge to the map of Asia than any other individual of our time'. But this time it was not Nain Singh who won the acclaim and admiration of fellow explorers.

Only twenty-one and the youngest of the pundits when first recruited by Montgomerie some six years previously, Kishen Singh – code name 'A.K.' – had already completed two successful missions when he was dispatched by Walker, now a General, on what would turn out to be a marathon route survey of nearly three thousand miles. His target was the then unknown north-eastern corner of Tibet around Koko Nor lake, close to the Chinese and Mongolian frontiers. Delayed for a whole year at Lhasa while waiting for a caravan bound for this barren wasteland (their owners being unwilling to reveal to strangers when they were planning to leave for fear of alerting bandits), Kishen Singh used this time to prepare by far the most detailed map of the Tibetan capital yet seen. He also studied Mongolian which was to prove valuable when finally he managed to attach himself and his servant-companion to a north-bound caravan of Mongolians, all heavily armed against expected attack by the inevitable brigand bands roaming this lawless region.

After travelling for several weeks across the utterly desolate

Chang Tang, Tibet's great northern desert, the party was suddenly attacked by a band of two hundred armed bandits. Although outnumbered by two to one, the Mongolians managed to drive off the marauders. But the unfortunate Kishen Singh, who was posing as a trader, lost all his baggage animals and most of the goods he had purchased in Lhasa for sale in the north. Miraculously his survey instruments survived. Although almost penniless, the pundit was determined to press on with his companion. Twice he was forced to enter service in order to eat, once looking after a Tibetan trader's camels and another time tending ponies and goats for five months. At times nearly destitute, he and his faithful servant-companion continued northwards, eventually penetrating as far as the Chinese oasis town of Tun-huang in the heart of the Gobi desert and well beyond the frontiers of Tibet. Here, among the dunes, lie the famous Caves of the Thousand Buddhas where Sir Aurel Stein was to stumble on a long-lost library more than a quarter of a century later. But at the time of the pundit's visit the caves were known only to Buddhist pilgrims. Not content with getting this far, and counting every pace of the way, Kishen Singh and his companion pressed on northwards into the desert towards Lop Nor where nearly a century later the Chinese were to test their first nuclear weapons.

Now for the first time their movements began to attract suspicion. Shortly after leaving Tun-huang they were overtaken by a horseman with orders from the Chinese governor to return. Although he never discovered their surveying instruments, he strongly suspected them of being spies and held them virtually prisoners for seven months. By a stroke of luck, however, a prominent Tibetan lama whom they knew arrived at Tun-huang as a pilgrim to the sacred caves. He managed to obtain their release by offering to take them with him as servants on his six-hundred-mile journey home. On reaching his monastery they had to wait two months before being paid for their services, but finally they arrived at the town of Tachienlu, on Tibet's eastern border. Here the two weary and penniless travellers were taken in by Catholic fathers who ran a small mission on the Tibetan-Chinese frontier.

Kishen Singh had concealed on him a letter of introduction from General Walker to the priest in charge of the mission. This priest, whom the pundit took into his confidence, gave his guests money and sent a message to Walker by a fellow priest who was visiting India to say that they were alive and well. The news was gratefully received by the pundit's anxious family, for it was now four years since they had heard from him, and a horrifying rumour had reached them, that he had been arrested as a spy by the Tibetans and had had both his legs amputated to curtail his activities. General Walker too had heard these reports and had been making enquiries through Nepalese and Kashmiri contacts in Lhasa when the priest's message reached him that the pundit was on his way back to India.

Continuing their still unbroken route survey along the Tibetan-Chinese frontier, the two men eventually reached the then little-known and wild south-eastern corner of Tibet where the great rivers of the uplands drop through the Himalayas to the plains below. At one point they found themselves within thirty miles of British territory, yet dared not cross. For this was the domain of the murderous Mishmi, a tribe with an evil reputation for treachery. They had killed the French missionaries Krick and Boury in 1854 after promising them safe passage, not the last travellers to perish in this lawless region. Instead, the pundit and his companion turned westwards and headed for northern India. But even now their troubles were not over, for shortly after passing a Tibetan penal settlement they were seized on suspicion, due to their ragged appearance, of having escaped. Once again they owed their release to the fortuitous arrival of an influential acquaintance prepared to vouch for them. This was the second time they had been arrested since their release from Tun-huang, for not long before they had been held on suspicion of being thieves. Only miscreants, they were told, travelled at this time of year. Enquiries had fortunately shown that no crimes had been committed which could be pinned on them, and they were freed.

Finally, some four and a half years after setting out on his marathon journey, Kishen Singh reached Darjeeling. Throughout a march of 2,800 miles the pundit had maintained an unbroken route survey covering vast, previously unknown and unmapped tracts of Tibet. This meant that Kishen Singh, with the aid of his rosary, had counted some five and a half million paces. It was an astonishing performance, calling for incredible determination and devotion to duty, not to mention extraordinary courage. General Walker recalled the return of Kishen Singh and his faithful servant Chumbel in a paper later read before the Royal Geographical Society.

'They arrived in a condition bordering on destitution, their funds exhausted, their clothes in rags and their bodies emaciated with the hardships and deprivations they had undergone . . . But, though worn and weary, they were triumphant.'

Not only did Kishen Singh return with all his route survey notes, despite the many tribulations which had befallen him, but also with his surveying instruments, including the bulky sextant, intact. But it proved to be a costly adventure for him personally. He got back to discover that his young son had died during his long absence and that his home had broken up. His health had suffered severely from the months of privation and hardship, and for a time it was doubted whether he would survive. As a final blow, the gold watch which the Royal Geographical Society had given him in recognition of his remarkable exploits was stolen. But perhaps the accolade which he would have most valued came years later when Colonel C. H. D. Ryder, who subsequently became Surveyor-General of India, travelled some one hundred and twenty miles along Kishen Singh's route survey and found, using more sophisticated instruments, that the pundit's results came within a mile of his own.

*   *   *

But for sheer devotion to duty nothing can eclipse the story of Kintup, or 'K.P.', who was sent into Tibet by Captain H. J. Harman of the Survey to try to establish once and for all whether or not the Tsangpo flowed into the Brahmaputra after it disappeared into the Himalayas. This was to be done by the simple expedient of floating specially marked logs down it and waiting to see where they turned up. For observations brought back by Nain Singh from his first journey into Tibet had pointed to the probability of the two rivers being one and the same. The results of Kishen Singh's survey virtually proved this, but when Kintup set out in August 1880 Kishen was still in Tibet, and by then presumed dead.

For reasons which are not clear, Captain Harman chose a Chinese lama living in Darjeeling to lead the expedition. Kintup, posing as his servant, was to accompany him as his assistant. Although he could not read or write he had twice accompanied other pundits in this role and had shown himself to be highly reliable and intelligent. Their instructions were to follow the Tsangpo as far eastwards as they could and then, starting on a certain date and at the rate of fifty a day, throw into it five hundred marked logs, each a foot long. But Harman, it quickly transpired, lacked Montgomerie's intuition when it came to judging men. For long before the two men reached the Tsangpo the lama had begun to fritter their funds away on women and drink, wasting four precious months in dalliance at one village alone. He also treated Kintup, himself a devout Buddhist, with contempt and at times brutality.

Eventually they arrived on the banks of the Tsangpo and began to work their way down it. The further eastwards they travelled the harder the going became. Before long the lama had secretly decided that he was not cut out for this sort of work. Telling Kintup he was going off for two or three days, he instructed his assistant to await his return at the home of the village headman. Before long, when the lama failed to return, Kintup discovered the horrifying truth. His colleague had sold him to the headman as a slave and was now on his way home to China.

After working for his new master for several months, Kintup managed to escape, immediately heading for the Tsangpo determined to complete his mission. But close to the monastery of Marpung he was overtaken by pursuers sent by the village headman with orders to drag him back. In desperation Kintup appealed to the abbot of the monastery, falling at his feet and pleading that he was a poor pilgrim who had been treacherously sold into slavery by his companion. The abbot took pity on him and bought him from the headman for fifty rupees, on condition that Kintup refunded this by working for him for an agreed period. He turned out to be a kindly employer, so after a while Kintup asked for leave to make a pilgrimage to a sacred mountain which he knew lay further down the Tsangpo. The abbot readily agreed.

When, many months later, Kintup reached the remote spot from where he and the lama were to have released the logs, he painstakingly set to work to prepare them. He had managed somehow to obtain a saw and also to secrete, despite his misadventures, the special tags with which Harman had provided them. Finally, after hiding them in a cave, he returned to his master. There was no point in releasing the logs until he could get a message to Harman warning him to have the Brahmaputra watched. The only possible way to do this was to send a letter from Lhasa. But how could he get there? After working patiently for a further two months, Kintup asked the abbot if he might go on another pilgrimage. Once again the abbot agreed, and Kintup set out for the Tibetan capital. On arriving there, being illiterate himself, he got a Sikkimese he knew to write the following letter to a pundit, now living in Darjeeling, with whom he had once worked. He asked that it be passed at once to the Head of the Survey of India.

'Sir [he reported], The Lama who was sent with me sold me to a village headman as a slave and himself fled away with Government instruments that were in his charge. On account of this the journey proved a bad one. However, I Kintup have prepared five hundred logs according to the order of Captain

Harman, and am ready to throw fifty a day into the Tsangpo from Bipung in Pemako from the fifth to the fifteenth of the tenth Tibetan month of the year called *Chuluk* . . .'

The letter was to be carried to Darjeeling by the wife of his Sikkimese friend, and Kintup returned to his master for a further nine months. Then, as the date approached when he was due to release the logs, he again asked if he might visit the sacred mountain by the Tsangpo. This time, gratified at the devotion of his servant, the abbot granted Kintup his freedom. Heading back to his secret store by the river, the pundit released the logs, fifty at a time, over ten successive days. He had now completed his mission in the face of every conceivable obstacle and was free to make his way back to India.

On reaching home after four years' absence, he was to receive a series of blows. First he learned that his mother had died, believing him also to be dead. Next he found that his message had never reached the Survey of India as the pundit to whom he had sent it had died. His months of devotion to his British masters had thus been in vain. The five hundred logs, so laboriously prepared, had merely floated unnoticed down the Brahmaputra and out into the Indian Ocean. In any case, the Tsangpo-Brahmaputra riddle had by now been solved. Worst of all, many people simply did not believe Kintup's amazing story, and he sank back into obscurity, his devotion unrecognised and unrewarded. But there remained in the files his dictated account of his travels, a mass of topographical detail. Nearly thirty years later, after travelling extensively in the little-known area which Kintup had described, a British frontier officer, Colonel Eric Bailey, realised just how accurate his account was. Convinced that Kintup had been telling the truth all along, Bailey managed to track him down, finding him working as a tailor in Darjeeling. He lobbied hard for him to be granted a pension. This was refused, but he was given instead a lump sum of a thousand rupees. Very soon after this Kintup died, still obscure but vindicated.

*   *   *

Nain Singh and Kishen Singh, the most successful of the pundits, were both awarded small pensions and grants of land. Nain Singh's pension cost the Indian Government little enough considering the value he had been to them, for he died in January 1882, not long after returning from one last secret journey through Tibet before his retirement. But Kishen Singh, despite his broken health, lived to enjoy for some thirty-five years both his pension and the revenues from the small Himalayan village of Itarhi. He died only in 1921 – 'accurate, truthful, brave and highly efficient', his personal file declares – the last survivor from this great era.

Just what would have become of these extraordinary heroes had they not been simple Indian hillmen but Englishmen? This question was asked, and answered, by a distinguished American scholar and traveller as long ago as 1891. William Rockhill, who was to make two adventurous and illegal journeys through Tibet himself, wrote in his book *The Land of the Lamas*: 'If any British explorer had done one third of what Nain Singh . . . or Kishen Singh [he lists others] accomplished, medals and decorations, lucrative offices and professional promotion, freedom of cities, and every form of lionisation would have been his. As for those native explorers, a small pecuniary reward and obscurity are all to which they can look forward . . .'

What then drove men like Nain Singh, Kishen Singh and Kintup to perform such prodigious feats and take such grave risks for their British masters? Was it simply the inspirational leadership of officers like Montgomerie and Walker? Was it perhaps the feeling of belonging to an élite of some kind which engendered an *esprit de corps* in these hillmen, each one of whom knew that he was hand-picked? It is unlikely that we shall ever know, for everyone connected with the pundits is now long dead. The last of these, Colonel Bailey, died in 1967. He had known several of the one-time pundits when a young political officer, and two of them had sat on the board which examined and passed him for his Tibetan language examination. Although in his memoirs he expresses great admiration for these explorer-spies – and no one was more qualified to appraise their work than he, in his day both explorer and spy – nowhere does he ask this question. Perhaps, as a man of duty himself, he just accepted it as normal.

But one man did raise the question – and attempt to answer it. He was Sir Richard Temple, a former Governor of Bengal and an experienced Himalayan traveller, who knew as much as anyone about the pundits. Following a talk by General Walker to the Royal Geographical Society on the achievements of Kishen Singh, he declared: 'Had he been an Englishman he would have possessed the stimulus afforded by a liberal education. Had he been an Englishman he would have looked forward to returning to his native land where the applause of the public, the thanks of Parliament and the gracious approval even of the Sovereign would have awaited him. But what had this poor man to look forward to?'

To his audience Sir Richard's answer was a comfortable one and no doubt sincere, even if it fails to be wholly convincing. Yet it is difficult to think what else it was that drove these men to perform such astonishing feats of endurance and loyalty. He went on: 'Not to those honours which afforded an honourable stimulus to British enterprise, but only this – his zeal for the department he served, his obedience to so good a superior as General Walker, his loyalty to the public service, his firm determination to do his duty according to his poor ability and, above all things, his reliance upon the British Government which he knew would reward him generously should he survive, and would take care of his family should he perish.'

What, one wonders, would Kintup, who for no reward besides his meagre pay, endured hardship and hazard so willingly and cheerfully, have made of that? Today, sadly, the pundits are all but forgotten, not merely in Britain but even, it seems, in their own homeland. When I wrote to the present Director of the Survey of India seeking further information about these one-time employees I received no answer. In my letter I explained that I hoped to honour the pundits' memory, if only in print, before a world that knew little, if anything of them. Perhaps my letter never reached Dehra Dun. On the other hand perhaps the pundits are something of an embarrassment to the Indians in the post-colonial era. For they were, after all, the heroes, not so much of India, as of the British Raj.

Whatever the true place of the pundits in Asian history, there is no doubt that their clandestine journeys across the roof of the world whet the appetite of other travellers. And before very long an international race was to begin for Lhasa, the most mysterious city on earth.

5. The Race for the
Holy City Begins

If the gatecrashers were determined to get in, the Tibetans were equally determined to keep them out. The dreadful retribution meted out to a Tibetan official who had unwittingly given assistance to one such intruder is grim proof of this. He was arrested, imprisoned, flogged, then flung – still living and with his hands tied behind his back – into the Tsangpo. The hands and feet of his servants had been cut off, their eyes gouged out, and they were then left to die in agony. Furthermore the official himself, a high-ranking lama at the head of a monastery, was condemned posthumously to eternal damnation – a punishment more to be dreaded than death by a devout Tibetan Buddhist. When, soon after his execution, his reincarnation appeared in a small boy, the child was callously abandoned. Frontier officials who had let the intruder past the check-point were also severely punished, and nineteen years later two other men who had been implicated were still in chains in a Lhasa dungeon.

The gatecrasher who caused all this trouble was Sarat Chandra Das, immortalised in *Kim* as Hurree Chunder Mookerjee. Posing as a pious Buddhist scholar, although actually on the British payroll and a Hindu, he twice visited Tibet, first in 1879 and again in 1881. Unlike the other pundits, he was a highly educated Bengali, and he brought back a wealth of political, economic and other intelligence, largely confided to him by unsuspecting Tibetan officials. But after his return to India the story of his subterfuge leaked out and the Tibetans soon learned of it – with the terrible results described above.

Until the British and Tsarist empires had begun to expand

into Central Asia, the Tibetans had never had cause to fear the white man. Those few European travellers who crossed their frontiers were regarded merely as objects of wonder, curiosity or simply of amusement. Of far more concern were the warlike Gurkhas from neighbouring Nepal, who by the middle of the eighteenth century were raiding across the frontier in search of plunder. But in 1792 this threat was removed for ever when an invading Gurkha army was put to flight and massacred by a seventy-thousand-strong Chinese punitive expedition.

Soon the map of Central Asia began to change, however. Not only was the Tsarist war machine swallowing up, one by one, the khanates around Samarkand and Khiva, but British India too was creeping northwards towards Tibet. The strategic aim of Britain, in fact, was relatively innocent – to form a series of buffer states, or a *cordon sanitaire*, between the wealth of India and possible trouble from the north. But it can hardly have seemed like that to the Tibetans who, when they realised what was happening all around them, began to feel gravely threatened by these great new Asiatic powers.

The Chinese, they knew, were in no position to help them against the modern weapons of these powerful newcomers, as they had against the primitively-armed Gurkhas. From now on, the Tibetans realised, they would have to protect their own frontiers. The foreigners, or 'fringies', the authorities in Lhasa warned their local officials, were up to every sort of trick. They insinuated themselves into a country on which they had their eye, stirred up trouble for the authorities, and then annexed it. The Chinese, themselves trying desperately to hold together a disintegrating empire and every bit as anxious about these new imperialists, deliberately played on these Tibetan fears, telling them that it was the British who had instigated the Nepalese invasion. It was after this that Lhasa decided to close its frontiers to all Europeans and non-Asiatics.

From now on Tibetan xenophobia began to feed on two principal fears. First there were their gold-fields, which the Panchen Lama himself had innocently drawn to the attention of

Warren Hastings, and on which Lhasa was now convinced the British had designs. Secondly, and far more alarming to the Tibetans, was the threat to their religion which, the Chinese told them, the British and Russians were aiming to destroy. This explains the Tibetans' obsessive fear of missionaries and their particular determination to keep foreigners out of Lhasa, their holy capital.

But none of this was to deter those adventurous travellers who, largely inspired by the success of the pundits, had set their sights on entering Tibet and, if humanly possible, on reaching Lhasa. Indeed, the more difficulties strewn in their path, the more alluring the challenge seemed to become. Among British frontier officers the desire to visit this mysterious but forbidden land on their very doorstep was to become 'an occupational disease', according to a historian of the period. Moreover, the hopes of all would-be travellers to Tibet must have been momentarily encouraged by the reassuring words of one misguided British consul based in western China. After reading an account of Nain Singh's secret journey in 1865, he wrote an angry letter to the Royal Geographical Society which appeared in their journal. In it he declared: 'It is to be regretted that the Topographical Department of India, under a mistaken supposition that the Chinese Government dislikes foreigners to travel in their country, have thought it necessary to send agents across the Chinese frontier to make surveys in a clandestine manner, instead of openly.'

He assured travellers that entering this region of the Chinese Empire (and it is clear that he meant Tibet) was 'perfectly easy and safe for British subjects', provided they possessed Chinese passports permitting them to do so. The infiltration of pundits in disguise, and without such passports – he added – 'must tend to excite suspicions in the minds of the Chinese injurious to the friendly and confidential relations which have now subsisted for several years between the British and Chinese governments.' That there was no love lost at this time between British officials in China and those of the Raj is well known. But in giving this most misleading advice to intending travellers, the consul had clearly swallowed the official Peking line – that the Chinese controlled Tibet.

The British Indian Government soon showed itself to be every bit as gullible. Following the murder by tribesmen of a British official travelling in Yunnan, the embarrassed Chinese had reluctantly agreed to grant passports for an official British overland mission to Lhasa. In fairness, it appears that even Manchu officials in Peking believed that their rule still prevailed across the length and breadth of Tibet. The fact that it no longer did was hardly something that the Chinese *amban* in far-away Lhasa was going to admit to Peking in a hurry, since this would have cost him his lucrative office, if not his head. If Peking was aware of the true state of affairs in barbaric Tibet, which officials regarded as a hardship posting, then it is just possible they never really believed that anyone could seriously want to visit Lhasa. If so they were in for a shock. For while the official British mission to Lhasa was to get no further than the frontier – for reasons which will be seen – there would be no shortage of contestants in the race for the Tibetan capital.

They came from nine different countries, and made their approaches from almost every point of the compass. All except one – a Japanese – were white, and all were individuals of exceptional determination and courage. Three of the most intrepid were women. None of them for a moment doubted their right to gatecrash Tibet – least of all the first contestant to cross the starting line, Colonel Nikolai Prejevalsky of the Imperial Russian Army.

A professional to his fingertips, he was to make two all-out attempts to reach Lhasa. Already, in the winter of 1872, while the pundits were still secretly filling in the blanks on British maps, he had made a first exploratory foray into the ill-guarded northern regions, penetrating as far as the headwaters of the Yangtze before being forced back by the rigours of winter. Harsh as this journey had proved (it cost Prejevalsky some fifty-five camels and twenty-four horses), the allure of this strange land and the bizarre adventures which befell him there made him determined next time to reach Lhasa.

On their very first day they had been charged by Chinese cavalry who were supposed to be engaged in hunting down bandits. When the Russians had stood their ground, and were seen preparing to shoot, the Chinese veered away, explaining afterwards that it had all been an unfortunate mistake. The following day the Russians spotted a hundred bandits lying in wait for them. Prejevalsky's Mongol caravan men wanted to turn back, but he had threatened to shoot anyone who did. His obvious lack of fear, and his modern weapons, so unnerved the ambushers that the explorer, a legendary marksman with a rifle, and his party had passed by unmolested.

Word soon spread that Prejevalsky was a *khubilgan*, or saint, on his way to see the Dalai Lama. As he entered one village, two hundred Tibetans had knelt in prayer, and the colonel was expected to bless the sick and predict the future. It was rumoured too that he had one hundred invisible warriors protecting him, and they had no further trouble with brigands. Prejevalsky had wanted to press on to Lhasa, but by now his party was suffering severely from exposure and hunger, and their clothing was in tatters. Finally they had only eight ounces of silver left, enough to buy one sheep. Prejevalsky wrote in his diary: 'We have absolutely no supplies left . . . The privation is terrible.' Sorrowfully, he decided to head for home. But next time he determined to head straight for Lhasa.

Six years were to pass before he set out on the first of his two attempts to reach the capital. This time he was well prepared. By now he was a legend in his own country, with high connections in St Petersburg, and for this expedition he had obtained the backing of the Tsar who personally ordered the Treasury to give him ten thousand silver roubles and as many paper ones. Nor was he going to take any truck from bandits this time, being accompanied by an escort of seven carefully chosen Cossacks, all expert rifle shots, who had sworn to go through 'fire and water' with him. Perhaps the foremost scientific explorer of his day, he took a mass of instruments and other apparatus with him, including more than a thousand sheets of blotting paper for preserving plant specimens. He also carried gifts for local officials whose goodwill they might need. These included coloured pictures of Russian actresses which went down particularly well with the recipients. Finally, before setting out in the Spring of 1879, the party spent some time in rifle practice and working out defensive tactics in case they were attacked. Each member of the thirteen-strong expedition was armed with a rifle and a revolver, and between them they carried nine thousand rounds of ammunition, plus loose powder and bullets for making more. If need be, they would shoot their way to Lhasa. But this, Prejevalsky was confident, would not be necessary. For he had obtained, through the Tsar's personal influence, a Chinese passport for Tibet.

The journey through Tibet's great northern mountain ranges and on to the high Chang Tang was uneventful. But once, when they failed to find a pass they wanted, we glimpse the imperious and ruthless Prejevalsky in action. He simply rode down two passing Mongol horsemen and threatened to shoot them unless they guided the party through the pass. Having served this purpose they were then set free.

By now alarming rumours had begun to reach Lhasa of the Russian expedition's advance towards the capital. Prejevalsky, these claimed, was coming, as spearhead of a Tsarist invasion force, to kidnap the Dalai Lama and carry him off. It was a somewhat less saintly role than that ascribed to him six years before when villagers had knelt in his path. But the mood of the Tibetans had changed much since then, and their xenophobia had become more intense. Their foreign policy, if it can properly be called that, now had two aims. One was to try to undermine any remaining authority of the Chinese *amban*, and the other to resist by every possible means any attempt by foreigners to enter the country. Indeed, the country's priestly hierarchy had sworn a solemn pledge to that effect, and the moment it was learned in Lhasa that the Russian party had crossed their northern frontier and was heading rapidly for Lhasa, they resolved to act first and notify the *amban* afterwards.

The first Prejevalsky knew that trouble lay ahead was when he learned from a passing caravan that there was uproar in the capital over his advance. Warrior monks, he was informed, had been mobilised with orders to bar his way, while villagers had been warned that anyone selling him food would be executed. By chance, the pundit Sarat Chandra Das was travelling in Tibet at this time and recorded the event in his secret diary. Three thousand warrior monks had been sent north to lie in wait for the Russians, he was told. As a learned man from India he was questioned as to whether he thought the Tsarists were planning to invade Tibet, and had tried to reassure his questioner, pointing out that such a move would involve the Russians in a war with the armies of the Chinese Emperor.

So it was that when only one hundred and fifty miles short of Lhasa, Prejevalsky was halted by two Tibetan officials who asked him to proceed no further but await instructions from the capital. Prejevalsky, armed with his Chinese passport and still believing that he would be able to talk his way past this obstacle, complied, setting up camp beside a stream. After a wait of nearly three weeks he was informed that a special envoy had arrived from Lhasa. But the news he brought was a bitter blow to Prejevalsky who had staked so much – not least his reputation – on this expedition. The orders from the Potala were that there could be no question of his being allowed to advance any further, and that he and his men must leave Tibet at once.

When Prejevalsky flourished his Chinese passport and protested that he had the Emperor's authority to travel to Lhasa, the Tibetans replied that they did not take their orders from the Chinese but only from their own Government. According to the Tibetan version, recently unearthed by an Italian Sinologist from among contemporary documents, the Russians had claimed that they were not westerners but 'subjects of the Heroic White Sovereign' – the Mongol name for the Tsar.

Their Emperor, they said, had informed the Chinese Emperor of their intention to visit Tibet. 'Why,' they had asked, 'do you prevent us?' The Tibetans had replied: 'All the laymen and monks of this Tibet of ours have frequently had sad experiences when we extended kindness to foreigners. Together we have sworn a sealed covenant not to allow foreigners to enter Tibet.'

The argument continued until sunset, the Tibetans repeatedly stating their case and the Russians theirs. But Prejevalsky now realised that he was beaten. Even with his crack Cossack escort and their high-velocity rifles he could not seriously expect to fight his way to Lhasa, still nearly a week's march to the south. He had no choice but to accept Lhasa's verdict. But first he demanded a written document signed by the Tibetan officials present, and stating their reasons for rejecting his Chinese passport and refusing to allow him to proceed to Lhasa. Only if they produced this would he agree to turn back. Otherwise, he warned, he would continue his march towards their capital the very next morning. According to the Tibetans he had added: 'Even if one thousand soldiers and ten thousand horses were pitted against us, we thirteen shall not be afraid.' But the Tibetan officials produced the document (even if it did not bear the signature of the Chinese *amban* as Prejevalsky had at first demanded) and the disappointed Russians struck camp and departed, vowing that they would tell the whole world how barbaric and unfriendly the Tibetans were.

Thus the great Prejevalsky had failed to achieve his dream of years, and the ill-armed Tibetans had successfully tweaked the nose of the Russian bear. It would not be Prejevalsky's last attempt to reach Lhasa, but that too was destined to end in failure. Just four years later, at the age of only forty-nine, the Russian explorer – by now a Major-General – would die after drinking typhoid-infected water. He was buried by his devoted Cossacks on the shores of Lake Issik Kol, high in the Tian Shan mountains, and the Tsar ordered the nearby town of Karakol to be renamed after him. And so it remains to this day – Prejevalsk – a memorial to this Central Asian Livingstone and immortal Russian hero. Meanwhile the race for Lhasa continued.

* * *

But if this great explorer, with his armed Cossack escort and the mighty backing of the Tsarist Government, had failed twice to reach Lhasa, what hope, it might be asked, had anyone else of getting there? However, this is to underestimate both the extraordinary allure of Lhasa and the determination of the men and women who set their hearts on reaching it. But these were early days still, and the race had not yet opened to all comers. Prejevalsky had been no Central Asian freebooter out for glory, but a government man, his intelligence reports read avidly by the Imperial General Staff back in St Petersburg. It was still the turn of governments. The Russians had tried and failed, and now it was the turn of the British, their principal rivals for the hearts and minds, and possibly the gold, of the Tibetans.

In 1876, it will be remembered, the Chinese had agreed to grant passports for a British overland mission to Lhasa – albeit with extreme reluctance. The agreement, signed at Chefoo in China, had envisaged the mission setting out the following year. However, nine years were to elapse before Calcutta finally decided to take up this option – the first serious attempt to break the century-old deadlock in Anglo-Tibetan relations since the Panchen Lama's overture to Warren Hastings in 1774. The decision had followed the return of the Bengal Government's Financial Secretary, Colman Macauley, from a fact-finding mission to the Tibetan-Sikkimese frontier. There, using Sarat Chandra Das as his interpreter, he had held talks with a local Tibetan official, the *jongpen* (magistrate), who had assured him that Tibetans were only too anxious to trade with their giant southern neighbour. British manufactured goods, including textiles and cutlery, would be welcomed in exchange for gold and raw wool. Only the most conservative elements of the lamaist establishment, Macauley was persuaded, would be likely to resist such a move, and they could be bought off with suitable gifts.

Macauley returned enthusiastically to Calcutta where he penned a glowing report on Anglo-Tibetan trade prospects. This appeared at the very moment when pressure was building up, particularly in the textile industry at home and also among the Himalayan tea planters, for an opening up of the Tibetan market. Although lukewarm about the idea himself, the Governor-General of Bengal, Lord Dufferin, had agreed – under pressure from his Government at home – to mount a combined economic and political mission to Lhasa. To lead it he chose Colman Macauley.

The mission, armed with its reluctantly supplied Chinese passports, gathered in Darjeeling early in 1886, ready to march through Sikkim and up the Chumbi Valley to Lhasa, a route regularly used by pilgrims and Himalayan traders. Accompanying it were experts in a number of fields – including a geologist to investigate the gold-mining prospects – while Macauley had taken the precaution of purchasing expensive and impressive gifts with which to help smooth the way. His interpreter once again was Sarat Chandra Das, a man of remarkable ability, but a tactless choice in view of Tibetan fury over his earlier activities in their country on behalf of his British masters. There was to be an escort of three hundred Indian troops, later considerably reduced, but too late to dispel Tibetan – and even Chinese – fears that this was the spearhead of a British annexation force. For at no stage had the Tibetans been consulted.

But the Macauley mission never left British India. On the very eve of its departure it was suddenly called off. Bitterly disappointed, Macauley, whose brainchild it had been, never recovered from the shock, dying four years later at the age of only forty-one, his health broken. The eleventh-hour decision to abort the mission was made by the Cabinet in London who now realised that it would be resisted by the Tibetans. Macauley, it seemed, had been hoodwinked by a minor Tibetan official who did not speak for Lhasa. Just what the latter's motives were will probably never be known, but he had certainly told the Englishman what he had wanted to hear.

Unhappily, events had now taken on a momentum of their own. When the authorities in Lhasa learned of the mission gathering on their doorstep, they had immediately assumed that the British were mounting the long-feared invasion which would destroy their religion and replace it with Christianity. For nobody had thought to inform them, it appears, that the enterprise had been called off. The state oracle in Lhasa was consulted with the result that troops were rushed to the frontier ready to repel the intruders. In fact, a deal had already been struck behind the scenes between the British and the Chinese whereby London agreed to abandon the mission in return for Peking accepting Britain's annexation of northern Burma. Although Lord Dufferin felt that this trade-off with the Chinese was the better bargain, British public opinion was outraged at the abandonment of the mission. For this, it was argued, would be interpreted by Lhasa as weakness.

As though to confirm this, the Tibetans now moved their troops forward to occupy a strategic hilltop some eighteen miles inside Sikkim, and actually visible from Darjeeling. This well-chosen position commanded the line of advance which Macauley's mission would have taken. In London and Calcutta this was viewed as a hostile and highly provocative act. To the Tibetans, however, Sikkim was a vassal state of theirs and they had every right to be there. Certainly they did not recognise any treaties signed between Sikkim and Britain as valid. Immediately, in press and parliament at home, there were angry demands that the Tibetans should be expelled by force from what was regarded as British suzerain territory. But because the British Government still regarded Tibet and the Tibetans as under Peking's control, attempts were made first to try to get the Chinese to force them to withdraw. When a year later the Tibetans were still occupying the hilltop, an ultimatum was sent to their commander warning him that unless he withdrew by a stated date he would be expelled by force. The ultimatum was returned unopened. A month before it was due to expire, a similar warning had been sent to the Dalai Lama. But there was no reply.

There was nothing for it now but to use force. For on receiving the ultimatum, the Tibetans had rushed two generals, a minister and nine-hundred reinforcements to the front line. The British, in their turn, assembled two-thousand troops and four field guns at Kalimpong. In the meantime, the Sikkimese ruler worked feverishly to try to avert bloodshed on his terri-tory. But his efforts were in vain, and on the eleventh day of the second month of the Earth-Mouse Year, on the Tibetan calen-dar – March 21, 1888 on our own – the first ever clash between British and Tibetan troops took place. Never before had Tibe-tans, largely armed with matchlocks and swords, had to face modern weapons in the hands of a highly trained and disci-plined enemy. Inevitably it was a rout.

The ill-led Tibetans were easily driven from their positions, fleeing back across the border. But although totally out-matched, they still had stomach for the fight ('truculence' and 'insolence' were the words used to describe their courage at the time), and twice tried to reoccupy their positions. The second time they managed, in one single night and under cover of darkness, to build a defensive wall some three miles long and three to four feet high, only to be driven back across the frontier the following morning. This time they did not return. British casualties were one officer killed and three other ranks wounded. The Tibetans lost some two-hundred dead and twice that number wounded. It was scarcely a victory the British could be proud of. Considering they had started out with the hope of winning Tibetan hearts and minds, not to say their trade, then everything had turned remarkably sour. But Calcut-ta did not press home its advantage, and Tibet was momentarily written off.

If the British now dropped temporarily out of the race, there was no shortage of unofficial contestants only too anxious to get there. In Peking at that moment, making careful preparations for his attempt, was an American whose dream it had been to reach the forbidden city ever since he was a schoolboy.

6. Four Dreams of Lhasa

William Woodville Rockhill decided that only by stealth would a westerner ever reach the Tibetan capital. To attempt to seek permission to go there from either the Chinese or the Tibetans would be clearly futile, as the luckless Macauley had discovered. Nor, as the Russians had found, would bluster get you there, even if this was backed with modern weapons. The only successful trespassers had been the pundits, and they had gone in disguise and only after two years of intensive preparation. Rockhill decided to do the same.

A young American attaché at the Legation in Peking, he had an unusual background. Brought up in Paris and educated at St Cyr, the military academy, he had served for a while as an officer in the French Foreign Legion. Already speaking Chinese, he now set about learning Tibetan. At first he had difficulty in finding a Tibetan in the Chinese capital willing to teach his language to a 'foreign devil'. But eventually he managed to win the confidence of a lama from Lhasa, and for the next four years – from 1884 to 1888 – he studied under him.

Rockhill was convinced that his best hope of crossing secretly into Tibet was from the remote north-east. Here the frontier with China was vague and ill-guarded and the population sparse. But to venture there would be to take his life in his hands. Unlike Prejevalsky, he would be only lightly armed and unable to defend himself if attacked by the bandits who made their living plundering caravans passing through this lawless region of desert and mountain. To try to enter the country from the south, on the other hand, would be hopeless. The Tibetans were by now fully aware of the past activities of the British pundits, and the passes from India were more closely watched than ever. However good his Tibetan, Rockhill knew he would never be able to talk his way past the border guards after the terrible punishments meted out to their unfortunate colleagues who had allowed Sarat Chandra Das to slip into Tibet. But even if he did manage to cross the unguarded northern frontier without being spotted, he realised that he would quickly be denounced and arrested when he entered more populated parts if it were suspected for a moment that he was a westerner. He had one trump card, however. Few Tibetans had ever seen a western face. He decided therefore to wear Chinese costume, hoping that his non-Asiatic features might be taken as belonging to one of China's many minority peoples.

So it was that in the winter of 1888 Rockhill resigned his post at the American Legation and set out on the first stage of his journey westwards. This was the gruelling, thousand-mile march to Lanchou, astride the ancient Silk Road, from where he hoped to embark on his clandestine crossing into Tibet. 'My outfit was simple and inexpensive', he wrote afterwards in *The Land of the Lamas*, his account of his journey. 'For dressing and living like a Chinaman I was encumbered neither with clothes nor foreign stores, bedding, tubs, medicines nor any of the other endless impedimenta which so many travellers consider absolute necessities.'

Taking with him one tried and experienced Chinese servant who the year previously had accompanied Lieutenant (later Sir) Francis Younghusband on his celebrated ride across the breadth of China, he left Peking by mule-drawn *mappa*, the country's high, two-wheeled cart. He got the owner to agree that for every day that the journey exceeded the normal thirty-four, a small sum would be deducted from the cost, while he would pay the owner the same amount for every day gained. In the event everyone was happy, Rockhill getting there two days earlier than he had expected.

Rockhill's westward march towards Tibet took him through

desperately poor parts of central China overrun by groups of
armed peasants driven to banditry by hunger. Everywhere he
came upon police posts and military patrols as the Manchus
struggled vainly to maintain law and order. The journey was to
provide the American with plenty of lurid material for his book,
today almost forgotten except among experts on Tibet. In one
small town he came upon a troupe of what he describes as
'sing-song girlies' who travelled from inn to inn entertaining
guests with their three-stringed Chinese banjos. The Chinese
euphemistically called these girls, most of whom had been sold
by their parents into slavery, 'wild flowers'. But they were
hardly to Rockhill's taste, being 'ugly, dirty, powdered and
rouged' and usually mere children.

At one point he halted briefly to allow a grisly caravan to pass.
Led by four mounted soldiers, it consisted of five open carts,
each bearing a heavy wooden cage. In each of these there
crouched a man – if the poor creature could be so described –
his hair long and matted and a chain around his neck and body.
All five were wearing red rags, a sign that they were destined for
execution. Two of them, Rockhill was told, had been brought
all the way like this from the furthest corner of Chinese Central
Asia, four months away, merely to be beheaded in their native
province. Another town he passed through was swarming with
convicts, iron collars around their necks and heavy chains
attached to their limbs. Several, who had tried to escape from
this curious open prison, had logs shackled to their legs.
Everywhere Rockhill saw people smoking opium in an attempt
to alleviate life's hardships. The American found himself
wondering whether in such a region as this the habit was
necessarily a bad thing. In a land where there was insufficient
food to go round, it seemed illogical to condemn it on the
grounds that it destroyed men's appetites.

Every night they halted at one of the many Chinese inns along
the road. These were invariably built to the same plan – a large
open courtyard where horses were unsaddled and carts parked,
and surrounded on four sides by buildings. Rooms for guests

took up two sides, stalls for horses and mules occupied the third, while the kitchen, restaurant and the innkeeper's quarters formed the fourth, usually fronting onto the street. Each room had a *kang*, the traditional 'stove bed' of China, heated from underneath by means of glowing coals fed in through an aperture in the outside wall. The noise when the inn was full was deafening, with everyone shouting orders from his room to the hotel staff who replied likewise. As dishes were cooked, the chef screamed out their names. Adding to the hubbub were the altercations of the carters, the squealing of pigs and other livestock in the yard outside, and the braying of the mules in the stalls.

Rockhill reached the walled city of Lanchou, from where he planned to begin his secret journey into Tibet, without misadventure. Here he paid off his carters and bought himself a pony. He also hired three mules to carry his baggage, in which was concealed surveying equipment. His Chinese servant, one can only assume, walked. On arriving at Sining, the last town in China, he received his first fright. Three policemen called unexpectedly at his inn and told him to report to the Chinese magistrate who he was, what his business was and where he was proposing to go.

Alarmed, Rockhill decided to move on as quickly as possible, for he knew that this magistrate, one Se-leng-o, had previously been the *amban* in Lhasa. Moreover, he was known to be strongly anti-foreigner. Were he to get an inkling of the American's intentions, then the whole plan to reach Lhasa would have to be scrapped. To confuse any pursuers, Rockhill added to his disguise by shaving both his head and face and donning a Mongol fur hat and gown before leaving the inn. But he need not have feared, for there was no pursuit, and soon he found himself entering a sort of no-man's-land between China proper and Tibet. Although nominally under Peking's authority, there was little sign of any Chinese presence. Rockhill's companions on the road were now sheepskin-clad Mongols on camels and horses, or lamaist priests in red or yellow robes. Everyone seemed to be heading towards, or coming away from, the great Tibetan monastery of Kumbum which lay just within the frontiers of China, or so the Chinese claimed, and near which the present Dalai Lama was born.

Apart from wanting to visit this famous lamasery, with its golden spires and roofs, Rockhill hoped to solve once and for all the mystery of its miraculous tree whose leaves, it was said, bore Tibetan characters of deep religious significance and after which Kumbum – meaning 'Ten Thousand Images' – is named. After visiting Kumbum nearly half a century earlier, the Lazarist priest Evariste Huc had written of this tree: 'Our eyes were directed with earnest curiosity to the leaves, and we were filled with an absolute consternation of astonishment at finding that, in point of fact, there were upon each of the leaves well-formed Tibetan characters, all of a green colour, some darker, some lighter than the leaf itself . . .'

But Rockhill was to be disappointed, for the tree was leafless. Huc had reported that its bark also bore Tibetan characters, but of these the American could detect no sign. Leaves which had been shed by the tree in the autumn were being sold to the pilgrims by the lamas, but these were so dried up and crumbling that Rockhill could make out nothing on them in the way of characters. Nonetheless he was assured by local Muslims – a reasonably neutral source – that images were indeed to be seen on the living leaves.

In all, the American stayed a month and a half at Kumbum posing as a pilgrim and gathering material on the Tibetans and their religion for his book before moving on towards his real goal. During this time no one had challenged his right to be there or questioned him about his country of origin. Although local people painted a harrowing picture of the desert road ahead, torn by sandstorms and plagued by murderous bands of Tibetans, Rockhill's prospects of reaching Lhasa now looked promising. They seemed still more hopeful when a lama whom he had known in Peking, far from denouncing him, introduced him to other monks who suggested that in view of his interest in their religion he must visit Lhasa. They assured him that once across the desert his problems would be over. His lama friend even agreed to provide him with a guide.

But suddenly his friends seemed to get cold feet. First, the guide found by the lama sent a message to Rockhill saying that he could not accompany him, but adding that a replacement would be arriving shortly. When the latter did turn up, however, he brought word from the lama warning Rockhill that even if he crossed the desert safely, the moment he and his men were discovered in Lhasa they would certainly be put to death. This disturbing message was delivered to Rockhill, perhaps deliberately, in front of the men whom he had just recruited, though only after great difficulty, to accompany him. 'It was a crushing blow,' he wrote, 'after what I had been telling them about the absence of danger.'

After several days of persuasion, the American managed to cajole them into coming with him, and the following week was spent hiring camels and purchasing stores for the arduous journey ahead. But then the guide himself informed Rockhill that he was not prepared to accompany him even on the first stage of the march, let alone all the way to Lhasa. The American did not attempt to argue with him but instead sent a message to the lama chiding him for 'sending an old friend such a white-livered wretch'. Undeterred by this setback, Rockhill now set out across the desert with what remained of his small party, but not before receiving a message from the lama (who seemed curiously reluctant to see him) informing him that his erstwhile guide had been beaten and incarcerated. While offering profuse apologies for the guide's behaviour, the lama offered no explanation for his own. As a peace-offering, however, he sent Rockhill some food and a huge Tibetan mastiff to protect him, but no guide.

For the next two months, in face of ever increasing obstacles, Rockhill pressed slowly on towards Lhasa, lying more than seven hundred miles away to the south-west. Everywhere people tried to discourage him from proceeding further. The last foreigner who had tried to reach Lhasa, the abbot of one monastery told him, had never been seen again. This tale, of which Rockhill heard more than one version, could only refer to Prejevalsky. But he was also assured, more worryingly, that a large party of Russians – seventy-five in all and led by a man with a long beard – had beaten him to Lhasa. He was never able to discover the source of this story.

Rockhill learned too of the British punitive expedition against the Tibetan force which had invaded Sikkim. To try to resist this, he was told, the authorities in Lhasa had recruited large numbers of peasants from Chamdo in eastern Tibet and rushed them south, assuring them that the bullets of the *Ingi-li* – the English – would not harm them because of the incantations which the lamas would be reciting on their behalf. In the first clash, Rockhill learned from his disillusioned informants, a number of these Chamdo warriors had been killed or wounded. The survivors, he wrote, 'had then and there started back for their homes, and left the lamas to fight their own battles as best as they could.'

Gradually the difficulties facing Rockhill accumulated to the point where they became insuperable. The harsh, north-eastern route to Lhasa may have seemed the most promising, but because of the enormous distances involved and the need to have one's own caravan, it also proved to be extremely expensive. At last, some six months after leaving Peking, and less than four hundred miles from his goal, Rockhill knew that he was beaten, for he did not have enough money left to continue towards Lhasa. Disappointed, he turned south and made his way home via the Chinese-Tibetan borderlands. Thus the first of the individual travellers had failed to reach the forbidden city. But Rockhill was not a man to give in easily. In less than two years he was to make another attempt to get there, again from the north-east. This time he was to get to within one hundred and ten miles of Lhasa – closer than Prejevalsky and his Cossack escort – before being turned back by the Tibetans. But neither of his journeys was wasted. From each he brought back a wealth of valuable material on Tibet and its people, and to this day his scholarship is greatly respected by Central Asian scholars. And if it was to be any consolation to him, like his Russian predecessor Rockhill was awarded the gold medal of the Royal Geographical Society for his daring journeys. Later, in a distinguished diplomatic career, he went on to be American Minister in Peking and subsequently ambassador to St Petersburg and Constantinople.

*   *   *

Meanwhile, in the winter of 1888–89, while Rockhill was still vainly trying to reach Lhasa, an adventurous English clergyman had arrived in Ladakh from where he hoped to gatecrash Tibet by means of a ruse. This new contestant was the Reverend Henry Lansdell, a veteran Central Asian traveller who had already visited Samarkand and Bokhara and itched to go east again. When the idea first occurred to him he was living quietly in Eltham, in south-east London, where he was vicar of St Peter's.

'How would it do,' he wrote in his book *Chinese Central Asia*, published on his return, 'if I asked the Archbishop of Canterbury to give me a letter to the Dalai Lama, then go to the frontier, pose as an English lama bearing a communication from the Grand Lama of the West to the Grand Lama of the East, and ask for permission to enter the country and deliver my message?'

The necessary funds were speedily raised by his parishioners and other enthusiasts for the idea of a one-man Church of England mission to Lhasa led by this experienced traveller. The Archbishop of Canterbury, also fired by the idea, wrote the following letter to his opposite number in the Potala.

'This is to certify that the Reverend Henry Lansdell, Doctor of Divinity and Fellow of the Royal Geographical Society, a learned and excellent clergyman of the Church of England, and a traveller of great distinction, is, with my full knowledge and approbation, undertaking a journey through the regions of Central Asia and China; his journey, however, having no political, military or commercial object whatsoever.

'If therefore it should be possible and agreeable to the authorities to grant Doctor Lansdell special facilities for visiting the ancient city of Lhasa and other places of interest and importance in Tibet, I shall esteem it a kindness, tending to promote the fuller knowledge of another's welfare which is to the good of the various nations of the earth.'

Lansdell had the letter, which bore the Archbishop's seal and signature, mounted on yellow satin. It was then rolled up like a scroll and placed in a satin-lined red morocco case. This, in its turn, was packed in a tin cylinder to protect it on its rugged journey to India and – hopefully – beyond. In November 1888, Henry Lansdell reached Leh, the Ladakhi capital, and immediately set about seeking a reliable native traveller who would undertake to carry the all-important letter and deliver it personally to the Dalai Lama. But he was out of luck, for everyone knew that to attempt what Lansdell was asking was to invite almost certain death.

Like most Central Asian travellers, Lansdell was not easily discouraged. He vowed 'not to stop till I am convinced that it is not God's will that I should go further.' Moving to Kalimpong, at the other end of the Himalayas, he tried again, but with no success. Nor was he any more successful in Kathmandu. So, after distributing quantities of Christian literature to the Nepalese, he moved on to Calcutta from where he took a steamer up the China coast to Tientsin. From here he travelled inland to Peking with the Archbishop's letter. Evidently the British Ambassador had been warned that this determined cleric was on his way, for Lansdell found a message awaiting him inviting him out to the embassy's summer residence in the Western Hills but warning firmly that 'it would be out of the question' to ask the Chinese for a passport for Tibet for him. Not that it would have got him within five hundred miles of Lhasa. The clash between British and Tibetan troops had only just taken place, and under no circumstances were the Tibetans going to allow an Englishman to cross their border, whoever he carried a letter from (and they could hardly have been expected to know who the Archbishop of Canterbury was).

Fearing perhaps that Lansdell might try nonetheless to reach Lhasa, it was firmly pointed out to him by the Ambassador that such an act might seriously worsen Anglo-Tibetan relations. With negotiations in progress over the future status of Sikkim, these were currently in a most delicate state, it was explained to him. This was too much for poor Lansdell. The hazards of Central Asian travel were something he had bargained for, but not this. If his own government was as opposed to his going to Lhasa as the Tibetans appeared to be then he might as well abandon the idea. 'I forthwith gave in and hauled down my colours, saying that of course I would desist,' he wrote afterwards. 'For if only as an Englishman I could not think of being so unpatriotic as to allow a little private scheme of my own devising to hamper or be a cause of hindrance to negotiations of such importance . . .'

The Ambassador, no doubt relieved to hear this, suggested that Lansdell should leave the Archbishop's letter with him. Once the Sikkim affair had been settled then he might be in a position to do something for Lansdell. In view of what followed, it would seem that he never had any serious intention of pursuing Lansdell's interests, but merely thought it wise to relieve him of the letter. For without this the clergyman was in no position to make any further attempt to reach Lhasa.

Lansdell travelled slowly homewards, every now and again writing hopefully to enquire how things were progressing. Here and there he picked up bits of news about the progress of the Sikkimese negotiations. In Hong Kong he was heartened to learn that British troops had now been withdrawn from the Sikkimese frontier. But there was still no word from Peking. It was only when Lansdell reached Jerusalem that his last hope of becoming 'the only European now living' to enter the Buddhist holy city was finally dashed. It came not from Peking but from

Calcutta, in the shape of a letter from the Viceroy's office. It informed him that although the Sikkim-Tibet troubles had been satisfactorily resolved, 'His Excellency did not consider the moment opportune for endeavouring to procure facilities for travelling in the latter country.' He therefore regretted that he was unable to be of any assistance to the vicar of Eltham. There was nothing for it now but for Lansdell to make his way homewards. It had been a singularly easy victory for the Tibetans, and the score now stood at three-nil in their favour.

*   *   *

Undaunted by the failure of a Russian, an American and an Englishman to reach their goal, a fourth contestant in the race for Lhasa was already on his way. This time it was a Frenchman, the seasoned Asiatic traveller Gabriel Bonvalot, and a far more determined gatecrasher than the easily rebuffed Lansdell. Although scientific geographers of the day did not take Bonvalot very seriously (at a time when route surveys were *de rigeur* his maps were extremely hazy) no one questioned his courage or enterprise. He had already made two major Central Asian journeys, visiting Samarkand and Bokhara and crossing the icy Pamirs into India. He now set his sights firmly on Lhasa, determined to be the only living white man ever to have been there. Like everyone else who aimed to visit the forbidden city, Bonvalot believed that only he knew the secret. His theory was that one's plans must at all cost be kept secret, not merely from the Tibetans, but also from the Chinese. To apply for a passport, as Prejevalsky had, was lunacy, for it simply alerted the enemy. As he explained afterwards in his book *Across Thibet*: 'The Mandarins would have given us the warmest letters of recommendation and then, as soon as our itinerary was known, would have sent orders for every sort of means to be used to stop us on the road and compel us to turn back.'

Accompanied by the young Prince Henry of Orleans, whose father had contributed handsomely to the expedition, and

Father Dedeken, a Chinese-speaking Belgian missionary, he decided to enter Tibet from the extreme north. This meant that they had first to storm the towering Altyn Tagh, part of Tibet's great northern bastion, before gaining the Chang Tang. Such was Bonvalot's obsession with secrecy that he kept their real destination even from his two companions. Prince Henry, a passionate sportsman, and Father Dedeken, himself no slouch with a rifle, thought they were embarking on an exploring-cum-shooting trip across northern Tibet, and would then make their way across China before catching a boat home.

Crossing the Altyn Tagh in mid-winter brought hardship and death to the expedition. Even before they had reached the altitude of Mont Blanc, almost everyone was suffering from mountain sickness, with several of the caravan men bleeding from the nose. The two-humped Bactrian camels, they quickly found, were unable to ascend sharp inclines when fully loaded, but kept sitting down and obstructing the narrow trail for those following behind. Thus the baggage at times had to be carried by the men themselves, while the protesting beasts had frequently and brutally to be flogged to their feet. In some of the steepest parts, they even had to be hoisted up bodily with ropes. The caravan men, unused to such conditions, soon began to express their fears, both for their own lives and for those of their valuable beasts. Cruel winds, blizzards and sub-zero temperatures brought continuous hardship to both Europeans and natives as they struggled ever on upwards towards the great Tibetan plateau.

One of the caravan men now became seriously ill and had to be strapped unconscious to a camel. Bonvalot knew that his only hope of survival lay in descending to a lower altitude, but there could be no question of this, for the way ahead climbed still higher. Although the man's fate was already sealed, it was hastened by a callous act of the caravan leader. In a fit of temper he released the ropes attaching the sick man to the camel, and as a result the man fell heavily onto the frozen ground. Furious, Bonvalot was momentarily tempted to shoot the caravan leader,

for the dying man was one of the most liked and best of his
party. Finally, at 17,000 feet and in the middle of a blizzard, the
man died. It was two days before Christmas 1889, and to keep
the wolves from eating his remains they managed to dig a
shallow grave in the rock-hard earth. As Father Dedeken
prayed over his lonely resting place, all three Europeans found
themselves crying over the loss of this simple, trusting companion, their tears freezing on their cheeks and forming icicles
on their beards.

By now they were through the Altyn Tagh and up on the
Chang Tang. Since they had no guide, Bonvalot's plan was to
follow the old pilgrim route, marked in some places only by
camel droppings or the skeletons of yaks from earlier caravans.
At times snow and rain reduced visibility to no more than a few
yards, and they had to steer their way forwards by compass,
hoping to pick up the trail further on. Now that they were safely
in Tibet Bonvalot broke it to his companions where their real
destination lay. Young Prince Henry had already guessed and
was full of enthusiasm. Father Dedeken, although doubtful
whether they would succeed, agreed to press on. In reality he
had little choice.

Despite all their hardships, they were still well supplied with
fresh meat, for there were enough wild yak and antelope about
for their needs. However, owing to the altitude, cooking had
become extremely difficult. But their biggest worry was fodder,
and some of the animals began to die from starvation and
exposure. At halts they had to hobble their famished camels to
prevent them from eating their saddles. It was now January
1890, and on one cruelly cold night Bonvalot recorded temperatures of forty-eight degrees below zero. Two of their horses died
and one of the caravan men developed frostbite, 'with one of his
big toes almost dropping off and his sores so dreadful that it is a
wonder he can keep on his horse'. Bonvalot knew that the man
was doomed.

Their advance towards Lhasa had so far gone unnoticed by
the Tibetans. Perhaps they had not dreamed that anyone might

be rash enough to try to cross the Chang Tang in mid-winter. But then, early in February, Bonvalot and his companions encountered their first Tibetans. Initially these were friendly although curious. They were fascinated by the ticking of Bonvalot's watch, and impressed by the party's revolvers. They tried to discourage Bonvalot from advancing towards Lhasa, but he ignored this and pressed on, having learned that it was only twelve marches away. But gradually resistance to their advance grew as the Tibetan intelligence system woke up to the fact that a foreign party was approaching. Had his men not been on their last legs, Bonvalot would have been tempted to make a dash for it. He wrote afterwards: 'If we had a few vigorous and determined men we might, by a *coup de main*, seize as many of the Tibetans' horses as we required, load them, and march direct on Lhasa.'

By February 12 things had got so bad that the three Europeans decided to do just that, although in vain. The Tibetans, realising what they were planning, galloped off, but too late to stop one of their horses and two of their men from falling into Bonvalot's hands. They also left their arms behind, so frightened were they by the sound of the Frenchman's revolver as he emptied it over their heads. He describes in his book how the elder of the two hostages, an old man, sat looking dazed and terrified. Periodically he would stick his tongue out at his captors, the traditional Tibetan greeting, and offer them gifts of powdered cheese and dried meat from his pathetic little store of provisions which he kept in innumerable small bags. To show him they meant him no harm, Bonvalot and his companions gave him sugar to suck. To judge from his obvious satisfaction, it was clear that he had never tasted it before.

The following day the frostbitten caravan man died, to the great sorrow of everyone. 'We all liked him,' wrote Bonvalot. 'For if he was rough of speech, he was good-hearted, plucky and a hard worker.' They buried him beside the trail, covering his grave with large stones to discourage the wolves from digging him up. Everyone shed tears as once again Father Dedeken prayed over the grave. Meanwhile, keeping the older man hostage, they had released their other prisoner after explaining to him that they wished to pay for the horse they had seized as well as to buy others. But soon realising that this was hopeless, they now decided to press on to Tengri Nor, a sacred lake only a hundred miles or so from Lhasa. The old man, laden with presents, was set free and the Tibetans' primitive arms were returned to them as a gesture of goodwill. Successfully reaching the lake, they again pressed on towards the capital, their caravan now reduced to only two horses. Ahead lay a mountain range, and Bonvalot wrote in his diary that night: 'We may well ask if we shall ever be able to cross this seemingly insurmountable barrier, and our spirits do not rise when night sets in and the wolves commence their sinister chorus.'

But the decision was not to be theirs, for some ten miles south of the lake they were finally forced to halt by a large body of armed Tibetans who included officials from Lhasa. The latter, despite Bonvalot's denials, seemed convinced that he and his companions were either British or Russian, whom they clearly regarded as their enemies. Days of parleying were to follow, with the Tibetans insisting they leave the country by the way they had come. Realising that any hopes of reaching Lhasa – whether by force, bribery or persuasion – were now futile, Bonvalot argued that with his men and beasts in such pitiful condition, it would be suicidal for them to attempt to retrace their steps across the Chang Tang. He proposed instead that they head eastwards towards China, though only if the Tibetans would first supply them with fresh horses.

The Tibetans finally agreed to allow him and his companions to leave for China via Batang, far to the east, and to provide them with fresh horses (trained, incredibly, to eat raw meat). Thus, exhausted and disappointed, they turned sadly away from Lhasa and made their way slowly eastwards. They had been beaten, just ninety-five miles from their goal. But Bonvalot at least had the satisfaction of knowing that he had got closer to the holy city than any of his rivals, even than the great

Prejevalsky with his formidable escort of Cossack marksmen. Considering how ill-prepared they had been for the cruel Tibetan winter, it was indeed an astonishing feat of courage and endurance by all three men, not to say by their stoical caravan men. But the Tibetans had won yet again.

*　　*　　*

In the summer of 1891, two young Indian Army officers set out from Ladakh to cross secretly and illegally into Tibet. Ostensibly – that is to all except certain senior officers in Calcutta – it was simply an adventurous journey by two soldiers who chose to spend their leave trailing dangerously and uncomfortably across the Roof of the World. But documents to be found today in the Foreign Office archives tell a very different tale.

The two travellers were Captain Hamilton Bower and Surgeon-Captain W. G. Thorold. It was not the first adventure to have befallen Bower in the wilds of Central Asia. Already, while still only a subaltern, he had twice in one year made a name for himself there. In 1889, while on a shooting expedition in Chinese Turkestan, he had been ordered to hunt down and bring to justice a huge Afghan who had brutally hacked to death the young Scottish explorer Andrew Dalgleish on a lonely mountain pass. Native agents recruited by Bower had eventually trailed the killer to Samarkand where he was apprehended. But in the course of the murder hunt Bower had learned of an ancient manuscript which native treasure hunters had found in a ruined mud temple. Bower purchased this and dispatched it to Calcutta where it caused an immediate sensation among scholars. For it pointed to the existence of a long-lost Buddhist civilisation lying beneath the deserts of Chinese Central Asia. It was this find – known to scholars as the Bower Manuscript – which led to the six-nation race for the Buddhist art treasures of the Silk Road.

Bower's Tibetan venture, ostensibly a shooting expedition like his previous Central Asian foray, with a little surveying

thrown in, was in fact sanctioned at the highest level in Calcutta – by none other than the Viceroy himself and also the
Commander-in-Chief. Its true purpose – to see what was really
going on in Tibet, and if possible Lhasa – was so secret that
even the British Minister in Peking, Sir John Walsham, was not
told the truth when he was asked to obtain Chinese passports for
Bower and Thorold for areas abutting on Tibet. A letter from
the Viceroy to Sir John, now in the Foreign Office archives,
explains the purpose of Bower's mission to him thus: 'Russian
and other foreign travellers have shown much activity of late in
this direction, and it is considered desirable to obtain information regarding their proceedings as well as a knowledge of the
country itself.'

Nowhere does the Viceroy even hint that the two officers
would be heading straight for Tibet (which makes one wonder
why they wanted a Chinese passport), or that they would be
accompanied by a trained pundit, Atma Ram, whose task it
would be to pace every yard of their journey across Tibet. The
Minister was requested to tell the Chinese 'as much or as little
regarding Mr Bower's movements and intentions as may
appear, in your judgement, to be expedient.' In other words, as
little as possible. Considering how little he himself had been
told, this was not difficult. When eventually he discovered the
truth he was understandably angry, for at the best of times there
was little love lost between Whitehall's representatives in China
and those in India. One can only assume that he was deliberately kept in the dark because, had he known what was afoot, he
would have moved heaven and earth to prevent this two-man
invasion of Tibet from going ahead with its potential threat to
Anglo-Chinese amity.

But whatever the explanation, on July 3, 1891 the two officers
crossed unnoticed into western Tibet accompanied by Atma
Ram, an orderly, a cook and six locally recruited caravan men.
It had not been easy to find the latter because of Bower's
unwillingness to reveal their destination. He knew that once
word reached the Tibetan traders in the bazaar at Leh that he

was proposing to cross into Tibet the game would be up.

The days and weeks which followed, as they rode ever eastwards across the desolate Chang Tang towards Lhasa, were filled with incidents and misadventures of the kind so familiar to all Tibetan travellers. Perpetually soaked to the skin – although it was mid-summer – from blizzards, hailstorms, sleet and rain, they were deserted by their guides, lost animals from exposure, got lost themselves, suffered from hunger and thirst and from the uncomfortable effects of the great altitude. At times the heavy snowstorms made all movement impossible, while at others visibility was so poor that they had to steer by compass. But although stretched to the absolute limit, Bower and Thorold pressed determinedly and uncomplainingly onwards as one would expect from military men. Beside them all this time walked Atma Ram, the pundit, patiently counting his paces as he had been taught at Dehra Dun. For none of this part of Tibet had been surveyed before, the existing maps merely showing it as a huge blank expanse with the one word 'unexplored' written across it.

Since crossing the Tibetan frontier, now some seven hundred miles to the west, they had encountered no signs of resistance to their advance. For the last four hundred miles they had not seen another soul, so barren was this great plateau. Rarely had they camped below 16,000 feet. But towards the end of August, as they found themselves at slightly lower altitudes, they encountered a group of Tibetan nomads from whom they tried to buy meat, since their own food supplies were running perilously low, and also to hire guides. But the Tibetans were suspicious, and the two caravan men Bower had sent forward to negotiate returned empty handed. At one point, the nomads had opened fire on them with their matchlocks, luckily hitting no one – except one of their own horses. However, the two men returned with an important piece of intelligence. Lake Tengri Nor, from where Bower hoped to strike south to Lhasa and where Bonvalot had been turned back some eighteen months earlier, was now only ten days' march away. But without accurate maps or the help of guides the problem was to find their way there.

A day or two later they ran into another party of herdsmen. Although they flatly refused to supply guides, explaining that they would be severely punished if they did, they agreed to sell supplies to Bower's men, provided they were satisfied that there were no Europeans in the caravan. To be quite sure of this, two of the Tibetans rode over to Bower's camp with the sheep and other provisions. Fortunately one of the caravan men managed to ride ahead of them in time to warn the two Englishmen to don their disguises. 'By the time they arrived,' wrote Bower afterwards, 'Dr Thorold, in ragged native garments and holding a pony, looked as unlike a member of the medical profession as it is possible to look.' Bower, with similar alacrity, had transformed himself into a Muslim trader. Their Tibetan visitors then saluted them by thrusting out their tongues – 'a mode of salutation I had never seen before,' wrote Bower, 'but I promptly thrust out mine.' Having satisfied themselves that there were no Europeans around, the visitors handed over the supplies and departed. But after this close shave, Bower and Thorold decided from now on to travel in disguise.

Tibetan suspicions were now beginning to focus on this curious caravan heading towards their capital. One morning, as Bower and Thorold were breakfasting English style, a strange Tibetan appeared unexpectedly in the camp. The two officers at once dived into their tent, fortunately without being seen, while the intruder was hurried off to the tent of the *caravanbashi* where he was plied with tea. But he asked a lot of awkward questions, and they now found themselves being shadowed by small groups of Tibetans as they travelled. Annoyed, Bower halted and told them through one of his men who spoke Tibetan that he had a passport (not saying that it was not for their country), and added sternly that they must not follow him any further. This appeared to succeed, though not before he had ascertained from them which trail led to Lhasa – or so he thought. It was not until the following day that they realised they had been fooled, and put deliberately on a trail leading away from the holy city and out of the country.

They regained the Lhasa trail only to be stopped by three horsemen, one of whom appeared to be a minor official of some kind. He told them that an English invasion was expected and said that they were suspected of being its advance guard. After trying to question the two Englishmen he asked them to halt while he contacted his superior for instructions. Bower refused and pressed on towards Lhasa. From now on they found themselves shadowed by more and more horsemen, just as Bonvalot had been as he approached the capital. When Bower sent two of his men to ask them what they wanted, a message came back that this was their country and they were moving about in it – 'an answer', Bower had to admit, 'to which it was impossible to take exception.'

It was now becoming increasingly clear to Bower and Thorold that it was not going to be easy to get to Lhasa. After pressing on forcibly for three days, they finally agreed to halt and await the imminent arrival of a more senior official. Within an hour he rode in accompanied by a colleague. 'Intellectually and physically they were fine men,' wrote Bower, 'and about both there was an air of pronounced individuality.' Seated in his tent, they began to question him. Realising there was no fooling them, Bower admitted: 'We are English, we have come from Ladakh, are going to China, and here is our passport.' In reply, they were told that they would have to await the arrival of more senior officials from Lhasa who would decide their case. If they continued to advance they would be stopped by force. If this failed, then they – the Tibetans – would be beheaded by their own authorities. Bower wrote later: 'If we fought and killed them, it was just as good as being killed in Lhasa. They were absolutely immovable in this resolve, and I have not the slightest doubt would have attempted to stop our progress by force had we resolved to go on at all hazards.'

Unwilling to risk bloodshed (for which Calcutta would hardly have thanked him), Bower agreed to wait at a spot where there was good pasturage for his animals, some of which had been reduced to little more than living skeletons. In the meantime the Tibetans were to provide him with meat, flour and butter, and to guarantee his party's safety. After keeping them waiting there for three weeks, during which time both men and beasts regained their strength, a high dignitary finally arrived from Lhasa riding on a mule and holding aloft a large red umbrella – whether to keep off the rain or the sun not being clear, 'there being no signs', Bower noted, 'of either at the time.'

Discussions were held in Bower's tent, at the latter's insistence. In response to the official's questions, Bower told him that they were English travellers who had intended to pass more to the north, but had been forced south when they began to run short of provisions 'confident that, owing to the friendship existing between the British and Lhasa governments, we should receive every assistance.' To this the Tibetans answered that their country was forbidden to all strangers and they had no choice but to send Bower back by the route he had come. 'As for the friendship existing between the two governments,' they added, 'that was no reason why the people of both nations should not stick to their own countries.' Negotiations soon became deadlocked, with Bower threatening to proceed to Lhasa 'to discuss the question there'. He knew perfectly well, however, that no amount of threatening or persuading would weaken the Tibetans' resolve to prevent him from advancing on the capital. He was going to have difficulty enough in persuading them to let him continue travelling eastwards across Tibet and thus enable him to complete his clandestine map. To set foot in Lhasa was not that essential to his mission.

Finally, after an enforced halt of nearly a month, the Tibetans agreed – encouraged by a *douceur* of a thousand rupees – to allow Bower to continue eastwards and leave Tibet via its eastern frontier with China. But they insisted that he first go back eight marches, like a game of snakes and ladders, so that they could truthfully report to Lhasa that the foreigners had left by the way they had come. So it was that he and his party, after numerous misadventures – including having their sheep eaten by wolves and ponies freezing to death – crossed into China in January 1892 only just in time before the pass was blocked for the winter by a heavy snowstorm. There, so far as the public was concerned, their epic journey ended. Bower and Thorold, like Prejevalsky, Rockhill, Lansdell and Bonvalot, had failed to see the golden domes of the holy city, although as a feat of scientific exploration their crossing of Tibet was hailed as a triumph. Bower's gold medal, presented to him by the Royal Geographical Society, was well earned, while his narrative of their adventure – *Diary of a Journey Across Tibet* – enjoyed a huge success.

But, as we know, there was considerably more to this journey than met the reader's eye. Bower had spent those seven hazardous months crossing Tibet for the satisfaction of neither the Royal Geographical Society nor the British public. He was there, as the Foreign Office archives show, to gather as much intelligence as he could about India's shadowy northern neighbour on behalf of Colonel Ellis, his chief in the Intelligence Branch at Simla, from where all the information-gleaning north of the Himalayas was organised. But, knowing this, today's reader of his travel narrative might be excused for wondering how on earth this officer, however resourceful, managed to gather any military or political intelligence at all during his gruelling journey. Just how and when he did it remains his secret, and possibly that of Colonel Ellis too. But to see just how much he did bring back one must turn to file number FO 17 1167 in the Foreign Office records at Kew. There can be found Bower's slim, blue-covered official report entitled *Some Notes on Tibetan Affairs*. A brief forward by Colonel Ellis points out that the material in this report was deliberately omitted from Bower's published narrative because it was 'politically undesirable' to include it. The file copy, which bears the word CON-FIDENTIAL in red letters, had been sent to the Political and Secret Department of the Foreign Office, by Field Marshal

Lord Roberts, Commander-in-Chief in India.

In this ten-page report Bower explains how Tibet is governed, its Dalai Lamas chosen and other details of Lhasa's rule. Of the Tibetan army he notes: 'Nominal strength of six thousand, of whom half are supposed to keep themselves ready for service, and half engaged in agricultural and other pursuits.' Their armaments were limited to 'sword, spear and matchlock – the latter having a prong attached to serve as a rest when being fired.'

Bower goes on to assess Tibet's vulnerability to invasion, pointing out that Lhasa could easily be seized by 'a very small force' entering from the south or south-west, since it would be passing through populated areas and thus be able to obtain supplies. Thus, he argues, an invading force from India would have an overwhelming advantage over a Russian one from the north, as it would be able 'to strike the enemy in his most vital part without being cut off from its base.' Pinpointing three possible lines of approach from the north, Bower remarks: 'All these roads are difficult, and we may be certain that, however feasible it may be for exploring parties to cross them, no army could possibly do so, and a force destined to operate against anything more than the Lhasa army [he is presuming here that Peking would resist such an invasion] would assuredly come to grief.'

Tibet's northern defences – the Kun Lun and Altyn Tagh bastions and the largely waterless Chang Tang plateau – were, he declared, 'the strongest in the world'. However, Tibet's martial strength he dismissed as 'nil'. The Chinese, he reported, had made a policy of assuring the Tibetans, still reeling from their painful clash with British troops in Sikkim, 'that we are a poor race of barbarians that could never stand up for a moment before the braves of the celestial Empire'. Yet even in those parts of the country lying close to China's frontiers, he argued, 'Chinese power is merely nominal'. In conclusion, Bower wrote: 'At present China and Lhasa are playing a game which suits both. The Chinese are keeping up an appearance of dominating Tibet, while the Lhasa Government are avoiding having to treat with a foreign power.'

That the Foreign Office liked neither the hawkish tone of Bower's report nor its message is apparent from two footnotes neatly inscribed on the letter accompanying it. One dismisses his views on the Chinese in Tibet as 'somewhat crude'. The other, in red ink, observes that he appeared to be 'a sort of damn them all' man. They may not have liked what he had to say (for the Foreign Office was still under the delusion that Tibet was controlled by Peking) but events were soon to prove Bower right. Whitehall's disdain for his views, moreover, was to cause no injury to his career, for Bower went on to become a Major-General and to be knighted, only dying in 1940.

Meanwhile, on Tibet's borders, travellers with widely differing motives were already positioning themselves for fresh assaults on Lhasa. The first of these was a middle-aged Englishwoman.

7. Death of an Explorer

With the score now standing at five-nil to the Tibetans, this challenging land – and particularly its holy city – began to cast its spell over men and women other than professional explorers. For several years small numbers of missionaries had maintained a precarious toe-hold in the Chinese-Tibetan borderlands far to the east of Lhasa. Now some began to cast evangelical eyes on the forbidden land itself. Among them was the diminutive Annie Taylor, whose dream it had become to preach Christ's gospel inside the heathen capital. For beyond those protecting mountains lived a uniquely religious people awaiting – surely – rescue from their barbaric beliefs and practices, and ready for conversion.

It was, after all, the early Christian missionaries who had first discovered Tibet, even if they had failed to find there the legendary Christian Kingdom of Prester John. Though they had won no converts, they had at first been well received by the friendly Tibetans. But then, as we have seen, Lhasa's attitude to this alien creed suddenly changed. Fearing for their own faith, and encouraged in this by the Chinese, the Tibetans took fright. Both the English and the Russians, the Chinese warned them, were intent on destroying their ancient religion and forcibly replacing it with Christianity. There was, of course, a grain of truth in this – even if the Chinese did have devious motives for fostering such fears.

From then on, Christian missionaries were even less welcome in Tibet than other gatecrashers. The Tibetans' fear of them was to become almost pathological. In 1887, they attacked a French mission station on the Chinese-Tibetan frontier, razing it to the ground, slaughtering its native converts and forcing its white priests to flee for their lives. But this in no way lessened the evangelical zeal of those missionaries bent on converting the Tibetans, although some were to lose their lives in the attempt.

It would certainly have taken much more than this to weaken the resolve of Annie Royle Taylor, a Presbyterian of thirty-six, who was bent on carrying the gospel to the Dalai Lama himself. The daughter of a well-to-do Cheshire businessman, and one of ten children, Annie was born with a heart condition which led doctors to believe that she would never live to reach maturity. Brought up by nannies and governesses and pampered by her parents, she grew into a wilful teenager. But at the age of sixteen she suddenly felt the call of a religious vocation which was soon to cause a growing rift between herself and her father. She gave up going to dances and to the theatre, 'having ceased to find any pleasures apart from Jesus', and refused to go riding with her father on the Lord's Day. When she went into mission work in London's East End, her father begged her to give this up 'and go into Society like your sisters'. But instead, at the age of twenty-eight, she sold her jewellery to pay for her lodgings and took an elementary medical course, for she had heard that 'the Lord wanted women for China'. Accepted as a missionary by the China Inland Mission, she set sail for Shanghai in the autumn of 1884, and for the next eight years she worked in China and in India, always hovering on the Tibetan border-lands. For 'Tibet, not China, was my goal', she wrote years afterwards.

Annie now set about to realise this dream, learning Tibetan and acquiring a faithful follower, a Tibetan called Pontso, who was to serve her for twenty years. She chose the old walled city of Tao-chou, on the Chinese-Tibetan frontier not far from Kumbum monastery, as the starting point for her journey to Lhasa. It was there that she met a ruffianly (as it turned out) Chinese named Noga who, with his Tibetan wife, was planning to visit Lhasa. He agreed to accompany Annie as her guide.

Her caravan consisted of herself, disguised as a Tibetan,

Noga, his wife, Pontso and two servants. She took sixteen horses, some for riding and others to carry their tents and bedding, enough supplies for two months and gifts which she hoped would smooth their way. Her plan was to slip away from the town at dawn, the moment the gates were opened, then head for the frontier, hoping that the border guards would still be half asleep at that hour of the morning. She then proposed to make straight for Lhasa, trusting that her disguise would not be penetrated before she reached the capital where she intended to hurl herself on the mercy of the Dalai Lama. Hers was perhaps the most naive of all the attempts to reach Lhasa, but what she lacked in professionalism she more than made up for in courage and determination. Even had she known what a harrowing time she was destined for, it seems unlikely she would have held back for a second. Her trust in the Almighty, and her commitment to evangelising the Tibetans, was absolute.

Annie and her companions left Tao-chou on September 2, 1892 and crossed into Tibet without arousing anyone's suspicion. But from that moment onward her troubles never ceased. Continually harassed by bandits she quickly lost all her spare clothes, her tent, camp bed and most of her horses. One of her servants decided to return home and another died, leaving her and the gentle Pontso to the mercies of Noga who soon began to demand money from her, threaten her and steal from her. Quarrels broke out among her men, and between Noga and his wife. They were attacked by huge mastiffs, battered by ferocious winds, and held up for days by swollen rivers and blizzards. But every night, whatever had befallen them, Annie would write in her little black-and-red-diary, an account of their day's adventures or – more often – misadventures.

Never once did she complain. Unshakable courage and absolute faith shine forth from every page of her battered journal. As they progressed conditions gradually worsened. One day, six weeks after leaving Tao-chou, they were warned that five hundred Tibetan soldiers were on the rampage ahead robbing passing caravans. Annie was advised to turn back. She wrote: 'I am all for going on, but the others want to return.' She added: 'The Lord will open up the way somehow.' He miraculously did, dispersing the rampaging soldiers. That same night, however, her sick Chinese servant died as Noga read to him from the Koran. Annie had tried to convert the poor man but his last word, she records, was 'Allah!' A large, strongly-built man, he had more than once protected her from Noga's violence and rages. After they had buried him Annie noted down: 'The Master has called to account the strong, and left the weak to go on and claim Tibet in his name.' The following day she lost her dog. 'Now they are both left behind,' she wrote, adding: 'May the Lord spare the rest of us.'

Annie's own health was now beginning to suffer, and at times she was too weak even to control her own horse. Then the faithful Pontso would take the reins and lead her until she could ride no further. One day they watched in silence as eagles gorged themselves on a corpse which had first been cut up in accordance with Tibetan custom. They also talked with a man recently in Lhasa who told them that 'the war with the English' was not yet over. Noga now began to threaten to denounce Annie for what she was. 'May the Lord preserve us from all his wickedness', was her only comment.

As they got nearer to Lhasa, Noga's behaviour became more and more alarming. During a row with his wife he threatened to report her for smuggling an Englishwoman into the country, bragging that they would punish her but would reward him. Annie observed calmly in her diary: 'The Lord will take care of us. I do not fear.' During another violent outburst Noga threatened to kill both Annie and the gentle Pontso. Hurling a heavy cooking pot at Annie, he tried to draw his sword but was restrained by a friendly Tibetan, who had attached himself to the party and who later offered to kill the miscreant and blame it on robbers. Annie declined his well-meant offer. Next day she learned that the treacherous Noga had done what all along she had feared: he had spread word abroad that she was an Englishwoman in disguise. Surprisingly, his denunciation seems to have caused no immediate alarm among the local Tibetans, who continued to befriend her.

Annie prayed that Noga would leave them. He did, but only to travel ahead to Lhasa to alert the authorities there, taking two of her horses and other valuables with him. Almost destitute now, Annie and Pontso spent twenty nights sleeping in the open in glacial conditions. However, on December 20, in the midst of all her difficulties, she nevertheless managed to make a Christmas pudding 'of some suet that I begged, a few currants, some black sugar, and a little flour'. She also noted in her diary that 'the cold is extreme'. On Christmas Day the naive but indomitable Annie put her pudding on to boil, but found after two hours that in the middle it was still stone cold. Tea, too, if not drunk instantly, was soon covered in ice. 'This is a strange climate,' was her puzzled comment.

By now the bedraggled party, so reduced in numbers and in belongings, was on the celebrated Tea Road, the main caravan trail between Szechuan and Lhasa. But ahead still, between Annie and her goal, lay the Dam-jau-er-la,* one of the highest of Tibet's passes. Grimly noting the skeletons of earlier travellers and their pack animals which signposted the trail, they toiled painfully over this and, safely and thankfully, down into the valley beyond. Now they were nearing the sacred Tibetan province of U, in which Lhasa stands, and at whose approaches, they learned, troops had been posted the previous year to prevent Europeans from trying to reach the holy city. But, to Annie's relief, there was no sign of them, and she pressed on as quickly as she could. She knew she was now closer to Lhasa than any of the other travellers who had attempted to reach it. Less than one week's journey ahead, her evangelical goal seemed at last to be within her grasp.

But then, on January 3, 1893, her hopes were dashed. At a spot only three days' march from the capital, her party was suddenly confronted by two armed soldiers who ordered them

---

* *La* in Tibetan means pass.

to halt, saying that they were under arrest. As she had feared, Noga had informed the chief of the district that an English-woman was approaching Lhasa. Orders were given for her to be stopped and held. Weakened by hardship and fatigue and hardly able to walk more than a few yards at a time, Annie knew that she had no choice but to obey. Pontso and her other servant spent the night in terror, aware that death by beheading was the fate of all those who brought foreigners into the country (though why they had not thought of this before is rather puzzling). After two days the commander of the nearest garrison arrived with an armed escort. He was courteous, and listened to all that Annie had to say, but insisted that she must return the way she had come.

She argued with him that this was impossible, pointing out that she had neither food nor money, that her horses were totally exhausted and that she was too enfeebled to survive the journey. 'To return,' she told him 'simply meant to die on the road.' But this extraordinary woman, he quickly discovered, not merely argued fearlessly, but was also demanding. 'I demanded justice,' she wrote in her diary. 'I had to be very firm since our lives seemed to rest on my taking a firm stand.' She insisted on seeing the local magistrate so she could lay serious charges against Noga who, she complained, had stolen two of her horses and tried to murder her. She got her way, and ten days after her arrest a senior official arrived from Lhasa together with Noga. Annie spent much of the night before her case was heard in prayer.

The following day she was brought before the official and seated on a mat in front of him. 'He asked many questions,' she recorded in her diary that night, 'and wanted to know why I had come to their country within three days of Lhasa. I said that I wished to cross it to get to Darjeeling.' She wisely made no mention of why she was really there. Her diary continues: 'He said that the Tibetans were at strife with the English, and that the war question was not settled, also that Noga denied having any of my things, except the horses which he alleged I had given him.' She insisted that she had not given them to him. Noga was then brought in, but denied everything. 'I had never heard such lying', Annie noted.

The Tibetan official then told her that soldiers would escort her back the way she had come. 'I said they might carry my corpse, but they would not take me against my will', she recounts. When he told her frankly that he preferred Noga's case to hers, pointing out that he was Chinese and she was English, Annie stormed at him: 'Is this Tibetan justice? Noga has done a great wrong to me, yet you say you cannot punish him . . . You want to send me on the road with horses that cannot go, and without a tent, knowing that in a few days we shall have to stop in a place where there is no chief, a place swarming with brigands, and thus seek to be rid of me, not killing me yourself, but getting me killed by others. I can only say that if you do not help me to return I must stay where I am until the *amban* is informed.' At this point the Tibetan was forced to admit that he did not know how to deal with her. Finally, after six days of argument and negotiation she won from him the promise of an escort, fresh horses, a tent, warm clothing, blankets, and food and other necessities sufficient to get her party as far as the Yangtze.

Thus, on January 18, 1893, Annie was sent back over much of the same grim route which it had taken her four months to traverse. Her disappointment must have been hard to bear. Had she not chosen Noga as her guide she would very likely have reached Lhasa, though only to have been expelled from there – or perhaps worse. For the Japanese traveller Ekai Kawaguchi, who did reach Lhasa several years later, and whose own misadventures we shall hear more of, was to meet the very official who had been sent to try Annie Taylor's case. This man, by now the country's Finance Minister, had remarked: 'Dear me! The English people are odd creatures.' He added that Annie would certainly have been executed had the chief in charge of the district where she was halted not been a man of particular compassion. Indeed, much as one may admire Annie

Taylor's astonishing courage (and her journey out of Tibet was to prove even more harrowing than her entry), one is also struck by the remarkable forbearance of the Tibetans toward those foreigners who repeatedly tried to gatecrash their sacred places. However, if Annie Taylor and those who had preceded her were lucky, very soon there were to be others who would prove less fortunate.

*   *   *

The first to suffer violence at the hands of the Tibetans was a French explorer named Jules Dutreuil de Rhins. A former naval officer who had already travelled extensively in the Congo, he now turned his energies to the scientific exploration of Central Asia. Financed jointly by the French Government and by the Academy of Inscriptions and Letters, he left Paris for Chinese Turkestan in February 1891 with a younger colleague, an orientalist named Fernand Grenard. The remainder of that year and much of the following was spent exploring the Kun Lun and Karakoram ranges. This done, they now set their sights on Lhasa, which Dutreuil de Rhins was determined to win for French exploration.

On September 3, 1893, accompanied by thirteen locally-hired caravan men, interpreters, servants and others, the two explorers left the small oasis town of Cherchen and, full of optimism, struck southwards through the mountains towards Tibet. 'Who foresaw then,' Grenard wrote afterwards, 'that a day would come when the entire mission would be dispersed, sacked, almost annihilated without a trace?'

Four gruelling months after leaving Cherchen (during which time they went sixty days without seeing another soul), they reached a point just six days' march from Lhasa. But here, like Prejevalsky, Bonvalot, Bower and Annie Taylor before them, they too were halted. The Tibetans, as ever, were courteous but firm, putting the blame on the Chinese, while the *amban*'s men accompanying them assured the explorers privately that but for the barbaric attitude of the Tibetans they would have been welcome to visit Lhasa. It was, in any case, 'a horrible place', the Chinese insisted, inhabited by savages.

The usual demand was made that they return the way they had come. Dutreuil de Rhins adamantly refused to do so, insisting that they must travel to Lhasa to resupply their much depleted caravan. He pointed out that of the sixty-one pack animals they had set out with, no fewer than thirty-six had been lost during their punishing winter journey. Even as they argued, others were dying, and soon the area around the camp had become a charnel house, with vultures gorging themselves on the corpses and giant crows feasting on the open sores of the surviving beasts. Before long several of the men, including Dutreuil de Rhins himself, were ill, while a number of others decided they had had enough and deserted.

Unmoved by all this, or by the Frenchmen's arguments, the Tibetans stolidly insisted that if they allowed them to press on towards Lhasa they themselves would be thrown into the Lhasa river with their hands and feet bound. Finally, after fifty days of negotiation, Dutreuil de Rhins was forced to abandon his attempt to reach the holy city. The best he could achieve was a compromise whereby instead of returning the way they had come, they were allowed to leave Tibet via Sining, on the north-eastern frontier with China. The Tibetans agreed, moreover, to supply them with fresh animals and food.

On January 20, 1894, little realising that their troubles had scarcely begun, the two explorers started on their long trek out of Tibet. For one of them it was destined to be his last journey. At the small town of Nagchuka they were forced to halt for a month, living in a dark, verminous house while they waited for both the weather and Dutreuil de Rhins' health to improve. Much of the time the temperature lay at thirty degrees below zero, and soon their interpreter, weakened by months of hardship and malnutrition, also fell ill. Before long they had to bury him, protecting his frozen corpse from wild beasts by means of heavy stones. It was while making enquiries about the long route ahead that they came across a man who had made the sixteen-hundred-mile journey there and back no fewer than five times. On his last journey, from which he had just returned, his legs had been badly frost-bitten and gangrene had resulted. 'Hideous sores had formed,' Grenard wrote, 'and the front portions, almost completely severed, hung down like horrible rags.' Parrot-fashion he recited for them the names of the eighty-eight halts where the caravans camped. The explorers knew from ancient Chinese documents that once there had been a shorter route, but this had been abandoned so long before that no one knew of it any longer.

By March 6 the weather had improved, albeit only momentarily, and accompanied by their remaining men and a caravan of slow moving yaks they set out for Sining. Ten weeks later, after crossing the frozen headwaters of both the Salween and the Yangtze, and exploring the source of the Mekong, they reached the village of Jyekundo. It was here that they had their first hint of serious trouble. One of their men, whom they had sent ahead to make contact with the authorities, was angrily driven off with stones, while the head lama forbade the villagers to sell them supplies or even talk to them. Forced to press on without a guide, they eventually reached the small village of Thom Bundo. Here, too, they found all doors barred to them. Worse was to follow.

Dutreuil de Rhins was by now in considerable pain, the heavy rain having done nothing to improve his bronchitis or, for that matter, his temper. Angry at their treatment by the villagers, he forced his way into a cattle enclosure containing an empty stone shelter where they spent the next two nights while waiting for the rain to stop. On the morning of the third day a bright dawn tempted them to set out once again. It was then that they discovered that during the night two of their horses had been stolen. Furious now, Dutreuil de Rhins sent two armed men out to search for them, but in vain. He ordered his men to seize two horses belonging to the villagers, saying that he would hand them back as soon as his own were returned.

Perhaps this was the excuse the Tibetans were looking for. As the caravan left the shelter of the walled cattle enclosure and began to advance in single file along a narrow pathway, the villagers opened fire on them through the loopholes of a nearby building. Several of the pack animals were struck immediately, and falling, blocked the way of those behind. Dutreuil de Rhins immediately began to return their fire while Grenard, whose rifle was with one of the leading animals, ran forward to retrieve it and also to try to move the caravan out of range of the Tibetan matchlocks. It was then that he heard a cry of pain from his leader. On reaching him he found to his dismay that his compatriot had been struck in the stomach by a crude bullet. 'The sight of the wound,' he wrote afterwards, 'left me no hope.' Their ambushers had momentarily stopped firing and Grenard managed to drag his friend to temporary safety behind a wall where he tried to improvise a stretcher from one of the camp beds. But unable to lift or carry his wounded colleague by himself, Grenard set out to look for some of their caravan men, all of whom had fled when the shooting began.

The hillside was now swarming with armed Tibetans who began to fire at him from all sides, cutting him off from the spot where Dutreuil de Rhins lay. 'I was in a painful dilemma,' he wrote afterwards in his account of the affair. 'Was I to leave our chief to his now inevitable fate, and to save that by which he set store above all else, the scientific results of his mission, or was I to sacrifice everything to an honourable but useless attempt to snatch from the enemy's hand a man whose life had perhaps already left his body?'

The matter was soon settled for him. He had now used up all his ammunition and the Tibetans made a rush for him, firing off their matchlocks and yelling '*song*! . . . *song*!' ('go! . . . go!'). Seizing him, they began to beat him with the flats of their swords, at the same time rifling his pockets. He was now convinced that his last moment had come as the screaming mob drove him forward with their swords and lances, angrily prodding and striking him. But instead of killing him they escorted him as far as the village boundary where they turned back, leaving only the children to hurl stones at him with their slings. Badly bruised and shaken, but luckily without any serious injuries, Grenard managed to stagger to a village nearby which proved to be less hostile. Here he and four of his terrified men were given shelter.

Grenard remained in the village for three weeks, endeavouring, through middle men, to negotiate for the return of his leader's body and also for their baggage. From one of their servants he learned of Dutreuil de Rhins' fate. According to this man, the Tibetans had bound the explorer's hands and feet and flung him, still living, into the river. There he had been seen desperately trying to keep afloat. This latter detail Grenard found difficult to believe, for when he had last seen his compatriot several hours before, he had already been very close to death.

Eventually, after recovering some of their scientific papers and part of their baggage – one missing manuscript was later to turn up, somewhat mysteriously, in St Petersburg – Grenard made his way sadly on to Sining without further mishap, and thence a further fifteen hundred miles to the Chinese capital. It may have been of some satisfaction to him to learn later that a Chinese punitive expedition had been sent to the village of Thom Bundo, following pressure from the French Minister, and four of the men involved in the attack executed – the head of one of these being stuck on the main gateway to Sining for all to see.

But for Grenard the affair was not yet over. Back in Paris, where news of the tragedy had preceded him, he found himself having to defend both himself and his dead leader against charges that they had brought the whole thing upon themselves by their high-handedness. Indeed, years later, some support for this view was to appear in a curious little book of memoirs written in broken English by a Ladakhi caravan man named Rassul Galwan.

In *Servant of Sahibs*, published in 1923, Rassul quotes an

eye-witness version of the tragedy as told to him by one of the
expedition's servants. Dutreuil de Rhins, if this man can be
believed, was a man of hasty temper. Fearful lest they be
attacked by the already hostile villagers, the servant had begged
him to return the confiscated horses, only to be accused of
cowardice. He told Rassul that the village headman and the
owner of the horses had come to Dutreuil de Rhins and warned
him that unless the animals were returned: 'When you start
from here, you look. Now your life will be finished very soon.'
He claimed, furthermore, that it was not Grenard but himself
who had dragged their wounded leader out of the line of fire,
alleging that Grenard had run away. It should be added that in
Grenard's own account of the affair, he had equally unflattering
things to say about this particular servant, claiming that he had
fled at the first hint of danger and only reappeared several days
later.

The true story will never now be known. However, another
attempt to reach Lhasa – the seventh in twenty-two years –
had been defeated. Prejevalsky, Rockhill, Lansdell, Bonvalot,
Bower, Annie Taylor and now Dutreuil de Rhins and Grenard
had all failed to reach this irresistible goal. But to some this only
served to heighten Lhasa's allure, for within a year, an English
country gentleman, his somewhat delicate wife, their nephew
and their small dog were on their way there.

                    *   *   *

One might be excused for thinking that this homely-sounding
trio would have been better suited to a day on the Sussex downs
than facing the physical hell of the Chang Tang. However, one
should not be deceived by their amateurish appearance.
Already Mr and Mrs St George Littledale – not forgetting their
terrier – were seasoned Asiatic travellers who had earned the
respect of geographers and fellow explorers as a result of their
two earlier Central Asian journeys.

'My scheme,' wrote Littledale, a wealthy Berkshire landowner, 'was to strain every nerve to reach Tibet and, if possible, Lhasa, with plenty of food and animals to carry it.' Most of the other attempts had failed, he argued, 'owing to their arriving in a more or less destitute condition.' This had meant that the Tibetans were then able to dictate their own terms. The Littledales intended to arrive in a position of strength. He admitted candidly: 'We also relied upon bribery, and went well prepared for wholesale corruption.' Their nephew was a young rowing Blue from Oxford, six-foot-three in height, named William Fletcher. Both he and Littledale were noted rifle shots.

After crossing Russian Central Asia, they reached Kashgar, in Chinese Turkestan, in January 1895, where Fletcher's height caused a stir in the bazaars. Next, after travelling eastwards along the old Silk Road to Cherchen (where less than two years earlier the ill-fated Dutreuil de Rhins had prepared his caravan) they struck southwards into Tibet's northern ramparts on April 12. With them they took seven locally-hired caravan men – including Rassul Galwan, who was later to record his experiences in *Servant of Sahibs* – and an escort of three Pathan ex-soldiers armed with the latest Colt lightning-repeater rifles. Their caravan consisted of an astonishing two hundred and fifty animals, including ponies, mules and donkeys, more than half of which were to be sent back after the party had got safely through the mountains with the eleven tons of fodder and six months' provisions which they carried. A small flock of sheep provided a mobile larder of fresh meat.

But before long, although it was spring, they ran into heavy snowstorms which obliterated all signs of grazing and fuel, and on the sixteenth day they lost the first of their ponies. The Europeans kept up their own morale and strength with tins of Silver's self-heating soup, with which they had thoughtfully provided themselves, but without fuel for turning snow and ice into cooking water the natives in the party appear to have fared less well. Perhaps it was this which caused some of their caravan men to deceive them, persuading them that they had already reached the edge of the Tibetan plateau. As a result, many of the pack animals were sent back and their owners paid off before the Littledales realised their error. It took them a further ten days to discover a pass which finally carried them on to the Chang Tang, though not before they had lost half a dozen of their donkeys and two more ponies.

Here they also nearly lost one of their men, who, as an inducement to accompany them, had been paid several months' wages in advance. He was planning, they found, to slip off home under cover of darkness. Littledale recounts: 'As we were terribly short-handed we took the liberty of decorating him for a few nights with a pair of handcuffs', adding that: 'He afterwards proved to be quite one of our best men.' Progress now became slow, for the animals were suffering from the effects of the altitude and harshness of the climate, as well as from lack of nutrition. One morning they awoke to discover that their nineteen surviving sheep had strayed during the night, and each had had its throat bitten through by marauding wolves. Their animals, including the ponies, were now dying off at such a rate that Littledale and his nephew had to walk, converting their own riding ponies to pack animals. Only Mrs Littledale continued to ride.

'Our animals were dying in an ominous way,' wrote Littledale, 'and the survivors were so weak that when they fell or lay down we had to lift them on to their legs again.' They even tried making protective clothing for the suffering animals from whatever spare materials they had, but to little effect. 'Not a day passed,' Littledale recalled, 'but several animals had to be shot or abandoned.' To lighten the loads of their remaining beasts they decided to leave behind everything that was not absolutely necessary. This included clothes, camp furniture, scientific specimens, horseshoes, even books. Where the contents of the latter were essential, their bindings were torn off and tossed away.

'Our men,' Littledale recounts, 'seeing new clothes thrown away, wished to exchange their own rags for them. We told them they might take what they liked, but if anyone took a coat, for instance, he must leave his own in exchange.' He added lightly that it was 'a little difficult to arrange an exact equivalent for some ladies' garments.'

The journey had now begun to take on a pattern only too familiar to those who had previously attempted to approach Lhasa from across the barren, storm-swept northern plateau. The Tibetan spring had turned out to be far more severe than the Littledales had anticipated. But then, after they had been on the march for more than a month, and just as their situation was becoming desperate, their luck turned. The weather suddenly grew milder, and much-needed showers of rain provided them with water for cooking and drinking. They now found themselves in a valley containing grazing and water sufficient to restore strength to their skeletal animals. Here they camped for a week while the unfortunate beasts gorged themselves from dawn to dusk. The morale of the men, too, rapidly recovered. As Rassul Galwan noted in his own account of the expedition: 'We take in a day three time foods.'

When both men and beasts had regained their strength, the caravan moved forwards again, for the Littledales were still as determined as ever to reach Lhasa. They soon began to come across traces left by other caravans, but it was not until June 26 that they spotted the first human beings they had seen since leaving Cherchen one and a half months earlier. These were Tibetan nomads with large flocks of sheep and herds of yak. Littledale climbed a hill to observe them surreptitiously through a telescope as they quarried salt from a lake for sale in Lhasa. Rassul Galwan quotes him as warning the men: 'We do not want any Tibetan look at us. If they see us, then they will report to the government of Lhasa.' He continued to keep a careful watch on the Tibetans to make sure they had not been observed, and that night they set off by a route which would take them clear of this potential danger. However, they had not gone far when the caravan got stuck in a swamp. 'There was every prospect of our having to remain there all night and being discovered in the morning,' Littledale recounts. Fortunately they managed to struggle clear just as the moon set and darkness fell.

Travelling only by night they continued, unobserved, towards Lhasa, always sending scouts ahead to ensure that the way was clear. Littledale describes one anxious moment. 'Just at one critical time, when passing at night close to an encampment, the donkey carrying our pet cock and hen chose to tumble, and there was a great cackling and fuss.' A moment later one of the mules trod on a dog which gave a piteous howl. Fortunately they attracted no untoward attention, passing no doubt for a native caravan. Since it would have been unwise to light a lantern, Littledale was obliged to read his compass by the glow of a patent luminous matchbox. Deliberately he kept their marches short, not merely because of the difficulty of travelling by night, but to ensure that their beasts got ample grazing and rest. Littledale was determined to keep up the strength of their remaining animals as these were so vital to any hopes of success.

But they could hardly hope to remain undetected for ever, and as they drew gradually closer to the capital they encountered more and more Tibetan encampments. On one occasion they found that they had no choice but to pass boldly through a camp of some thirty tents. By bunching the pack animals together, and themselves walking in the midst of them, the three Europeans managed to get through unnoticed. But the following day they were finally spotted by some shepherds. Littledale wrote: 'The men, on seeing us, pluckily bolted up the mountains, leaving their wives in charge.' But the Littledales' secret was now out, and the Tibetans, who appeared good-natured enough, asked the party to halt while they sought instructions from their chief.

Realising from the experience of those who had preceded them that this would be fatal, the Littledales now pressed on as fast as their revitalised men and animals were able. They could reach Lhasa, they estimated, in eight hard marches. Littledale had held in reserve sixteen donkey-loads of fodder for such a contingency, thus saving vital time which would otherwise have been spent in grazing the animals. As they rode, local Tibetan officials begged them to advance no further, pleading that they themselves would be executed if the caravan did not halt. Hardening their hearts against such entreaties (or perhaps not believing them) the Littledales pressed determinedly on. 'Our object', Littledale wrote afterwards, 'was to push on so fast that they would not have time to collect their militia in sufficient numbers to stop us.' The Tibetans now began to change their tactics. One man – 'a determined, picturesque-looking individual' – seized Littledale's bridle, but immediately let go when the latter drew his revolver and flourished it at him.

By now, according to Rassul Galwan's account, some three hundred tribesmen armed with matchlocks had fallen in on either side of the caravan. To try to dissuade the Littledales from proceeding, a bribe of three hundred rupees was offered them by the Tibetans. When this was rejected, similar inducements were offered to their caravan men, the Tibetans claiming that they had bought off previous European-led expeditions in this way. The Tibetans now began to enquire about the party's weapons. Rassul Galwan boasted to them with relish that just one of Littledale's rifles could kill a thousand men. When the Tibetans enquired what was in the boxes they carried, he told them: 'In these boxes we have enemy killing thing. If put fire to a box, then burn all men of country.' He added contemptuously: 'They are jungly men, believe to that matter.'

Next morning, to the Littledales' surprise, there was no sign of any of them. It could only mean that the Tibetans had gone ahead and were lying in wait for them. This proved to be so. 'We found them occupying both sides of a narrow ravine, lying down behind stones, with only rows and rows of black heads visible', wrote Littledale. As the caravan approached the spot, half a dozen Tibetans came forward to meet it. Unless the foreigners halted, they warned, they would be forced to open fire. Littledale then produced his passport, telling them that it was given him 'by a greater man than any at Lhasa', but the Tibetans brushed it aside. Littledale now gave orders for his men to load their rifles. He himself was armed with a Mann-licher, the three sepoys with Colt repeaters, while Fletcher and three of the caravan men had Express rifles. Meanwhile the theodolite and camera tripods were hurriedly stuffed into rifle covers to make them appear as warlike as possible, and Mrs Littledale was ordered, protesting loudly, to the rear of the column with the baggage animals. 'Mrs Littledale,' her husband noted, 'was very indignant with me because I would not let her have a rifle.'

He now cast an eye over his men to see which of them seemed willing to fight if it became necessary. With satisfaction he observed the three sepoys 'nursing their rifles, looking at me with murder in their eyes, impatiently awaiting the signal to begin.' He added: 'Here were these men who had been through the Kabul war, and knew what fighting meant, ready to face hopeless odds simply because their sahib ordered them.' Little-dale was banking on the Tibetans giving way in face of such determination. His bluff worked. The tribesmen held their fire and the caravan proceeded past them towards the capital, now only two days' march ahead. Lhasa at last lay within Littledale's grasp. For when challenged, it seemed, the Tibetans would back down rather than risk bloodshed.

Only one towering pass – the 19,000-foot Goring La – now stood between them and the holy city. Crossing this by night was to prove a harrowing experience. The weather was appalling and there was no wood or other fuel for drying out their sodden clothes or for cooking. In the darkness, men and animals slid and stumbled on the icy track, and some had to be left to follow as best they could. Finally, soaked to the skin, hungry and utterly exhausted they reached the fertile valley beyond. Mrs Littledale, Rassul noted, was in tears. Here they learned from a Ladakhi traveller that they were now just one day's fast pony ride from Lhasa. But, tantalisingly, they could not see the holy city, for yet one more ridge still lay between them and their goal.

Ill-luck now struck them, for they discovered to their dismay that all the party's food was with the animals still snowbound on the pass. 'All idea of a rush for Lhasa had to be abandoned,' wrote Littledale. When the stragglers finally caught up they were so exhausted that the caravan had to halt for a further day.

That fatal delay, although he did not then realise it, very likely cost Littledale the race. For, before long, the first of a succession of Tibetan officials began to turn up, each accompanied by an armed retinue. Their instructions, they said, were at all costs to prevent the party from proceeding towards Lhasa. Failure in this meant that they would be beheaded. 'The numbers opposing us increased rapidly', Littledale wrote, and soon the area around the English camp resembled a small town of tents. The usual long-drawn-out negotiations now began, with letters going back and forth to Lhasa. But Littledale was confident that time was on his side. His aim was to wear his opponents down by the force of his unquestionably powerful will. His careful planning, unlike that of his predecessors, had ensured that the party had ample provisions for a longish siege. He wrote: 'The lamas were at their wits' end. We had food for a couple of months, so they could not boycott us.' Moreover, it was nearly September, and shortly the passes behind them would be blocked by snow. This would make it impossible for them to return, as the Tibetans were insisting, by the way they had come.

Littledale knew that he must impress the Tibetans with his importance, and refused to negotiate with any but the most senior official, or, by letter, directly with the Dalai Lama. He had instructed Rassul Galwan to lie, if necessary, to further their cause. 'You tell all that matter which make better for us. In this, lie or true does not matter,' Rassul recalls him saying. Mrs Littledale, the Tibetans were told, had been sent by her sister, Queen Victoria, to greet the Dalai Lama. They were warned that if they impeded the expedition there would follow 'a greater battle' than the one which had resulted in their being driven from northern Sikkim. 'That battle was for little men,' Rassul quotes Littledale as threatening. 'We am big men.' No doubt Littledale had phrased it a little differently, but at this stage he was clearly prepared to try anything. He himself recounts: 'Everything promised well, for they had no resources left but force, which they palpably dared not use; and, absurd as it may sound, so insecure did they feel of their position that, though there were upwards of five hundred men camped just below us, and more above, they actually had destroyed all the bridges between us and Lhasa.'

But now misfortune struck. Mrs Littledale fell ill. The nature of her illness is not disclosed by Littledale, although he admits that she had been 'more or less indisposed for some months'. Her symptoms, whatever they were, now became 'alarming'. Camping as they were in constant rain, and at more than sixteen thousand feet, Littledale realised that his wife's life was at serious risk. They could no longer consider sitting it out for two months in this bleak spot. The Tibetans, learning of his wife's illness, were quick to take advantage of the formidable Englishman's first sign of weakness. They pressed home their demands that the party should return immediately the way they had come.

Aware that he was near to defeat, Littledale now tried one last card – bribery. He sent a message to the Regent in Lhasa offering a 'donation' of five hundred pounds in silver if he would allow them to pass through the capital and travel on to Sikkim where his wife would be able to receive medical treatment. But the terrified lamas refused even to carry such a message. Finally, after Littledale had threatened to fight his way through, the lamas suggested a compromise. Instead of returning by the gruelling way they had come, the Littledales would be allowed to travel westwards to Ladakh, where there was a Moravian mission hospital. Despite her illness, Mrs Littledale protested vigorously against their capitulating, but her husband knew that they had no other choice. 'It was heartbreaking', he wrote, 'having to turn back when so near our goal, but it had to be done.'

Thus ended, just forty-nine miles from Lhasa, the most

determined – and most nearly successful – attempt so far to reach the Tibetan capital. It earned for St George Littledale the gold medal of the Royal Geographical Society. Their gallant fox-terrier, Tanny, was awarded an honorary Fellowship (entitling him to place the letters FRGS after his name) and given a special silver collar. Mrs Littledale recovered from her illness and lived into her ninetieth year. Their nephew William distinguished himself in the Boer War, only to die from gassing in the First World War.

The score now stood at eight-nil to the Tibetans. However the contest was not quite over. Already preparing to gatecrash the Forbidden Land and in pursuit of the prize that so many Asiatic explorers coveted was one of the most controversial travellers of all time. His name, once on everybody's lips but now long forgotten, was Henry Savage Landor. The story he had to tell, on his somewhat hurried return, was to dumbfound the experts, thrill the public, and blow up into a monumental row.

8. The Bizarre Adventure of Henry Savage Landor

If Henry Savage Landor's story is to be fully believed, then alongside it the adventures of most of his rivals pale into insignificance. This colourful individual had first set his sights on Lhasa while passing through China in 1891. In his memoirs – characteristically entitled *Everywhere* – he recounts: 'I had been told of the terrible trials one had to endure to reach it. The natives of Tibet were fanatically barbarous. A white man going into that country had no chance of coming back alive. All that gave me an invincible desire to visit that strange country.'

That this grandson of the cantankerous Victorian poet Walter Savage Landor was born with more than a normal streak of perversity in him was something that he would hardly have denied. Typically he tells us: 'It was, in my day, impossible to penetrate into Tibet from the south through India. Strong guards were placed on the principal Himalayan passes. It was from there that I made up my mind to enter.' Headstrong and arrogant like his grandfather (who is alleged once to have thrown his cook out of the window), he chose to make a living by seeking out the world's more outlandish spots and writing about his adventures there. His undoubted talents as an artist and photographer he used to dramatic effect in illustrating his books which enjoyed a considerable public. Tibet – remote, forbidden and thoroughly mysterious – was tailor-made for Henry and his readers.

His is a most extraordinary tale, and the reader must make up his own mind whether to believe all, or merely some of it. There can be no question that the broad outlines are true, as will become evident later. But for the details, always lurid and frequently bizarre, one has to rely upon his own written narrative.

Accompanied by thirty native carriers, he successfully crossed into Tibet on July 13, 1897, via the 18,000-foot Lumpia Pass. He had first tried to enter by the nearby Mangshan Pass, reaching an altitude, he subsequently claimed, of 22,000 feet before being forced back by altitude sickness. The going was punishing, and within five days of entering Tibet all but nine of his men had deserted him. The rest of the party pressed determinedly on, struggling waist-deep through icy torrents, evading Tibetan patrols and camping at extreme altitudes. These hardships, together with the fear of what would happen to them if they were caught smuggling an Englishman into the country, soon proved too much for five of his nine remaining men, and Savage Landor was forced to pay them off. After a further three marches, two others deserted during the night, taking with them vitally needed supplies and equipment. Worse, they began to spread word around that an Englishman was heading for Lhasa.

Their departure now left Savage Landor with only two men. One was his personal bearer, Chanden Singh, who had endeared himself to his employer, when first taken on, by presenting arms with an old cricket stump whenever he entered his master's tent. The other was a coolie named Man Singh, who turned out to be suffering from leprosy. Considering what they were to go through, these two native servants proved extraordinarily loyal and amazingly courageous. The temptation to turn back with the others must have been very strong, and both must have cursed themselves frequently during the days ahead for embarking on so rash an adventure. At least for Savage Landor, provided he survived to tell the tale, there would be a best-selling book and a hero's welcome at the end of it all.

The Tibetans were now out in force searching for the Englishman as he and his ragged party worked their way furtively eastwards along the course of the Tsangpo towards the holy city. It was while they were crossing one of the river's tributaries that misfortune struck them. One of the yaks carrying their remaining food, some three hundred rounds of ammunition and other vital stores went under, spilling its load. Savage Landor dived repeatedly into the glacier-fed torrent in a desperate attempt to retrieve part of the load, but in vain. Stranded now without food in this sterile landscape, he decided that they would have to try to buy supplies from the first Tibetan encampment or village they came across, and face the risk of being held. Three days later, exhausted and half starving, they reached the tented hamlet of Toxem. Here, much to their relief, they were well received – or so they believed. They managed to buy from the Tibetans sufficient food to keep them going for several weeks, as well as ponies for the two native servants, who by now were on their last legs.

'The demeanour of the Tibetans was so friendly, and they seemed so guileless, that I never thought of suspecting them', wrote Savage Landor afterwards. That was evidently what they intended. His two servants had been putting the new ponies through their paces before parting with any money, and had just called out to their employer for his verdict. Unwisely leaving his rifle behind in his tent, the Englishman walked over to where one of the ponies stood. 'I had just stooped to look at the pony's forelegs,' he recounted, 'when I was suddenly seized from behind by several persons who grabbed me by the neck, wrists and legs, and threw me on my face.' He fought tooth and nail to free himself from his assailants, but within seconds he was held by some thirty men. Describing the attack in his two-volume account of the affair, *In the Forbidden Land*, he wrote: 'I fought to the bitter end with my fists, feet, head and teeth each time that I got one hand or leg free from their clutches, hitting right and left at any part where I could disable my opponents.'

The struggle continued for some twenty minutes, during which the Englishman's clothes were torn almost to shreds. Finally the Tibetans managed to lasso their struggling captive with ropes, all but strangling him in the process. 'I felt as if my eyes would shoot out of their sockets,' he recounts. He was dragged, suffocating, to the ground, where the Tibetans kicked and trampled on him with their heavy, nailed boots, before binding his wrists, elbows, neck and ankles.

Meanwhile, a few yards away, Chanden Singh had been putting up a tremendous fight against some fifteen or more Tibetans, several of whom he had succeeded in injuring, before he was finally lassoed and brought to the ground. While Savage Landor was battling with his assailants he had heard his bearer repeatedly crying out to Man Singh, the leper, '*Banduk, banduk. Jaldi Banduk!*' ('Rifle, rifle. Quick, the rifle!') But four Tibetans had already seized the coolie who was too weak to put up much of a fight, pinning him to the ground. As their assailants fell upon the three of them, Savage Landor had heard a whistle blown. Now he saw what this signal meant. Some four hundred Tibetan soldiers, who had been lying out of sight around the camp, sprang to their feet and surrounded the three bound prisoners, their matchlocks pointed menacingly at them.

Months later, still furious at the indignity of their capture (and, perhaps, at his own failure to foresee it), Savage Landor wrote: 'When I realised that it took the Tibetans five hundred men [including the villagers] all counted to arrest a starved Englishman and his two half-dying servants, and that even then they dared not do it openly, but had to resort to abject treachery; when I found that these soldiers were picked troops from Lhasa and Shigatse despatched on purpose to arrest our purpose and capture us, I could not restrain a smile of contempt for those into whose hands we had at last fallen.'

To be fair to the Tibetans, it was not unreasonable to mount a force of this strength to find and intercept an Englishman, presumably armed with modern weapons, who had illegally entered their country accompanied by some thirty men. After all, they remembered only too well what had happened in Sikkim just nine years earlier when their own troops, armed only with matchlocks, had been routed by British-trained Indian soldiers using modern rifles. Ever since then, moreover, their country had been repeatedly gatecrashed by Europeans trying to reach Lhasa. Until now the Tibetans had shown considerable restraint in rounding up and turning back these individuals. The fate which had befallen Dutreuil de Rhins could hardly be laid at the feet of the authorities in Lhasa. Now, it seemed, their patience was at an end. Their anger was to be vented on the unfortunate Savage Landor.

First the Tibetans searched his baggage, soon finding his watches and chronometer whose ticking caused both alarm and wonder. 'They were passed round and round and mercilessly thrown about from one person to the other until they stopped,' Savage Landor recounts. They were then declared 'dead'. His compasses and aneroid barometers 'having no life in them' were tossed aside. The Tibetans were particularly apprehensive about his rifles lest they somehow discharged themselves. When the eight-hundred silver rupees which he had in his jacket pocket were discovered, immediately 'officers, lamas and soldiers' dived for their share, as they did every time more coins came to light.

The Tibetans were intrigued by an inflated rubber cushion which Savage Landor used as a pillow. 'The soft, smooth texture of the india rubber seemed to catch their fancy,' he noted, 'and one after the other they rubbed their cheeks on the cushion, exclaiming at the pleasant sensation it gave them.' One of them succeeded in unscrewing the valve and releasing the air with a loud hiss. There was momentary panic, followed by speculation among the Tibetans as to what evil powers this bizarre contrivance might or might not possess. Finally they came across his maps and sketch-books which aroused immediate suspicion. All his possessions were now bundled into bags and blankets and loaded onto yaks. Then, attaching the ends of the ropes which they looped around their captives' necks to their own saddles, they rode back to the settlement, dragging the three men after them.

It was here that the prisoners' long ordeal began. Before very long the Englishman, who had been separated from his two servants, was summoned by a soldier from the tent where, still firmly bound, he was being held. While preparing for his journey to Tibet, he had taken lessons in elementary Tibetan, and now overheard his escort, who first passed his hand meaningfully across his throat, tell the soldiers guarding him: 'They are going to cut off his head.' Savage Landor, however fearless, must have been apprehensive about what lay in store for him. But he had decided that it would greatly increase his and his servants' chances of survival if he managed to display a complete lack of fear, whatever trials might lie ahead.

'I had on many previous occasions found that nothing carries one further in dealings with Asiatics than to keep calm and cool,' he wrote afterwards, adding: 'I saw in a moment that if we were ever to get out of our present scrape it would be by maintaining a perfectly impassive demeanour in face of anything which might take place.' He was next led to a position from where he could see what appeared to be some kind of court, composed of shaven-headed lamas standing in a large open-fronted tent. His bearer, Chanden Singh, was now dragged forward to face them. But Savage Landor was not allowed to witness what followed, merely to listen to it.

From the mud hovel into which he was dragged, he first heard his servant being interrogated, the accuser angrily and shrilly charging him with bringing an Englishman into the country. There followed a noisy clamour from the crowd of soldiers and villagers grouped around the tent, and then silence. A few moments later he was horrified to hear the sound of a lash, followed by moans. 'I counted the strokes, the sickening noise of which is still well impressed on my memory, as they regularly and steadily fell one after the other to twenty, to thirty, forty and fifty,' he recounted.

Now came Savage Landor's turn. Half dragged, half pushed before the court, he found himself facing an effeminate looking official dressed somewhat like a clown, who turned out to be both a Grand Lama and a provincial governor with, as Savage Landor puts it, all the powers of a feudal king. He was seated, while crowded around him stood an assortment of lamas and other officials. 'As I stood silent, with my head held high before him, two or three lamas rushed at me and ordered me to kneel,' he wrote. They forced him to his knees, but Savage Landor endeavoured to keep his head high and look into the Grand Lama's face. Appearing angry, the Tibetan gestured towards the Englishman's left. As soldiers and lamas stepped aside, he saw there the unfortunate Chanden Singh, lying face downwards, stripped and bleeding. Two lamas, both burly men, now began to lash his bearer with leather thongs.

'Each time that lash fell on his wounded skin,' wrote Savage Landor, 'it felt as if a dagger had been stuck into my chest.' However, aware that this exhibition of cruelty was being put on for his benefit, he decided that under no circumstances could he afford to show any fear or pity since this, he felt, would only prolong Chanden Singh's torture. The Tibetans were unsettled by the Englishman's apparent nonchalance, and several standing near him shook their fists in his face, declaring that his turn would come next. To this he merely answered '*Nikutza, nikutza*' ('Very good, very good'), before being dragged away from the Grand Lama's presence.

But instead of being flogged, he now found himself confronted by the two priestly torturers clutching his notebooks and maps. If he told the truth, they assured him, he would be unharmed. Otherwise he would first be flogged and then beheaded. Telling the truth, it soon transpired, meant blaming everything on Chanden Singh. All he need say was that the latter had not only led him into Tibet but had also drawn all the sketches and maps. If he would agree to this then he would be escorted to the frontier unharmed and Chanden Singh would be executed instead of him.

'I explained clearly to the Lamas,' Savage Landor wrote, 'that I alone was responsible for the maps and sketches, and for finding my way so far inland. I repeated several times, slowly and distinctly, that my servant was innocent, and that therefore there was no reason to punish him.' If anyone was to be punished it must be himself. His servants had merely obeyed his orders.

This infuriated the two lamas, one of whom struck Savage Landor a heavy blow on the head which he tried to appear not to notice. Obviously the two men had their orders to obtain this face-saving 'confession' from the Englishman which, after he had seen his servant flogged, they must have assumed, would prove to be little more than a formality. In feudal Tibet, servants were used to accepting the blame and punishment for their masters' wrongdoings, but the lamas had not reckoned with Victorian England. However, if that was to be his attitude, they warned him, 'then we shall beat you and your man until you say what we want.' They began at once on the unfortunate Chanden Singh.

At this point one is justified in asking whether Savage Landor might not have spared himself and his servants – particularly Chanden Singh – a great deal of suffering if he had taken a somewhat more conciliatory approach to the Tibetans. After all, he must have realised why they were so angry with him – the ninth European in succession to force his way uninvited and illegally into their country. He must also have known that there was no possible hope now of their reaching Lhasa. Retreat was the only option. But while there could be no question of his allowing Chanden Singh to be beheaded in his stead, it would appear that in making this offer the Tibetans were – by their own standards – being conciliatory. They were indicating to Savage Landor that they had no wish to injure him, despite their anger, if some way round could be found.

Had he expressed appreciation of their proposal, and in return suggested some other face-saving formula involving no further harm to anyone, he might perhaps have saved the day. An explanation to the Grand Lama of just why he had so wanted to set eyes on their beautiful and world-famous holy capital, followed by a fulsome apology, and perhaps even an offer to demonstrate some of his European magic (with maybe the gift of a rifle), might well at this stage have resulted in the three of them merely being expelled. Of course, it might not have worked. But at least he could have tried to use diplomacy. As it is, one has the suspicion that his uncompromising and arrogant stand, however brave, was largely to blame for what followed. And here another, less charitable, thought occurs to one. Savage Landor was there to gather material for a best-seller. Mere expulsion would have provided a far less lurid tale for his eager public than that which, in the event, his hair-raising experiences at the hands of his captors did yield.

But whatever his reason, the die was now cast. While Savage Landor looked helplessly on, the flogging of his bearer was resumed, the unfortunate man biting the ground to try and stifle his cries. 'Chanden Singh behaved heroically,' wrote Savage Landor. 'Not a word of complaint, nor a prayer for mercy, came from his lips. He said that he had spoken the truth and had nothing more to say.' Feigning lack of concern at the fate of his servant, the Englishman was finally dragged away by the Tibetans to a spot from where he could hear the cross-examination continuing and 'those dreadful sounds of the lash still being administered'. Then, mercifully, it suddenly began to rain heavily. At once the flogging ceased as the Tibetans ran for shelter in the tents, dragging their captives after them.

It was here that Savage Landor found himself in the charge of a Tibetan officer of fairly senior rank. This man, he tells us, treated him with unexpected compassion, telling him: 'I am a soldier, not a Lama. I have come from Lhasa with my men to arrest you, and you are now our prisoner. But you have shown no fear, and I respect you.' To underline this, he pressed his forehead against Savage Landor's and thrust out his tongue in traditional Tibetan greeting. If Savage Landor is to be believed (and there is no way of knowing how good his Tibetan was) they then had a long and friendly conversation about the soldiers of their respective lands. The Tibetan assured the Englishman that the matchlock was more efficient than the modern rifle, pointing out that provided you had powder left you could fire almost anything from it. 'Pebbles, earth or nails did as good work as any lead bullet,' he insisted. But if that were so, Savage Landor asked, why then had some Tibetan soldiers they had briefly encountered earlier in their journey run away. 'Yes, I know that they ran, but it was not through fear,' his captor replied. 'It was because they did not wish to hurt you.' When the Englishman enquired why in that case they had run so fast, the officer roared with laughter, patting his prisoner delightedly on the back.

But this light relief was to be short-lived, for very soon his new friend was summoned by the Grand Lama, and a replacement guard took over. They proved to be extremely hostile, knocking Savage Landor from his seat and on to a heap of dung stored in the tent for fuel. His feet and knees were bound together so tightly that the pain kept him from sleeping, and before long his clothing was invaded by vermin which were not to allow him a moment's peace for the remainder of his captivity.

During the night the friendly officer returned and to Savage Landor's astonishment began to loosen his bonds under the pretence of tightening them, abusing the soldiers angrily for their carelessness. Covering the Englishman with a blanket, he whispered quickly: 'Your head is to be cut off tomorrow. Escape tonight. There are no soldiers outside.' He then extinguished the butter lamp and lay down not far from his prisoner. Wrote Savage Landor: 'It would have been comparatively easy, when all the men had fallen asleep, to slip from under the tent and steal away. I had got my hands easily out of the ropes, and should have had no difficulty in undoing all my other bonds, but the thought that I should be leaving my two men at the mercy of the Tibetans prevented my carrying the escape into effect.' The officer then rose to check that his soldiers were asleep, returning to whisper urgently to the Englishman: '*Palado!*' ('Go!'). Savage Landor thanked him but explained that he could not think of deserting his two men.

One finds oneself wondering whether once more the Tibetans

were not trying to find a way out of the impasse, with the friendly officer acting on the Grand Lama's instructions and not merely out of the kindness of his heart. For without food or transport of any kind, and with every man's hand against him, Savage Landor would not have got very far, unless the escape had had official sanction. It may have been no coincidence that the officer had been to see the Grand Lama shortly before making the offer. Moreover, unless the plan had official approval he himself would undoubtedly have paid for Savage Landor's escape with his life. The officer, Savage Landor tells us, was apparently 'much disappointed' at the rejection of his offer, but 'treated me with ever-increasing respect and deference', even feeding his captive from his own *puku*, or wooden bowl.

Following their officer's example, the Tibetan soldiers also began to feed their trussed charge, who had not eaten for some thirty-six hours, from their own rations. 'Their hands, it is true,' Savage Landor observes, 'were not over clean, but on such occasions it does not do to be too particular, and I was so hungry that the food they gave me seemed delicious.' But having given the Englishman one, and possibly two, chances to extricate himself, the Tibetans were now in no mood to make further concessions to this madman. Before long a soldier entered the tent and informed Savage Landor that he was to be flogged, both his legs broken, his eyes burned out and, finally, his head would be cut off.

He was next dragged outside where heavy iron handcuffs were substituted for the ropes binding his wrists. Clearly wishing to avoid another fight, the Tibetans had resorted to guile in persuading him to be handcuffed. 'We have ponies here, and are going to take you back to the frontier,' they assured him. 'But the *Pombo* [provincial governor] wishes to see you first. Do not make any resistance. Let us exchange the ropes round your wrists for these iron handcuffs. You will not wear them for more than a few moments while we are leading you to his presence. Then you will be free.' But once he was securely shackled, the fury of the onlooking crowd was turned against the Englishman. 'They spat upon me and threw mud at me,' Savage Landor recounts. 'The lamas behaved worse than any of the others, and the one who had sworn that I should be in no way ill used if I would submit quietly to be handcuffed was the most prominent among my tormentors, and the keenest in urging the crowd to further brutality.'

But before any real violence could begin the friendly officer arrived and had him removed to the safety of a mud hovel. Ordering everyone else out of the room, Savage Landor recounts, the officer 'laid his forehead upon mine in a sign of compassion, and then sadly shook his head.' Then he whispered: 'There is no more hope. Your head will be cut off tonight. The lamas are bad and my heart is aching. You are like my brother, and I am grieved.' Moments later the mob burst into the room and Savage Landor was dragged once more outside. There he was spotted by Chanden Singh, obviously badly injured after his flogging. Crying out 'Sir, sir, I am dying!', he started to drag himself on his stomach towards his master. 'His poor face was hardly recognisable,' wrote Savage Landor, 'it bore the traces of such awful suffering.' The unfortunate man was seized by his guards and flung roughly back. Savage Landor, whose legs had been unbound, momentarily shook free of his captors in an attempt to reach his bearer, but the Tibetans quickly seized him too, dragging him towards a pony standing nearby.

His horrified eyes then fell on the wooden saddle on the animal's back. Projecting forward from the rear of this was a row of vicious-looking iron spikes, clearly designed to catch the rider in the small of the back – unless he was able to maintain a forward seat, difficult enough over rough, undulating country, and doubly so with no stirrups and with his hands manacled behind his back. As he studied the bizarre-looking saddle, Savage Landor was swept bodily off his feet by the soldiers and dumped unceremoniously on the pony's back. Then, escorted by thirty armed men on ponies, and accompanied by Man

Singh, his leprous servant, mounted on an unsaddled beast, they set off at a furious pace across country.

'But for those awful spikes,' Savage Landor wrote, 'the ride would not have been so very bad, for the pony I rode was a fine spirited animal, and the country around was curious and interesting.' Eventually they reached their destination, where some two hundred horsemen, including lamas, officers and soldiers, were drawn up with the *pombo*, or governor, at their head. The precise purpose of this parade, apparently in the middle of nowhere, is not clear from Savage Landor's account. But the next moment his pony was lashed by a soldier and sent speeding past the spot where the *pombo*, dressed in a yellow silk jacket and trousers and pointed hat, sat astride his mount. As he drew level with the governor, Savage Landor saw a man armed with a matchlock kneel down and take careful aim at him. Fortunately – or perhaps intentionally – the shot missed its target. However, terrified by the sound of the explosion, Savage Landor's pony began to buck, forcing the spikes agonisingly into his back. But – if his story is to be believed – this was merely the first entertainment to be provided for the amusement of the *pombo* and other Tibetan officials present.

The Englishman's pony was now recaptured, and rider and mount were led before the governor. 'I pretended not to feel the effect of the spikes tearing the flesh off my backbone,' Savage Landor recounts, 'and when they led me before the *pombo* to show him how covered with blood I was, I expressed satisfaction at riding such an excellent pony. This seemed to puzzle them,' he adds. By now the reader may have begun to wonder whether, in relating his misadventures, he was not guilty of gross exaggeration. However medical and other evidence was largely to bear his story out. But if not a liar, he was certainly a glutton for punishment, all but deliberately provoking his torturers into testing him to the limits.

A rope made from yak hair, some fifty yards long, was now attached to his manacles, while a mounted soldier held on to the other end. Then yelling, cat-calling and shouting war cries, the

Tibetans drove Savage Landor's mount ahead of them. 'In order to accelerate our speed,' Savage Landor wrote, 'a horseman rode by my side lashing my pony to make it go its hardest. Meanwhile the horseman who held the cord did his utmost to pull me out of the saddle, no doubt in the hope of seeing me trampled to death by the cohort behind me. As I leaned my body forward so as to maintain my seat, and with my arms pulled violently backwards by the rope, the flesh was rubbed off my hands and knuckles by the chain of the handcuffs. In places the bone was exposed, and, of course, every tug brought me into forcible contact with the spikes and inflicted deeper wounds.' Then, suddenly, the yak-hair rope broke, flinging the soldier holding it off his pony, and almost unhorsing Savage Landor. However, the rope was reattached and the game continued.

Then, some way ahead, he spotted a soldier with a matchlock obviously lying in wait for him at the foot of a sand dune. 'My pony,' Savage Landor wrote, 'sank deep in the sand, and could not travel fast here, which, I suppose, was the reason why this spot had been selected.' As he drew level with the soldier, the man fired. Once again the shot missed – by sheer luck, Savage Landor insists, but more likely by intent. All this time the Tibetans were travelling eastwards, although to where Savage Landor had no idea. Finally, towards sunset, they came to a large monastery on a hilltop, at whose foot they halted. He was now dragged from his saddle, weak with pain and loss of blood, and it was here that the final act of this bizarre drama was to take place.

During the next few days, he tells us, he was subjected to a series of extremely unpleasant ordeals intended presumably to break his spirit and to discourage other foreigners from gate-crashing Tibet's frontiers in future. First, Savage Landor tells us, he was taken to what he describes as 'the execution ground', for it was here, his captors assured him, that he would shortly be decapitated. He was first made to stand on a log with his legs wide apart. Then, he recounts, 'several men held me by the body while four or five others, using their combined strength, stretched my legs as wide apart as they could go.' His ankles were then bound tightly to the log with cord made from yak hair, 'so tight that they cut grooves into my skin and flesh'. Lined up in a row before him, there stood what Savage Landor describes as 'the most villainous brutes I have ever set eyes upon'. One of them held 'a great knobbed mallet used for fracturing bones', another a large, two-handed execution sword, while the rest carried 'various ghastly instruments of torture'. A crowd, 'thirsting for my blood', looked on expectantly, while three musicians playing horn, cymbals, and drum 'added to the horror of the scene'.

Before him stood the *pombo* himself. In his hand was a red-hot iron bar with a wooden handle. The crowd, according to Savage Landor, began to shout angrily: 'We will burn out your eyes!' To this, as he moved towards the Englishman brandishing the glowing iron, the governor added: 'You have come to this country to see. This, then, is the punishment for you . . .' He now thrust the red-hot bar towards his victim until it was only an inch from his eyes. Precisely how close it was Savage Landor could not see, for instinctively he shut both eyes tightly. 'Though the time seemed interminable,' he wrote afterwards, 'I do not think that the heated bar was before my eyes actually longer than thirty seconds or so.' But it was near enough to scorch his nose, and cause intense pain in his left eye. When finally he opened his eyes he saw to his relief, albeit through a red haze, that the horrifying implement had been dropped and lay sizzling away on the damp soil.

The crowd, Savage Landor tells us, soon began to get impatient, screaming demands for his death. 'Kill him, kill him! We cannot frighten him! Kill him . . .' He recounts what followed: 'A huge two-handed sword was now handed to the *pombo*, who drew it out of its sheath . . . A lama held his sword, while he turned up one sleeve of his coat to have his arms free, and the lamas turned up the other for him. Then he strode towards me with slow, ponderous steps, swinging the shiny, sharp blade from side to side before him, with his bare arms out-stretched.'

A Tibetan soldier who was holding him by his hair, which had now not been cut for several months, was ordered to make him bend his head forward. But this he refused to do, resisting with what little strength he had left. '. . . never until I had lost my last atom of strength', he wrote, 'would these ruffians make me stoop before them.' The *pombo* was not put out by this, however. 'The executioner, now close to me, held the sword with his nervous hands, lifting it high above his shoulder. He then brought it down to my neck, which he touched with the blade to measure the distance, as it were, for a clean, effective stroke. Then, drawing back a step, he quickly raised the sword again and struck a blow at me with all his might.'

It missed – deliberately – for this was part of the ritual of a Tibetan execution, Savage Landor tells us. The *pombo* now lifted his sword again, bringing it flashing down towards the other side of his victim's neck. 'This time the blade passed so near,' he wrote, 'that the point cannot have been more than half an inch or so from my neck.' The next blow he assumed would be the last, for by now the crowd was demanding that the decapitation should be carried out without further ado. But then something extremely curious happened. The *pombo*, if Savage Landor is to be believed, appears to have lost his nerve, refusing to carry on with the execution. For a while the lamas angrily remonstrated with him, but the Governor 'kept his eyes on me in a half-respectful, half-frightened manner, and refused to move.'

In the middle of all this Man Singh, the leper, arrived with his escort, having repeatedly fallen from his saddleless pony and thus dropped far behind the main party. He was now bound by the ankles to the same log as his master. '. . . the coolness and bravery of the poor wretch during these terrible trials,' wrote Savage Landor, 'were really marvellous.' By now both men were terribly hungry, and the Englishman, in his pidgin Tibetan, asked a passing lama for some food, pointing out that unless they were fed they would die of starvation which would deprive them of the satisfaction of torturing their captives further, or even of executing them. For that, they had been assured, would be their fate the following day. The result was that food was brought for them. 'I have hardly ever enjoyed a meal more,' Savage Landor wrote afterwards, 'though the lamas stuffed the food down my throat with their unwashed fingers so fast that they nearly choked me.'

Further rough handling followed, including being stretched on a Tibetan-style rack for what Savage Landor described as 'the most terrible twenty-four hours I have ever passed', and during which his limbs gradually lost all feeling. But then, quite fortuitously, came the turning point in his fortunes. It happened as the *pombo* and his men were rifling through his boxes of scientific instruments 'with an amusing mixture of curiosity and caution over everything they touched'. Eventually they came upon the cases of undeveloped photographic plates. The *pombo* noticed that on being exposed to the daylight these gradually turned yellow, and nervously asked Savage Landor why this was.

'It is a sign,' the Englishman warned him, 'that you will suffer for what you are doing to me.' Immediately the *pombo* ordered a hole to be dug in the ground some distance away and all the plates to be buried as quickly as possible. At first the soldiers refused, but eventually were forced into acquiescence by the lamas. This evil omen was soon followed, as luck had it, by another. At the bottom of one of Savage Landor's cases they came upon a small flat object which he immediately recognised as his large bath sponge which had become greatly reduced in size by the weight of the photographic plates on top of it. After being handled cautiously, for some of the Tibetans thought it might be explosive, it was finally tossed aside. It had been raining not long before, and by chance the sponge fell into a puddle. Noticing that it was beginning to swell rapidly as it absorbed the water, Savage Landor began to address the sponge in English, or so he tells us. 'As I spoke louder and louder to the sponge,' he recounts, 'it gradually swelled to its normal size.' The Tibetans, he adds, 'became so panic-stricken at what they believed to be an exhibition of my occult powers that there was a general stampede in every direction.'

The last straw, so far as the Tibetans were concerned, occurred when one of them picked up Savage Landor's Martini-Henry rifle and inserted a cartridge in the breech. When the Englishman warned him that he had not closed the bolt fully, and therefore was likely to injure himself if he pressed the trigger, he was struck on the head with the butt for his pains. The lama now pointed the rifle at one of the Englishman's yaks, some thirty yards away. When he pressed the trigger, the weapon exploded. Savage Landor wrote: 'The rifle, flying out of his hands, described a somersault in the air, and the lama fell backward to the ground, where he remained spread out flat, bleeding all over and screaming like a child. His nose was squashed, one eye had been put out, and his teeth shattered. . . . The injured lama, I may say, was the one at the head of the party that wanted to have my head cut off, so that, naturally enough, I could not help betraying my satisfaction at the accident.'

Even the *pombo*, Savage Landor noted, 'could not help joining in my laughter at the lama's sorrowful plight,' adding: 'I believe he was rather glad that the accident had happened. For, if he had until then been uncertain whether to kill me or not, he felt, after what had occurred, that it was not prudent to attempt it.' That evening, after the *pombo* had talked with his senior lamas and officers, soldiers were sent to free Savage Landor from 'the stretching log', although his handcuffs were left on. Unable to stand without support, Savage Landor lay on the ground waiting for the life to return to his limbs. At first he feared that necrosis had set in and that he might have lost the use of his feet for ever, but after two or three hours the circulation began to return, causing excruciating pain.

Now, almost as though anxious to make amends, the *pombo* laid on an extraordinary display of horsemanship and marksmanship with prizes presented to the winners. Although the standard of shooting was abysmal, some of the feats of horsemanship impressed Savage Landor. One of the most spectacular of these consisted of a rider galloping at full tilt towards a man standing on the ground and sweeping him on to his saddle. Finally, the *pombo* himself stepped down from his throne and performed a strange, snake-like dance, apparently under hypnosis.

Although the governor had clearly made up his mind to spare Savage Landor's life, there was still strong feeling among many of the lamas that he should be beheaded, and there was even an attempt by the latter, he claims, to poison him. It was finally agreed that the decision should be left to the oracle, who called for a lock of the Englishman's hair and clippings from his finger and toe nails. It was when removing a small piece of finger nail that one of the lamas appeared startled by the sight of Savage Landor's hands, at once calling others to come and look. The *pombo* himself was summoned, and after one look immediately declared that the issue was settled. Suddenly and unexpectedly their captivity and ordeal were over. When, together with Chanden Singh and Man Singh, Savage Landor was taken under escort to the Indian frontier and freed, he was told by the soldiers the reason for this amazement at the sight of his hands. 'My fingers happen to be webbed rather higher than usual, and this is most highly thought of in Tibet. He who possesses such fingers has, according to the Tibetans, a charmed life, and, no matter how much one tries, no harm can be done to him.'

There, somewhat condensed, is Henry Savage Landor's long, bizarre and sensational tale. The moment he had recovered sufficiently from his mishandling, he burst into print with his highly colourful, two-volume work entitled *In the Forbidden Land*. Published by the respected firm of Heinemann, his extraordinary story at once became a best-seller, going into numerous editions and translations. But, some of his readers must have found themselves wondering, was it all true? As though anticipating that doubts might be cast on his tale, the author took the precaution of including some forty pages of appendices at the end. These comprise statements and affidavits sworn before the Indian Government magistrate sent to investigate the whole affair.

Perhaps the most important of these is the deposition of Dr Hakua Wilson, a missionary, who examined Savage Landor's injuries soon after he reached safety, and who had known and travelled with him earlier. He told the examining magistrate: 'I could hardly recognise Mr Landor: he looked very ill and seemed nearly exhausted. I examined his injuries and found that his forehead had the skin off and was covered with scabs. His cheeks and nose were in the same state. His hair had grown long. He was unshaven and unkempt. He was in rags and dirty, covered with swarms of lice. His hands, fingers and wrists were swollen and wounded. On his spine at the waist he had an open sore, and the parts around were swollen and red. His seat was covered with marks of wounds caused by spikes. His feet were swollen, and so were his ankles. The flesh about the latter was much hurt and contused, showing marks of cords having been tightly bound round them. He was in a very low condition.'

Wilson added: 'I am confident, if he had been a few days longer in the hands of the Tibetans . . . he would have died.' Attached to his sworn statement was a detailed list of Savage Landor's injuries. These included 'five large sores along the spinal column', and the observation that the spine itself had sustained 'severe injuries'. In addition to the mass of wounds and other injuries, especially to the limbs, Wilson observed 'burns, etc' on Savage Landor's face, which might appear to confirm the incident involving the red-hot iron bar. Wilson also reported on Chanden Singh's injuries, noting: 'So severely appears the punishment to have been administered that large patches of skin and flesh have been torn off by the lashing.' He described him as being 'in very poor health', although the flogging had taken place three weeks earlier.

Included in the appendices were sworn statements by Chanden and Man Singh. The latter confirmed that the Tibetans had been 'on the point of beheading my master', had 'tried to burn out his eyes', 'fired at him twice to kill him' and had 'tried to pull him off his horse to have him trampled upon.' Chanden Singh confirmed that when finally he had been reunited with his employer 'he was handcuffed with enormous cuffs, clothes torn to rags, bleeding from the waist, feet and hands swollen.' He also confirmed seeing his master being lifted onto a spiked saddle and tied by a long rope the other end of which was held by a horseman.

Furthermore, an Indian Government frontier officer, one Kharak Singh, told the examining magistrate that several Tibetans he had spoken to had actually admitted taking part in the tortures, and had agreed 'that all of Mr Landor's story was true'. But they argued that they had been justified in treating him so, indeed that it was 'their duty'. But, surprisingly perhaps, it was not over the question of whether or not he was tortured that a row now broke, but over his geographical claims, in particular his assertion that he had ascended, without ropes or climbing boots, to an altitude of twenty-two thousand feet on the Mangshan Pass during his first attempt to cross into Tibet. These claims, by a man whom they regarded as an upstart, greatly upset the mountaineering and geographical establishment of the day.

His scientific results, including route surveys, were in turn challenged in both the *Alpine Journal* and the *Geographical Journal*. Writing in the latter, Sir Thomas Holdich of the Indian Survey charged that the maps which Savage Landor had brought back with him (they had surprisingly been returned by the Tibetans) 'do not differ materially in topographical detail from those with which he was supplied on his outward journey. . . .' To the chagrin of the geographers, these maps were being currently exhibited in a Bond Street gallery where they were described as 'the latest and only accurate maps of South-Western Tibet, by A. H. Savage Landor, from his own surveys.'

The row now became public, spilling angrily onto the pages

of *The Times* in a letter from one of the most distinguished explorers and climbers of his time, Douglas Freshfield, a Royal Geographical Society Gold medallist and later its President. Writing from the Athenaeum on January 3, 1899, and devoting some twenty column-inches to his victim, Freshfield accused him of failing to produce any evidence 'to convince competent judges that his "results" are of any scientific value.' He added, furthermore, that 'no mountaineer can accept the marvellous feats of speed and endurance Mr Landor believes himself to have accomplished.' Savage Landor's 'very sensational tale', he charged, 'affects the credit, both at home and on the Continent, of English travellers, critics and scientific societies.' In other words, he called Henry Savage Landor a liar and a bounder.

Savage Landor was hardly the man to take such accusations lying down. He hit back with a blistering attack on Freshfield, challenging the latter's right to consider himself 'an expert', and accusing him of inaccuracy 'beyond belief' and with altering and distorting his words 'to prove his allegations'. On the question of his own claim to have reached twenty-two thousand feet, he declared 'The altitude reached was on the Mangshan Mountain, and not on the Pass, as Mr Freshfield misstates.' Just because certain peaks 'are not marked on the maps consulted by this gentleman', he went on, did not mean that they did not exist.

'As for the nailed boots, ropes, etc, to which Mr Freshfield attaches so much importance, and which are in my mind the principal cause of most Alpine accidents, I have stated before that I have never required them, nor have I seen any mountaineer in the Himalayas use them. I have, however, often heard of scores of amateur Alpine climbers being dragged together into precipices and killed owing to the use of these "safety" articles.'

After citing various authorities who, he claimed, accepted the scientific results of his journey, Savage Landor pointed out that 'all my maps, sketches, photographs, collections, clothes, which I brought back from Tibet, and the very boots which I wore on my ascent and descent of the Mangshan Mountain' were on exhibition at 160, Bond Street, so that 'the public may see, examine, and judge for itself.' Today's reader, too, must decide for himself whether Savage Landor's narrative carries total conviction, or whether he deliberately exaggerated or embroidered it in order to produce a more exciting book.

Even now the strange affair was not over, for the irate traveller was hell-bent on obtaining satisfaction from the Tibetans for the suffering they had undoubtedly caused him and his two native servants. But the Viceroy of India, Lord Elgin, strongly advised the British Government against sending a punitive expedition into Tibet, or even of seeking reparation, for a traveller who had sought neither British nor Chinese approval for his journey. It is interesting to note, though, that nowhere in the file on the affair in the India Office Library, confidential as it then was, does anyone cast doubts on the truth of Savage Landor's story.

Lord Curzon, then Under-Secretary at the Foreign Office but soon to become Viceroy himself, agreed with Elgin's recommendation, declaring: 'Tibet is not open to foreigners, and anyone attempting to enter the country does so at his own risk entirely.' Before long – when it suited him – he was to change his tune dramatically. And then, as we shall see, the Tibetans would more than pay for their inhumanity to Henry Savage Landor.

9. The Nightmare
of Susie Rijnhart

But one heartrending tale still remains to be told – that of Charles Rijnhart, the youngest of all Tibetan travellers. He was only eleven months old when his missionary parents set out for Lhasa in the spring of 1898. Of all the attempts by westerners to reach the holy capital, theirs was perhaps the most foolhardy. Certainly it was the most heroic.

When Dutch-born Petrus Rijnhart and his Canadian wife Susie set their hearts on getting there it seems likely that they were unaware of the mishandling which Savage Landor had suffered only a few months earlier. Otherwise they might have thought twice, particularly as they had a young baby who obviously could not be left behind. For at that time they were living in a remote area of the Chinese-Tibetan borderlands, cut off from all news of the outside world. This newly-wed couple, not sent by any missionary society but financed by the donations of friends and from their own savings, had left home in the autumn of 1894. Their first goal was the remote but famous monastery of Kumbum where, six years earlier, William Rockhill had spent a month, disguised as a pilgrim, before making his unsuccessful attempt to reach Lhasa.

Their arrival in the region had coincided with the Moslem uprising of 1895. Susie Rijnhart was a doctor, and she and her husband had endeared themselves to the local people by treating the wounded as well as victims of smallpox and diptheria. The abbot of Kumbum monastery, fearing for their safety, had invited them to move into the lamasery. Here the Rijnharts had set up a small medical centre, sharing months of terror with the inhabitants whose friendship and confidence they thus managed to win. But Lhasa was really their goal, and before long they felt the call to move on. They transferred their base to the village of Tankar, some twenty-five miles to the north-west and astride the great caravan route to Lhasa. Here, in addition to the Chinese and Tibetan they already spoke, they learned Mongolian. Here, too, their only child Charles was born.

The Rijnharts' plan was to move once more, this time as near as possible to Lhasa, settle there for a year of medical and evangelical work, and only then try to reach the holy city. Their Tibetan friends had warned them that although they might safely venture to within a day's march of the capital, they must not try to enter it because, as Europeans, they would defile it. But the Rijnharts were determined to reach Lhasa, though they confided this to no one. 'We knew,' wrote Susie Rijnhart in her remarkable account of their experiences, *With the Tibetans in Tent and Temple*, 'that if ever the gospel were proclaimed in Lhasa, someone would have to be the first to undertake the journey, to meet the difficulties, to preach the first sermon, and perhaps never return to tell the tale. . . .' The message of Christ, she added, could hardly be preached in the Buddhist stronghold 'without some suffering, some persecution, nay without tears and blood'. Before their journey was finished, the Rijnharts would suffer all these. They had lived on the edge of Tibet long enough to realise the grave risks they were taking, not merely with the authorities in Lhasa but more immediately with the bandits who roamed the lawless region through which they must first pass. One could be excused for wondering whether the Rijnharts were not bent on martyrdom.

They left Tankar on May 20, 1898, taking with them their dog Topsy, three native servants, five riding ponies and twelve more to carry their baggage and stocks of food. From the experience of earlier travellers they knew that hostile chiefs might well refuse to allow them to buy supplies, so they took with them sufficient to last, if necessary, for two years. Some they sent ahead by camel to a Mongol settlement through which they would pass in about a month. The Rijnharts wore Tibetan costume for the journey, while their baby son – 'little Charlie', they called him – was dressed in western-style baby clothes plus a tiny fur coat and boots, and, for special occasions, a Tibetan gown and sash.

During the following three gruelling months they passed safely through bandit-infested regions (where not long before rustlers had carried off some 50,000 cattle and sheep), crossed the treacherous Tsaidam marshes and toiled over stormy passes strewn with the skeletons of luckless pack animals. Whenever they came upon nomads or villagers as they pressed steadily onwards towards Lhasa, eight hundred miles to the south-west, they handed out their evangelical tracts, printed in Tibetan, while every night Petrus Rijnhart recorded the day's happenings in his diary. On June 30, Charlie celebrated his first birthday, his mother making a birthday cake for him. A local chieftain, invited to the party, had a salute fired in his honour. Susie Rijnhart recalled afterwards: 'How thoroughly baby enjoyed those days, when he made the tents ring with joyousness from his musical laughter, his shouts and the beating of our Russian brass wash-basin which he used as a drum. Then from sheer weariness he would fall asleep, leaving the camp pervaded by a stillness, made sweet by the fact that he was still there.' Their progress was slow but they were full of optimism.

Then suddenly their fortunes began to turn. Two of their three men deserted, and soon afterwards, during a storm, five of their best ponies were stolen. In the middle of this, little Charlie started teething. His mother noticed that a gland in his neck was swollen, but by August 21 she observed with relief that his eight teeth were finally through the gums. The weather turned fine again, the worst of the passes had been crossed and they were now only two hundred miles or so from Lhasa. The hillsides were ablaze with wild flowers and they picked these as they travelled. 'We all sang for very joy,' wrote Susie Rijnhart. But this happiness was to prove short-lived. She recounted afterwards: 'The morning of the darkest day in our history arose, bright, cheery and full of promise, bearing no omen of the cloud that was about to fall upon us. Our breakfast was thoroughly enjoyed, Charlie ate more heartily than he had done for some days, and we resumed our journey full of hope. Riding along we talked of the future, its plans, its work, and its unknown successes and failures.'

Together they discussed little Charlie's future, with Petrus insisting that he must have as normal a childhood as possible once they had returned safely from Lhasa, declaring: 'He shall have all the blocks, trains, rocking horses and other things that boys in the homeland have, so that when he shall have grown up he may not feel that because he was a missionary's son he missed the joys that brighten other boys' lives.'

But little Charlie was not destined to reach boyhood, nor even to see out that day. He was riding, as usual, in his father's arms when, as often happened, he appeared to fall asleep. On halting, Rahim, their servant, gently took him from Rijnhart's arms so as not to awaken him before the tent was pitched and his food prepared. His mother describes what followed: 'Rahim very tenderly laid our lovely boy down and, while I knelt ready to cover him comfortably, his appearance attracted my attention. I went to move him, and found that he was unconscious. A great fear chilled me and I called out to Mr Rijnhart that I felt anxious for baby, and asked him quickly to get me the hypodermic syringe. . . . In the meantime I loosened baby's garments, chafed his wrists, performed artificial respiration, though feeling almost sure that nothing would avail . . .'

With terrible poignancy she describes their prayers – 'to Him who holds all life in His hands, to let us have our darling child'. In this bleak spot they must truly have felt that God had forsaken them in their hour of direst need. 'Could it be possible,' she wrote, 'that the very joy of our life, the only human thing that made life and labour sweet amid the desolation and isolation of Tibet – could it be possible that even this – the child of our love should be snatched from us in that dreary mountain country – by the cold, chill hand of Death?'

But both of them knew, and so too did their sobbing servant Rahim, that there was no recalling the lifeless child in their arms. Little Charlie, aged one year, one month and twenty-two days, was fated to travel no further. 'We realised that we clasped in our arms only the casket which had held our precious jewel,' his mother wrote. 'The jewel itself had been taken for a brighter setting in a brighter world, the little flower blooming on the bleak and barren Dang La had been plucked and transplanted on the Mountains Delectable to bask and bloom forever in the sunshine of God's love. But oh! what a void in our hearts! How empty and desolate our tent. . . .'

It then struck the Rijnharts that were the Tibetans to discover that they were harbouring a dead child, Charlie's body might be taken from them and forcibly disposed of according to local custom. This would mean cutting it up before laying it, stripped of clothes, on the bare mountainside to be torn to pieces by wolves, vultures and other creatures of the Tibetan wilds. To avoid any risk of this, for there were nomads hovering near their encampment, the sorrowing couple decided to bury little Charlie at once. In the privacy of their tent they emptied one of their medicine boxes and lined it with towels. Then Charlie's father and the faithful Rahim went outside and together dug a grave. In her book, Susie Rijnhart recalls those final moments: 'With hands whose every touch throbbed with tenderness, I robed baby in white Japanese flannel and laid him on his side in the coffin where he looked so pure and calm as if he were in a sweet and restful sleep. In his hand was placed a little bunch of white asters and blue poppies which Rahim had gathered from the mountainside, and as the afternoon wore away he seemed to grow more beautiful and precious. But night was coming on and dangers threatened, and the last wrench must come. Many of his little belongings were put into the coffin, accompanied by our names written on a piece of linen and on cards. Then came the agony of the last look. Our only child, who had brought such joy to our home, and who had done so much to make friends for us among the natives – to leave his body in such a cold, bleak place seemed more than we could endure.'

The three of them stood beside the grave and lowered the little coffin gently into it, while Rijnhart read the burial service, translating it for Rahim, a Muslim from Ladakh, to understand. Thus Charles Carson Rijnhart became the first, and perhaps the last, western baby ever to be buried in Tibet. Quite possibly, too, his is the first Christian grave there, for the unfortunate Dutreuil de Rhins has no known resting place. To make certain that wild animals would not dig up his pitiful remains, Rijnhart and Rahim rolled a heavy boulder over the grave. Finally, to deter inquisitive natives, they obliterated all signs of the earth ever having been disturbed.

That night was spent camped beside their child's grave. Heavy rain, turning to snow, fell as they lay, unable to sleep, knowing that next morning they must move on, leaving Charlie for ever. Of that stormy night, Susie Rijnhart wrote: 'We could only think of our precious one, and be thankful that the body from which the vital spark had fled had no power to feel the chill of the mountain blast.' Curiously, although a doctor, she makes no mention of the cause of their baby's death, and one can only assume that the high altitudes at which they were travelling – often between sixteen and seventeen thousand feet – had proved too much for his tiny lungs.

The next morning, with no baby to dress and feed, Susie Rijnhart felt desperately aware of their loss, no doubt blaming herself for exposing him to such risk. But they had to move on, and her husband lifted her gently into her saddle. Then the three of them, with tears on their cheeks, rode away from the lonely grave which they would never see again. But little did they realise how grateful they would soon be to the Almighty for sparing their child the misery and suffering which they themselves were going to have to endure.

Their final march towards Lhasa now took on a familiar pattern. They came upon the first Tibetan encampment, were intercepted, successfully evaded their guards, were halted by a stronger force and instructed to stay put. The *pombo* (a friendly one, fortunately) then arrived, and they were ordered to leave by the way they came. They refused and began to negotiate. Being able to speak fluent Tibetan, and familiar with the courtesies of the people, the Rijnharts encountered none of the hostility which Savage Landor had provoked. Indeed the Tibetans were fascinated by these foreigners who could speak their language, who wore their clothes and had even read their scriptures. The Rijnharts explained to the *pombo* that they did not wish to proceed any further towards the holy city, but sought permission rather to set up their medical mission at this spot. They hoped thereby (though they did not tell him) to win the confidence of the people and eventually to be allowed to enter Lhasa. But their request was rejected out of hand. Considering they were Christian missionaries (although the Tibetans may not have fully realised this) they had got off very lightly in simply being turned away. Yet their disappointment, after losing their child in the attempt, must have been bitterly intense. However, even now the Rijnharts' tragedy was far from over.

After two days of negotiation, they managed to reach the usual compromise with the Tibetans. Instead of having to leave the country by the way they had come, it was agreed that they might take a shorter, more easterly route. They were given fresh ponies, all the food they required and a three-man armed escort as far as Tashi Gompa, a large monastery some fortnight's journey away. It was here that the Rijnharts hoped to persuade the abbot to allow them to spend the winter, as they had done at the great lamasery of Kumbum three years previously. It was secretly agreed between the Rijnharts and the faithful Rahim that he would make his own way westwards across Tibet to his home in Ladakh. He would accompany them for the first day, then slip quietly away from the party and head home independently. The Rijnharts rewarded him liberally in silver for his loyalty and devotion, presenting him also with a carbine and ammunition, a pony, and as much food as he was able to carry. It was a sad moment when they shook hands with him before parting forever. They prayed for his safety on the long journey to his far-away home, though they never discovered whether he ever got there.

During the days that followed, the Rijnharts passed heavily-laden tea caravans – some consisting of as many as two thousand yaks – crossed torrent after torrent, struggled through blinding snow-storms, and distributed Christian tracts in the villages through which they passed. Everywhere they were warned about the bandits who, in small armies sometimes fifty strong, were terrorising the region, murdering and rustling and driving people to seek refuge in the hills. On September 15, 1898, a particularly beautiful day, the couple celebrated their fourth wedding anniversary. 'For a time,' wrote Susie Rijnhart, 'we forgot about robbers.' She prepared a special dish – rice pudding and sultanas – which they shared with their Tibetan guides. That day, she recalled afterwards, they talked of 'all the joys and sorrows that had come to us since hand-in-hand we had gone forth to fulfil the mission to which we had been called.'

By now they were nearing the Tashi Gompa lamasery, and began to enquire from villagers where exactly it lay. They were told that it stood on the banks of the nearby Tsa Chu, head-waters of the Mekong, from which the monks drew water for preparing their butter tea. That night they pitched their tents beside the river, expecting to reach the monastery the following day. As they did so they noticed two armed horsemen on the far bank who, after observing them for some time, rode off. The Tibetan guides immediately warned the Rijnharts to expect an attack, these men almost certainly being scouts for a larger band of brigands. Their target would be the ponies. The Rijnharts and the three Tibetans prepared themselves as best they could to fight off an attack, Petrus himself sleeping in the tent doorway clutching two revolvers. The Tibetans slept in the open. To give early warning if anyone approached, Topsy, the Rijnhart's dog, was tied up near the ponies, which they hobbled. The night, however, passed peacefully.

The next morning, following the somewhat imprecise directions they had received from villagers, they continued their search for the monastery. At midday they found themselves on a narrow and precipitous yak trail ending eventually in a cul-de-sac formed by a vertical cliff face and a stretch of the river too swollen and fast-flowing for safe crossing. They retraced their steps therefore to a grassy spot where they halted to make tea before taking another trail which would bypass the cul-de-sac. It was here, as the kettle was being boiled, that the attack came.

Rijnhart had at that moment called for silence, saying he thought he could hear whistling. Almost as he spoke, marksmen hidden among the rocks above them opened fire, wounding one of the escort in the arm as all five of them dived for cover beneath the overhanging cliff. 'Immense boulders,' Susie Rijnhart recalled later, 'were hurled down from the heights, any one of which would have crushed us beyond recognition.' These, plus the hail of bullets, were accompanied by the blood-curdling cries used by Tibetan brigands to terrify their victims. But it was the ponies, not their owners, that the brigands were interested in, and the attack ended as swiftly as it had begun. It left the Rijnharts with only one pony, an old and rather feeble grey. The others had either been driven away by the rustlers, or left dead or dying to prevent pursuit. One had been deliberately shot through the spine and was trying pathetically to struggle to its feet. Topsy, too, was missing, and it was the last they were to see of the dog which had travelled so far with them and shown such fortitude. However, their Tibetan escorts, at considerable risk to their own lives, had managed to save three of their own horses. The brigands, they warned the Rijnharts, would very likely return to take their remaining valuables, 'kill us all, and throw us into the river.' They announced, therefore, that they would ride as fast as they could to the monastery, where there would be soldiers, to get help. They rode off just as the vultures were beginning to tear apart the first of the dead horses. The Rijnharts never saw them again.

That night they moved their bedding and valuables to the water's edge, intending tó try and escape across the river in the darkness if they were attacked. The night was eerie though uneventful, but they decided against risking another one there. When their escort had not returned by early afternoon, they abandoned hope of ever seeing them again, and decided to try to make their own way to the lamasery or to a village where they could buy fresh ponies. They buried what valuables they were unable to carry and left the tents and other baggage neatly stacked to await their return, although fairly certain it would be plundered the moment they turned their backs on it. Then, leading their grey pony, they set out in the direction in which they believed the monastery to lie.

Their plan was to follow the river, on whose banks the lamasery was said to stand. If they failed to find it, then, with the aid of a compass they would head back to the main caravan route from which they and their three guides had turned in search of the Tashi Gompa. They struggled on for two days, sleeping in the open, crossing turbulent rivers and once stumbling on the fresh footprints of three ponies and a dog which, for a moment, they thought might belong to their three guides returning with Topsy to bring help. Otherwise they saw no trace of any human being in this desolate region from whom they could ask the way to the monastery. However, on the third day, they spotted through their telescope a large tented encampment in the distance, on the opposite bank of the Tsa Chu. 'What rejoicing it brought us!' wrote Susie Rijnhart. 'It seemed as if our difficulties were all ended. . . .'

They decided to follow the river until they were opposite the camp. Then, keeping his wife in sight, Rijnhart would swim the river and approach the Tibetans, from whom he would try to buy fresh ponies. That night they camped in a snowstorm, sleeping in a shelter improvised from their rubber groundsheet. Although help now seemed at hand, nonetheless both of them

1 The pundit Nain Singh

2 Colonel Nikolai Prejevalsky

3 Capt. T. G. Montgomerie

4 The pundit Sarat Chandra Das

5 The pundit Kishen Singh – codename 'A-K' – in old age

6 Ekai Kawaguchi

7 Dr Susie Rijnhart in Tibetan costume

8 Annie Taylor and her servant Pontso

9 William Rockhill

11 Jules Dutreuil de Rhins

10 Gabriel Bonvalot

12 The Thirteenth Dalai Lama

13 Potala and the Lhasa valley. Note the banner unfurled on the frontage

14 Alexandra David-Neel in disguise (centre) and Yongden (left) in front of the Potala.
One critic claimed that the photograph, from David-Neel's
My Journey to Lhasa, was a fake

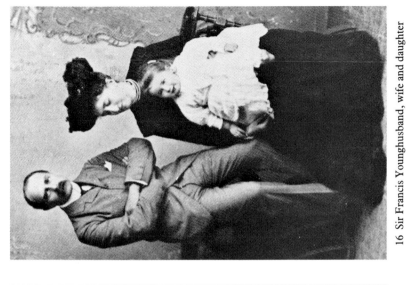

15 Henry Savage Landor with his leprous servant Mansing (left) and (right) Chanden Singh

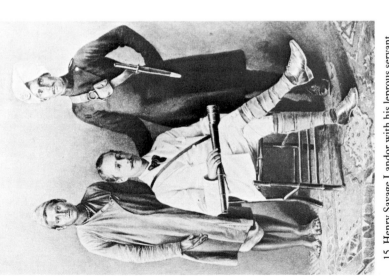

16 Sir Francis Younghusband, wife and daughter

17 British troops entering Lhasa in 1904 through the West Gate

18 Lhasa street scene, taken on Younghusband's expedition

felt uneasy. 'An indescribable feeling of uncanniness seemed to seize us both, so that we scarcely spoke above a whisper', Susie Rijnhart wrote afterwards. They found themselves wondering whether this spot might not once have been the scene of some horrible crime. The following day, after trudging through thick snow, they reached a point within hailing distance of the Tibetan encampment. But although the Tibetans called back, none would come near enough for the Rijnharts to be able to converse with them. It was now getting late and they decided to leave the river crossing until the morning, since it would have been dark by the time Rijnhart returned to his wife's side. That night was to be the last they would ever spend together.

Next morning, taking with him a revolver, six ounces of silver and some dry clothes wrapped in half a rubber groundsheet, Rijnhart entered the river and began to wade across, watched anxiously from above by his wife. Then, suddenly, when he was half way across and preparing to swim the rest, he stopped and unexpectedly turned back. Reaching the bank, he shouted something to his wife which she failed to hear, and then began to walk upstream in the opposite direction to the Tibetan camp. A moment later he vanished from sight around some high rocks. She never saw him again.

The story of Susie Rijnhart's lonely and dangerous journey to safety, during which she was continually abused, threatened and cheated and forced to surrender her few remaining possessions – even her husband's Bible and diary and small mementos of her dead child – is too long to relate here. But her explanation of how her husband probably met his fate on that chilly morning of September 26, 1898 is worth looking at briefly. When she failed to see him re-emerge in the water beyond the rocks, she clambered down to a spot from where, through her telescope, she could see both banks. It was then that she saw there was another encampment, just beyond the projecting rocks, on her own side of the river. It was this, she at once realised, that her husband had spotted, causing him to abandon his river crossing in mid-stream. Comforting herself with the thought that he was already in one of the tents, negotiating with the occupants for fresh ponies and discovering the precise whereabouts of the elusive lamasery, she innocently awaited his return. But when by the following morning he had still not appeared the frightful truth suddenly dawned upon her.

This second camp almost certainly belonged to the men who had attacked them and stolen their ponies. When they saw Rijnhart approaching, they at once assumed that the foreigner was coming to demand the return of his ponies. So to avoid any trouble they had killed him before he had time to use his revolver, and probably flung his body into the river. She realised that the same fate would befall her if she were spotted by the rustlers.

Emaciated and with frost-bitten feet, two months later she stumbled into a mission station on the Chinese-Tibetan frontier. Following pressure from the Dutch and British ministers in Peking, the Chinese sent officials to the spot under armed escort but they failed to come up with a satisfactory explanation. No culprit was ever found, and Susie Rijnhart made her way sadly back to her home in Canada, the sole survivor of this ill-fated expedition. She had lost her only child, her husband, not to say the race for the holy capital. The only thing she had not lost was her faith. Indeed, she was to remarry and return as a missionary to the Tibetan borderlands, although, sad to say, to die just three weeks after giving birth to another little boy.

*   *   *

There now enters the story a foreigner who succeeded not only in reaching Lhasa but also in living there undetected for more than a year. Yet, although he did this at considerable risk to his life, he could not really be said to have won the race. For Ekai Kawaguchi, who entered Lhasa on March 21, 1901, was a Japanese, the abbot of a monastery, and as an Asiatic and a Buddhist he enjoyed obvious advantages over his rivals from the West. But as an alien, he was no more welcome in Lhasa than any other gatecrasher, and had his disguise as a Chinese physician been penetrated, he would almost certainly have been put to death. As it was, he was eventually forced to flee for his life, and certain Tibetans who had unsuspectingly helped him were to pay dearly for this, suffering mutilation and other ghastly retribution.

It took Kawaguchi the best part of four years to reach Lhasa, for he travelled by a long, roundabout route which included sojourns at numerous monasteries on the way and a pilgrimage to Mount Kailas, far to the west. His slow progress very nearly cost him his victory. For close on his heels was another, somewhat more shadowy Japanese, also disguised as a Chinese, about whom we know little. The two men, each unaware of the other's presence, were to reside simultaneously in Lhasa, albeit briefly. But why this Japanese interest in Tibet? To discover the answer one must first consider a major political upheaval which had occurred elsewhere in Asia while the Littledales, Henry Savage Landor and the ill-fated Rijnharts were striving to reach the Tibetan capital.

For some years the Manchu rulers of China had been steadily losing their grip on some of the furthest-flung parts of their empire, including Tibet. Then in the summer of 1894 they had suffered a terrible reverse at the hands of the Japanese who had seized virtually the whole of Korea, the naval bases of Port Arthur and Dairen, and eventually obtained possession of Formosa. This public humiliation of the Manchus by a tiny neighbour who previously had counted for little was to encourage anti-Chinese riots in Lhasa and uprisings among the tribes of eastern Tibet.

As a new and rising power in Asia, Japan now began to feel concern about the remorseless advance eastwards of Tsarist Russia. It was a fear which Britain had been voicing for more than half a century, as year by year the Russian armies edged towards India's northern frontier. And, as will shortly be seen, no one felt this threat more keenly than George Nathaniel Curzon who in 1899 had been appointed Viceroy of India. Like

Curzon, the Japanese strategists also found themselves needing to know precisely what the Tsar was up to in Central Asia.

Historians therefore have always assumed that Kawaguchi was a Japanese spy, sent to keep an eye on Russian activities in Tibet. In fact, after he had slipped through their fingers, the Tibetans themselves were convinced that he was a spy, albeit a British one, curiously believing him to be an Englishman. But recent discoveries by an American historian, Paul Hyer, in Japanese diplomatic files of the day have somewhat demolished the theory that Kawaguchi was a Japanese agent. For Hyer has unearthed the fact that there was indeed a spy sent by Japanese Intelligence to Lhasa, although not Kawaguchi. The real spy was thirty-seven-year-old Narita Yasuteru, the traveller referred to earlier as having followed Kawaguchi into the Tibetan capital. But he, for reasons which are not clear, spent only a fortnight there, against Kawaguchi's fourteen months. We know very little about him, least of all what intelligence he managed to gather for his spy-masters. But since he was beaten to Lhasa by Kawaguchi he plays no further part in this narrative. However, even if he was on the payroll of Japanese Intelligence, he was not alone in collecting information on Tsarist activities in Tibet. For Kawaguchi, the genuine Japanese holy man, was in fact doing likewise. Only he was not passing it on to the Mikado's intelligence services, but rather to his old Tibetan teacher – and one-time British spy – Sarat Chandra Das, now living in Darjeeling. There seems little doubt that the latter, in his turn, was passing it on to former colleagues in British Indian intelligence, who were always eager for any stray crumbs which might emerge from beyond the Himalayas. But we are at risk here of moving ahead of the story.

In addition to reporting on Tsarist manoeuvrings, Kawaguchi gives us an important graphic portrait of Lhasa during the reign of the thirteenth, and perhaps greatest, of the Dalai Lamas – one of the few Tibetan God-Kings to survive the poisoners and attain both temporal and spiritual power. In his misleadingly titled book *Three Years in Tibet* (he was in the country barely two) Kawaguchi describes in detail everything from day-to-day monastic life to methods of disposing of the dead, from the Tibetan custom of polyandry to the art of poisoning. On the whole he did not gain a very favourable impression of the Tibetans, particularly of their religious life. Although admiring a few individuals, he complained that the rest were lascivious – some monks even fighting over young boys – ignorant, cruel, dirty, greedy, lazy and dishonest. Contrary to the tenets of Buddhism, many of them (including the Dalai Lama himself) ate meat, while others, supposedly following a religious vocation, behaved more like mediaeval roisterers.

Of one religious convention of some twenty thousand monks which he attended, a shocked Kawaguchi wrote afterwards: 'Of the twenty thousand very few were regular priests, the rest being warrior-priests or loafers who came only with the mean object of filling their stomachs. Instead of reciting from the scriptures, therefore, they were openly doing all sorts of things during the meeting, such as singing profane songs or pushing each other about . . . [They] sat there making obscene jokes and often quarrelling with one another.'

There was plenty more to shock the pious Japanese priest, including the blatant infidelities of some Tibetan wives – and their fearful tempers. 'They rage', he noted, 'like beings possessed', adding that it was not uncommon for husbands to apologise on bended knee to wives 'furious with passion'. He was appalled, too, by the squalor he found in this sacred city of Buddhism, with men and women defecating publicly into open cisterns, and one chapter of his book is called *A Metropolis of Filth*.

But what horrified him most of all was the barbaric Tibetan system of punishing malefactors and torturing suspects. The commonest form of punishment was flogging, mainly awarded for fairly minor crimes. The victim, however, might receive anything from three hundred to seven hundred lashes, ending up torn, bleeding and often suffering from severe internal injuries. Before a flogging, the convicted man – or woman – was put on public exhibition, manacled, fettered and wearing a heavy wooden collar, some three feet square, bearing a slip of paper from which passers-by could learn of the victim's crime.

Kawaguchi once came upon as many as twenty Tibetans, all well dressed, thus awaiting punishment, some tied to posts. He learned that they were all accused of being minor accessories in a plot to assassinate, by means of sorcery, the Dalai Lama. Sixteen Bon priests, he was told, had already been executed for their part, and many other priests and laymen sent into exile. The principal suspect was still being tortured in an effort to make him incriminate the head of his monastery, but so far he had refused to do so. His wife had also suffered, and Kawaguchi was dismayed to see her – 'a beautiful lady' – wearing the dreaded wooden collar and with her hands manacled. Her eyes were closed, her face was deathly pale and she appeared to be unconscious. She had shortly before received three hundred lashes and was sentenced, after a week on public exhibition, to be exiled to a remote region where she would remain manacled and fettered. Her crime had been to bribe her husband's gaoler to let her visit him, but she had been discovered.

For many everyday offences the standard punishment was mutilation. Removal of the eyes was one common form of this, while graver crimes were punished by the amputation of both hands. 'Lhasa,' Kawaguchi noted grimly, 'abounds in handless beggars and in beggars minus their eye-balls', adding that the latter appeared to exceed the former. Other forms of mutilation – for both parties in cases of adultery – included the amputation of the ears and what Kawaguchi describes as 'nose slitting'.

Executions were carried out by stitching the condemned person up in a sack and throwing him into the river or, alternatively, binding his arms and legs before drowning. The body was then fished out and decapitated, the head being displayed for three days in a special building set aside for the purpose, known as 'the house of perpetual damnation'.

'Tortures', Kawaguchi reported, 'are carried to the extreme of diabolical ingenuity.' They were such, he added, 'as one might expect in hell'. One, he describes, consisted of placing so-called 'stone bonnets' on the victim's head, one after another. 'The weight at first forces tears out of the eyes,' he wrote, 'but afterwards, as the weight is increased, the very eye-balls are forced from their sockets.' It ought, perhaps, to be added that in neighbouring China and elsewhere punishments of equal, or even worse, cruelty were commonplace at that time.

During his first few months in Lhasa, Kawaguchi had been living as a pilgrim at the great Sera lamasery, famous for its teaching faculty and its fighting monks whom it hired out as bodyguards to the wealthy. Possessing a modest knowledge of medicine, he soon began to acquire a considerable reputation as a doctor, especially as he charged the poor nothing. Horses would sometimes be sent to rush him from the monastery to a patient's bedside several days' journey away. Eventually his fame reached the ears of the Dalai Lama himself and the somewhat alarmed Japanese was summoned to the holy presence. He had been disconcerted to learn that the twenty-six-year-old Grand Lama of Tibet spoke excellent Chinese, his own supposed mother tongue, and he feared that he might be addressed in that tongue. His own Chinese, he was painfully aware, would not fool anyone really familiar with the language. He decided that if this happened, and the Dalai Lama penetrated his disguise, he would throw himself on his mercy, pleading that he was a Buddhist priest from far away who had come to the holy capital to worship and study at this fountainhead of his faith.

His audience with the Dalai Lama, which was to be the first of several, took place at his summer palace, which lay a short distance out of town. There, behind a high wall and surrounded by the summer residences of senior court officials, the Tibetan ruler escaped the heat and discomfort of the capital. Kawaguchi's meeting with him was ceremonious but cordial. To the former's relief the Dalai Lama addressed him in Tibetan, commending him for his work among the sick and expressing the hope that he would remain in the capital. He then asked Kawaguchi about Buddhism in China, a question which the Japanese managed to answer convincingly.

The Living God struck Kawaguchi as an impressive figure, with searching eyes and sharp, commanding voice. 'I judge', he wrote after several such audiences, 'that he is richer in thoughts political than religious.' The Dalai Lama appeared to be obsessed, moreover, by fear of Britain's designs on his country. His other preoccupation was about being poisoned, the fate of so many of his predecessors. However Kawaguchi sensed that this shrewd man would always prove more than a match for his foes, and he was right, for – apart from spells of exile – the thirteenth Dalai Lama was to rule Tibet for a further thirty-two years.

It was during Kawaguchi's stay in the Tibetan capital that something approaching panic began to build up in London and Calcutta over a friendship which appeared to be ripening between the Dalai Lama and Tsar Nicholas II of Russia. In the summer of 1901 the Russian press had heralded the arrival in St Petersburg of 'an Extraordinary Mission of eight prominent Tibetan statesmen' led by a mysterious individual named Dorjief. Their object, it was reported, was 'to strengthen good relations between Russia and Tibet'. To Russophobes in Britain this suggested one thing – secret diplomacy. For it was the second visit by Dorjief to St Petersburg in less than a year, and on each occasion he had enjoyed an audience with the Tsar.

A Mongol from the Buryat region of Siberia, and therefore a Russian citizen, he had first arrived in Lhasa in 1880 as a pilgrim, one of many such Mongol Buddhists allowed to come and go freely. In the ensuing years he had, by exceptional astuteness, worked himself into a position of considerable influence at the Dalai Lama's court, for a while acting as the latter's tutor. By the turn of the century, although still a subject of the Tsar, he was occupying a high advisory position at the

Tibetan court. And now, to the dismay of Curzon and others, he was apparently acting as middle man between the Tsar and the Dalai Lama in what rumour suggested was a secret alliance being forged behind the backs of both Britain and China.

Precisely what details of Tsarist activities in Tibet Kawaguchi passed on in letters to Sarat Chandra Das in Darjeeling is uncertain. But if what he later wrote in his book is anything to go by, then it must undoubtedly have disturbed the Great Game spymasters in London and Calcutta who seized anxiously on any intelligence coming out of Tibet. In the Buryats, Kawaguchi declared, the Russians possessed a highly effective instrument for promoting their own interests in Tibet, for its monasteries were full of their priests and students. Dorjief he portrayed as an *éminence grise*, politically astute in addition to being an outstanding Buddhist scholar whose learning impressed the Tibetans. As the former tutor to the Dalai Lama, moreover, he enjoyed the sovereign's ear and confidence, while all the time his principal aim was to further Russian interests.

According to Kawaguchi, Dorjief had ingeniously elevated the Tsar's image among Tibetans by identifying him with an ancient Tibetan prophecy. This told of a mighty Buddhist prince living north of Kashmir who one day would subdue the entire world and convert it to Buddhism. Dorjief, Kawaguchi reported, had written a pamphlet in which he cleverly argued that Tsar Nicholas was that prince. Translated into Tibetan, Mongolian and Russian, it was treasured by those possessing copies as though it was a rare Buddhist text. Kawaguchi also claimed to have stumbled upon a secret caravan of arms arriving across the Chang Tang from Russia. It consisted of some two hundred camels, each carrying two small but heavy boxes. This, he was told, had been preceded by another arms caravan of three hundred camels. Kawaguchi tells us he even managed to inspect one of the weapons which, although coming from Russia, bore an American manufacturer's mark. The Chinese *amban* in Lhasa, Kawaguchi claims, was aware of what the artful Buryat was up to but was powerless to do anything about it because, since their humiliating defeat by the Japanese, the Chinese were no longer feared by the Tibetans. Moreover, with the Boxer uprising on its hands at this time, Peking had more pressing problems to contend with at home.

Time was now beginning to run short for Kawaguchi. The principal cause of his undoing was his success as a doctor, which had made him the object of both curiosity and jealousy. He had hoped to live a peaceful monastic life in Lhasa, unnoticed and devoting himself entirely to meditation and study. But while his medical skill had won him friendship with influential Tibetans, and several meetings with the Dalai Lama, it had also made him enemies among the untrained Lhasa doctors, some of whom had virtually gone out of business since his arrival.

All this time, at least two people living in Lhasa had known his secret, but had remained loyally silent. One was the young son of a Tibetan nobleman, the other a merchant called Tsa Rong-ba. Both had known him when he was living in Darjeeling before he adopted his Chinese disguise. All had gone well until the young noble was struck down with paranoia, and in his ravings denounced his friend as a Japanese spy. Most Tibetans ignored this accusation as the fantasy of a lunatic, although Kawaguchi's enemies took pleasure in spreading the story around. But then Tsa Rong-ba, who had helped smuggle out his letters to Darjeeling and elsewhere, unfortunately shared the secret with a friend. By ill-chance the man to whom he confided it happened to be a caravan leader to the Dalai Lama's own brother, a high court official, and Kawaguchi suddenly found himself in the gravest danger.

Aided by loyal friends who could have saved themselves from the most appalling punishments by denouncing him and handing him over to the authorities, Kawaguchi slipped hastily out of Lhasa under cover of a religious festival. All the time fearing pursuit, capture and dreadul retribution, he managed in eighteen days safely to reach the Sikkim border, thankfully departing from the Forbidden Land across the Jelap Pass on June 15, 1902. Later, comfortably installed in 'Lhasa Villa', the Darjeeling home of Sarat Chandra Das, he recounted his extraordinary adventures to his old friend. One modern historian, Tsepon Shakabpa, has accused Kawaguchi of supplying the former British pundit with false intelligence, leading his government to believe that Tibet was receiving arms from Russia – with the disastrous results which were shortly to follow. However, I have not come across any corroboration of this in the British Indian intelligence files of the period. In fact, it is far from clear how much weight, if any at all, was placed by Calcutta or Whitehall on Kawaguchi's information.

But what about the race for Lhasa – could Ekai Kawaguchi be said to have won it? The answer is complicated by his being an Asiatic, but it really boils down to no. For while never a race in any formal sense, it had from the start essentially been a rivalry between westerners, beginning with Nikolai Prejevalsky. After all, Sarat Chandra Das himself was already in Lhasa when the great Russian explorer was making the first of his two attempts to get there. If Kawaguchi is to be included as a contestant, then Sarat Chandra Das must also be. To exclude them, as I have, is neither to deny them their achievements nor to underestimate the risks they took. The vengeance meted out to those who aided them surely proves this. But being Asiatics unquestionably gave them an advantage over their western rivals when it came to the plausibility of their cover stories and their disguise. It was clearly far harder for a European, however good his Tibetan, to reach Lhasa than an Asiatic. So far as western travellers were concerned, therefore, the race was still on.

Even as Kawaguchi was living in Lhasa, yet one more European – this time the great Swedish explorer Sven Hedin – was making his way there across northern Tibet disguised as a Buryat pilgrim. If ever a man was capable of achieving the impossible it was he. But Hedin, like every one of his predecessors, was detected and forced back just five days short of his goal. He thus became the eleventh westerner to try, and fail, to reach Lhasa. Despite his brilliant successes as a Central Asian

explorer (which were to win him an honorary knighthood from
Britain and the gold medal of the Royal Geographical Society)
Hedin was a poor loser, given to belittling the achievements of
his rivals. Thus, after failing to reach Lhasa, he dismissed it as
hardly worth visiting anyway. However, this is not the last we
shall be hearing of him, even if he was destined never to see the
holy city.

But armed as they were only with matchlocks and swords, the
Tibetans could not hope to keep inquisitive westerners out of
Lhasa for ever. The next gatecrasher, and really the winner of
this extraordinary race, was to shoot his way there at the head of
an army.

10. Lhasa – At Last

At first glance Francis Younghusband could easily have stepped from the pages of John Buchan. Like Richard Hannay or Sandy Arbuthnot, this brilliant young Indian Army officer seemed to possess all the qualities required of a romantic hero of the late Victorian or early Edwardian era. Soldier, explorer, athlete and writer, he had already made a name for himself by the age of twenty-five. While still a subaltern he had carried out a number of daring and adventurous journeys in Central Asia, including a twelve-hundred mile crossing of China from east to west by a route never before attempted by a European. By the age of twenty-eight he was already a veteran of the Great Game, having completed several secret missions in those sensitive areas where the British, Russian and Chinese Empires jostled in dangerous proximity. These solitary travels through unmapped territory had won for him the gold medal of the Royal Geographical Society. In 1889, had his commanding officer not put his foot down, the twenty-six-year-old Younghusband would have been on his way to Lhasa disguised as a Turki trader. Born in the Himalayan foothills, and having a remarkably persuasive way with Asiatics, he might even have succeeded where all others had failed. As it turned out, a further fifteen years were to pass before he was given his chance.

By the summer of 1902, as the Tsarist Empire advanced eastwards at the rate of some fifty-five square miles a day, Lord Curzon's fears over Russian intentions towards Tibet, and ultimately India, were rapidly becoming pathological. The Viceroy was convinced that a secret treaty of some kind existed between St Petersburg and Peking over Tibet. He was determined, he wrote to London on November 13, 1902, 'to frustrate this little game while there is yet time'.

His conviction that such a deal had been struck behind his back rested almost entirely on reports today to be found in the Foreign Office archives. Among them is a letter from a Chinese – one Kang-yu Wai – who had been forced to flee his homeland for political reasons and was now living as a refugee in Darjeeling. Written in barely comprehensible English, it was addressed to the Lieutenant-Governor of Bengal. It purported to contain details of a secret treaty between China and Russia which the writer claimed to have received from a contact in Peking. According to his letter:

> Chinese Government seen his parties very weak and not so active, so he hand over Tibet to Russia Government and requested him for help. . . . The Russian Empire received the Tibet now and he helps the mother of Chinese Empire. . . . All the mines of Tibet is in charged to Russian, and he can open railways etc. . . . The Russian is allowed to put a fort at Tibet and also railway, but they are not to destroy those monastery of Tibet . . .

This curious missive was dated August 7, 1902. Four days later Curzon received the following telegram from London:

> His Majesty's Minister at Peking reports that the Russo-Chinese Bank has designedly circulated rumours in the press that Chinese interests in Tibet may be transferred to Russia if the latter will undertake to uphold integrity of China.

Shortly afterwards a report from the *China Times* was forwarded to Calcutta purporting to contain the precise terms of the secret treaty. Beginning with the words 'China, conscious of her weakness . . .', it appeared, from its phrasing and contents, to emanate from the same source as the version supplied by Mr Kang-yu Wai's contact in Peking. This was not to say that there was any truth in it, but there were those in Calcutta and London, including Curzon himself, who were prepared to believe almost anything of the Russians, however indignant St Petersburg's denials. Other intelligence reports of Tsarist skulduggery in Tibet reaching India that month actually included one from inside Tibet. This came from Captain Randall Parr, an Englishman employed by the Chinese Customs Service at Yatung, just inside the frontier with Sikkim. Similar reports, or rather rumours, were also beginning to filter out of the independent state of Nepal, whose ruler was every bit as apprehensive as Curzon about what the Russians were up to in Lhasa. But it was not reports of secret deals conducted behind his back which gave Curzon the excuse he needed to send for his chosen trouble-shooter, Major Francis Younghusband, but other developments on the Tibetan frontier.

After the forcible expulsion of Tibetan troops from Sikkim in 1888, two agreements had been signed between Britain and China. One, the Sikkim-Tibet Convention of 1890, delineated the frontier between these two territories, confirmed that Sikkim was a British protectorate and that Tibet – in theory anyway – remained under Peking's control. The other, signed three years later, was intended to facilitate the free exchange of goods between India and Tibet, and agreed to the establishment of a trade-mart at Yatung, six miles inside Tibet.

The Tibetans, however, protesting that they had not been consulted over either agreement, had promptly set about sabotaging them both by violating grazing rights, overturning boundary markers, erecting defensive walls, boycotting the trade-mart and charging an illegal (under the new trade regulations) tariff on all goods passing between the two countries. Although nominally the suzerain power, the Chinese had been forced to admit to Calcutta that there was little or nothing they could do to force the Tibetans to honour the agreements. Such was the situation when the new Viceroy arrived to take up his post in January 1899, just a few days before his fortieth birthday.

At first, despite a naturally hawkish nature, Curzon had taken a conciliatory line, merely dispatching two successive letters to the Dalai Lama expressing his concern over the situation. The first, warm in tone, was returned weeks later with its seals unbroken. The second, a somewhat sterner note, met with a similar fate, if only because no one dared deliver it. The new Viceroy had been greatly affronted at seeing his imperial authority thus flouted by a political nonentity. But he also feared that this rebuff might actively encourage the Russians in their obvious – to him – designs on India's northern neighbour.

By the beginning of 1903 he was convinced that the only effective course of action was for Britain to dispatch a mission to Lhasa – using force if necessary – to discover the truth, and to put relations with the Tibetans on a firm and proper basis. He had found the home Government, so recently embroiled in an unpopular war with the Boers, extremely reluctant at first to risk further hostilities in Asia, with the ever attendant danger of Russian intervention. But in April of that year, he managed to obtain the go-ahead from London for a small mission to visit Khamba Jong, just inside Tibet, to attempt to negotiate with the Tibetans.

So it was, in May 1903, while pretending to watch a gymkhana together beneath the deodors at Simla, Curzon briefed his old friend Francis Younghusband for his forthcoming secret mission to Tibet. One month later, accompanied by Claude White, political officer for Sikkim, as Joint-Commissioner, and the Tibetan-speaking Captain Frederick O'Connor as interpreter, Younghusband and an escort of two hundred Indian troops left Kalimpong for the Tibetan border. By July 18 the Tibet Frontier Commission, as it was officially called, had reached Khamba Jong and begun to talk about talks with the Tibetans. But they got precisely nowhere, for the Tibetans refused to negotiate except on the British side of the frontier. The Tibetan delegates then withdrew into the *jong*, or fortress, and proceeded to boycott the mission. A stalemate ensued, lasting several months, after which the mission was recalled ignominiously to India. But if the Tibetans believed they had beaten Curzon they were mistaken. For in the meantime he had been pressing London for permission to enter Tibet with a far larger escort and advance as far as the great fortress citadel at Gyantse, half way to Lhasa. It was unacceptable, he argued, for a British diplomatic mission to be snubbed before the entire world by 'a petty Power which only mistakes forbearance for weakness'. To Curzon's surprise and delight, London's approval for his plan reached him almost by return. But the mission, it was emphasised by telegram, must proceed no further than Gyantse. Its sole purpose was to obtain 'satisfaction' from the Tibetans, and as soon as this had been achieved the force should be withdrawn.

'It was a curious telegram which I never quite understood', Younghusband admitted afterwards. The 'obtaining of satisfaction', he believed, was the function of a punitive expedition. So far as he and Curzon were concerned, he was merely going to Gyantse to try 'to get the frontier defined and recognised, to have the conditions under which trade could be carried on determined, and to have the method of communication between our officials and Tibetan officials clearly laid down.' By now both the Chinese and Russian governments, who had been officially informed of Britain's intended move into Tibet, were loudly protesting. But these complaints were brushed aside, it being sharply pointed out to the Russian Ambassador that in no way was this temporary advance into Tibet comparable with his own government's permanent occupation of vast areas of Central Asia.

The time of year was far from ideal but delay was out of the question. Planning went ahead swiftly. This time Younghusband was to be the sole Commissioner, and to raise his status he was immediately promoted to Colonel. However, being on the staff of the Political Department and his role in Tibet being essentially that of a diplomat, he could not also be in command of the military escort. So the latter, consisting of more than a thousand soldiers, two Maxim guns and four artillery pieces, was put under the command of Brigadier-General J. R. L. Macdonald. A soldier of no distinction, nor any proven ability, his choice for this extremely challenging role was both puzzling and, as it turned out, unfortunate. In addition to the several officers seconded to the expedition, correspondents from *The Times*, *Daily Mail* and Reuters were also invited to join it, though not until the force was safely inside Tibet.

Thus on December 12, 1903, Younghusband and his mission crossed over the lofty Jelap Pass into Tibet, led by a mounted soldier bearing a Union Jack. Behind, in the snow, trailed a straggling column of 10,000 coolies, 7,000 mules and 4,000 yaks (not forgetting six camels) together carrying the expedition's baggage. A small signals unit, laying a land line as it advanced, accompanied the invasion force. All in all, the scene reminded one officer more of Napoleon's retreat from Moscow than the advance of a British army, as men and beasts struggled breathlessly to reach the head of the 14,000-foot pass before slithering down the far side into Tibet. So began what was to become one of the most contentious episodes in British imperial history.

To Younghusband's and Macdonald's relief the Jelap Pass was unguarded, for up there, amid the rarefied air and sub-zero temperatures, fighting against a determined and well-positioned enemy would have been hellish. This was the highest altitude at which a British army had ever operated (they would be going even higher), and rifle bolts were already showing signs of freezing. During the treacherous descent – 'as steep as the side of a house', recounts one officer – of some five thousand feet into the Chumbi Valley they had lost many baggage animals and ponies of the mounted escort. But now, in the less extreme, wooded valley they ran into their first opposition.

Waiting for them there was a Tibetan general, accompanied

by a local Chinese official and (no doubt feeling very uncomfortable) Captain Randall Parr, the Englishman in the Chinese
Customs Service. Younghusband was told that he and his men
must return at once across the Jelap Pass to the Sikkim frontier
where senior Tibetan and Chinese officials would come and
confer with him. Pointing out that he had listened to all this
before at Khamba Jong only a few months earlier, Younghusband told them firmly that he was proposing to press on via
Yatung and Phari as far as Gyantse. But what, asked the
Tibetan general, if he found the gate in the wall at Yatung
locked and barred against him? 'In that case,' Younghusband
assured him, 'we would blow it open again.' It appeared that
even after their disastrous defeat fifteen years earlier in Sikkim,
the Tibetans still did not appreciate the power of the modern
armaments carried by the invaders.

But the following day, as they cautiously approached
Yatung, Younghusband and his officers noticed that the gate in
the wall which stretched right across the valley had been left
open. After a token speech of protest by the Tibetan general,
and a half-hearted attempt to seize Younghusband's bridle as he
rode through the gateway, the leaders of both sides were invited
by Captain Parr to his home for a lunch consisting of Chinese,
Tibetan and English dishes. Encouraged by this show of bonho-
mie and lack of determined resistance, Younghusband pressed
on up the Chumbi Valley. Everywhere the villagers were
friendly, selling food to the mission and escort and even hiring
out mules and ponies. The women and children, who had run
away into the hills at their approach, soon returned to their
homes. Younghusband now began to feel optimistic about
achieving a settlement with the Tibetans without having to shed
any blood. Perhaps he had forgotten, however, that twice
before, in wars with the Sikhs and the Gurkhas, the Tibetans
had lured their enemies into the heart of the country and there
fallen upon them.

Some ten miles beyond Yatung the expedition halted for
several days to consolidate. Meanwhile Macdonald rode for-

ward at the head of a flying column to reconnoitre the small
town of Phari, thirty miles ahead, where he had heard that a
Tibetan force was lying in wait for them. The route to Phari –
at 15,000 feet said to be the most elevated town in the world –
took them through territory never previously traversed by a
European. As they approached it, they could see towering
massively above the desolate plain a huge *jong*, built of stone, its
walls some hundred and thirty feet high. But it surrendered to
Macdonald without a shot being fired. The *jongpen*, or garrison
commander, assured the British general that he had no intention of doing anything so unfriendly as to fight him. Macdonald
then ordered two companies of Gurkhas to occupy the fort.
They found it defended only by a handful of frightened old men
and women – looking 'like hideous gnomes', one officer remarked.

Having thus secured the expedition's line of advance, Macdonald rode back to report to Younghusband. To his astonishment he found the latter furious, arguing that by seizing the
fortress they had shown bad faith to the Tibetans and through
this seemingly hostile act had prejudiced their claim to be a
peaceful mission. This, and his future disagreements with
Macdonald, only come to light in Younghusband's private
correspondence with his father, a retired Indian Army general
living in England. No hint of any such differences occurs in
Younghusband's own published account of the mission, *India
and Tibet*, or in the official Blue Books dealing with the
expedition. Much of the blame clearly lay with Curzon for not
making it clear to both officers who ultimately was in command.
Younghusband, senior in status but junior in rank, was in
charge of the mission, while Macdonald commanded the escort.
But the Viceroy had left it to the two men to work out for
themselves where their respective commands began and ended.
The situation was exacerbated by the fact that Younghusband
was a man of infinitely greater vision and ability than Macdonald. Macdonald, in fact, had not been chosen by Curzon at all
but by Lord Kitchener, Commander in Chief of the Indian

Army, with whom, as it happened, the Viceroy himself was privately quarrelling.

Despite all this, the expedition had now successfully overcome the first three obstacles facing it – the Jelap Pass, the wall at Yatung and the fortress at Phari – without spilling a single drop of blood, British, Indian or Tibetan. But then, all of a sudden, the friendly relations they had enjoyed so far with the Tibetans came to an end. Younghusband blamed this on the arrival from Lhasa of hostile monks who ordered the villagers to have no further dealings with the British, and particularly not to sell them any food or hire them animals. This was something of a blow to Younghusband and Macdonald, for an outbreak of anthrax among the yaks, together with the losses suffered on the Jelap Pass, was already affecting their lines of supply. Even so, Christmas Day 1903 was celebrated (by the British troops anyway) with turkey and plum pudding brought all the way from Darjeeling by special delivery. The only disappointment was the champagne which had frozen solid, and, on being thawed, proved undrinkable.

The weather now took a turn for the worse as the mission moved forward again through sub-zero temperatures and cruel winds past Phari towards the village of Tuna, nearly a thousand feet higher. To reach Tuna, where Younghusband proposed to sit out the rest of the winter before the final move on Gyantse, they had to struggle over the grim Tang La only three hundred feet lower than the summit of Mont Blanc. During the ascent the mercury dropped to minus fifty degrees Fahrenheit, freezing solid rifle bolts and the working parts of the Maxim guns. To try to prevent this the latter were stripped down at night and the working parts taken by officers and men into their sleeping bags. On January 8, 1904, they reached Tuna which they found undefended. It was, Younghusband wrote, 'the filthiest place I have ever seen'. At first they tried living in the stone-built houses, but were soon driven out by the vermin and stench, preferring their own tents in spite of the icy, penetrating winds which swept across the desolate plain. Here Younghusband and

Macdonald quarrelled once more, although there is no hint of it in Younghusband's book. Macdonald, clearly appalled at the prospect of spending any length of time in this miserable spot, and pleading inadequate fuel and food for his troops, demanded an immediate withdrawal to their original base-camp in the Chumbi Valley. He insinuated that if Younghusband wanted to remain there with his mission then that was his business.

'I told him I would never agree to retire,' Younghusband wrote to his father. The following morning Macdonald came to his tent again, arguing that they had only seven days' rations left and he had no choice but to withdraw. Younghusband pointed out that he was extremely familiar with this type of terrain from his earlier Pamir travels and was confident that they would be able to find not only fuel but also sufficient wild game off which to feed. Finally a compromise was reached. Younghusband and the mission would remain at Tuna protected by four companies of Sikhs, the Maxim detachment of the Norfolk Regiment and one six-pounder artillery piece, while Macdonald and the main body of the escort would retire across the Tang La. General Macdonald's original demand for a total withdrawal has been criticised as not merely unsoldierly and pusillanimous, but also as a dereliction of his duty as escort commander – particularly as a large Tibetan force was known to be gathering at Guru, not far off. Indeed, it was to earn him the nickname of 'Retiring Mac' among the junior officers. Younghusband, no doubt, was glad to be rid of him and left in the company of officers of like mind such as O'Connor. In fairness to Macdonald, it must be said that during the three months the mission spent at Tuna no fewer than eleven men went down with pneumonia, while a young British official of the postal detachment was stricken by frostbite and had to have both feet amputated. The stumps then became frostbitten and he died.

Edmund Candler, the *Daily Mail* correspondent with the mission, vividly describes one particularly grim day for those bringing supplies up to Tuna. 'A driving hurricane made it impossible to light a fire or cook food. The officers were reduced to frozen bully beef and neat spirits, while the sepoys went without food for thirty-six hours. . . . The drivers arrived at Tuna frozen to the waist. Twenty men of the 12th Mule Corps were frostbitten, and thirty men of the 23rd Pioneers were so incapacitated that they had to be carried in on mules. On the same day there were seventy cases of snow-blindness among the 8th Gurkhas.'

Full of admiration for the grit of the Indian troops and coolies born on the hot plains below who brought the supply convoys up from the Chumbi Valley amid such appalling conditions, Candler was at the same time scornful of those who feared a Russian annexation of this grim land. He wrote: 'The great difficulties we experienced in pushing through supplies to Tuna, which is less than 150 miles from our base railway station at Siliguri, show the absurdity of the idea of a Russian advance on Lhasa. The nearest Russian outpost is over 1,000 miles distant, and the country to be traversed is even more barren and inhospitable than on our frontier.'

But both Curzon and Younghusband, not to say millions at home, believed in the Tsarist spectre, and once the weather improved the expedition would press on to Gyantse – and perhaps beyond. For in their hearts neither Curzon nor Younghusband believed that in the end negotiations could be conducted with any lesser person than the Dalai Lama himself. And only in Lhasa could it be established once and for all what the Russians were really up to.

Meanwhile, the Tibetans, encamped in force at the village of Guru, some ten miles further on, resolutely declined all Younghusband's offers to visit them for discussions on their own ground. Conversations with stray Tibetan officials who visited the British lines always ended with the same refrain: 'Go back to the Sikkim frontier. Only there will we negotiate.' Frustrated beyond endurance not only by this but also by the five wasted months at Khamba Jong, Younghusband now determined to make a bold if risky attempt to confront the Tibetans at their own headquarters, and thus try to break the deadlock. Younghusband, to quote Curzon, knew the Asiatic 'by heart'. Relying on this intuition, and without consulting anyone, he now embarked on a course of action which could have had dire consequences.

Accompanied only by the Tibetan-speaking O'Connor and a young officer who was studying the language, he rode calmly into the Tibetan camp and, to the intense amusement of their ragged and ill-equipped troops, asked to be taken to their general. Passing numerous black tents from which peered incredulous soldiers, they were led to the Tibetan general's headquarters. Here they were courteously received with smiles and handshakes by the somewhat surprised general and his staff, and offered cushions to sit on. But while they sipped tea and exchanged courtesies with the Tibetan officers, they were painfully aware of the presence of three scowling and malevolent-looking monks from Lhasa who watched their every move. As Younghusband recalled afterwards: 'I could from this in itself see how the land lay, and where the real obstruction came from.'

Explaining that his was only an informal visit, Younghusband outlined the events which had led to his mission coming to Tibet, including the grievances which Calcutta felt against Lhasa. Now that they had met face to face he hoped that these differences could be settled and a lasting friendship forged between the two countries. The general and his officers listened to Younghusband's speech and asked questions, all quite civilly enough. But then, when Younghusband suggested that he should now return to his own camp, the three Lhasa monks – 'looking as black as devils' – announced that none of them would be allowed to leave until they had named a date when the British invasion force would withdraw from Tibet. Younghusband describes what followed: 'The atmosphere became electric. The faces of all were set. One of the generals left the room, trumpets outside were sounded, and attendants closed round behind us. A real crisis was on us, when any false step might be fatal.'

Smiling fixedly and keeping his voice studiously calm, Younghusband told the Tibetans that just as he realised that they had to obey the orders of their government in Lhasa, he too was no more than the emissary of his masters in London and Calcutta. He promised to signal their views immediately to the Viceroy in Calcutta, asking them in return to convey those of the British Government to Lhasa. If as a result he was ordered back to India, he personally would be grateful as he had a wife and child in Darjeeling whom he was anxious to see after so long a separation. This conciliatory speech seemed to lower the tension somewhat, although the three monks from Lhasa continued to demand a date for the mission's withdrawal from Tibet. The crisis was finally resolved when the Tibetan general proposed that they should await the British reply. The three officers, trying to preserve a nonchalant air, then mounted their ponies and rode off before the Tibetans had time to change their minds. 'It had been a close shave,' admitted Younghusband afterwards.

He was now more than ever convinced that any attempt to parley with the Tibetans anywhere short of Lhasa itself would prove quite futile. However, his orders were still to proceed only as far as Gyantse and to try to open talks there. But from now on, he and Macdonald agreed, any resistance by the Tibetans to the mission's advance would be brushed aside by force, albeit the minimum necessary. Whitehall, in sudden hawkish mood, signalled its approval of this. Yet because of Macdonald's cautious habit of providing his supply columns with heavy escorts (which consumed en route a sizeable part of the supplies they carried) the mission and main escort were not reunited and ready to move forward again across the snow-covered plain until March 31, 1904. That day would be one that no one who was present would ever forget.

Younghusband and Macdonald already knew, from patrols sent out the previous day, that some seven miles ahead, just short of the village of Guru, a force consisting of fifteen hundred Tibetan troops lay in wait for them. The question on everyone's

lips as they advanced on that bitterly cold morning was whether
or not the Tibetans would actually fight. Twice during the
march towards Guru, Tibetan emissaries rode forward to try to
persuade Younghusband, with alternate threats and pleas, to
turn back. He answered that if their officials would not come to
him, then he had no choice but to come to them.

Then, when they were just three miles short of Guru, they
suddenly spotted the Tibetan troops. Clearly visible, they were
massed together behind a hastily built wall, some two hundred
yards long, in the middle of the open plain. A few shells from
Macdonald's field pieces could have decimated them in minutes, but Younghusband at all costs wanted to avoid bloodshed.
As the British force swung into view, the Lhasa general,
resplendently dressed, rode forward with an armed escort of
some thirty men to make a last plea to Younghusband to turn
back. Once more Younghusband reminded him that his government had for fifteen years been trying to negotiate with
Lhasa, and that they had now lost all patience. There could be
no question of the mission halting, let alone of turning back,
before they had reached Gyantse and settled, once and for all,
and at the highest level, all outstanding issues. Moreover,
unless the Tibetan general removed his men from the British
line of advance within fifteen minutes, Macdonald's troops
would do so by force.

Fifteen minutes later the Tibetan soldiers were still in position behind the wall, brandishing swords and matchlocks as
well as a number of foreign (though none of them Russian)
rifles. Macdonald now began to issue his orders. Although the
Tibetans greatly outnumbered the British and Indian troops,
their combined fire-power was perhaps only one hundredth of
the latter's, if that. Macdonald's plan was to surround them
swiftly, and so convince them that resistance to his deadly
Maxim machine-guns, light artillery and modern Enfield rifles
would amount to mass suicide. Once the Tibetans had surrendered, it was proposed to disarm them and then allow them to
disperse. The general first sent his machine-gunners, with Sikh

infantry support, around the Tibetans' right flank, with orders to dig in some two hundred yards from the end of the defensive wall. Next the Gurkhas worked their way stealthily across the rocky terrain to the left, taking up a position almost opposite the Maxims. The mounted infantry then cantered around to the right, behind the Maxims, to form a cut-off party some six hundred yards to the Tibetans' rear. Finally Macdonald sighted his light artillery directly onto the Tibetan position, but ranged over the heads of his assault party. He now gave orders to the latter to advance slowly, and in extended line, towards the Tibetan soldiers huddled behind their wall.

If ever the discipline of native troops was tested, it was surely here at Guru, at the highest altitude at which a British army had so far fought, and in one of the most bizarre actions in history. Macdonald had given the Sikh assault party – and indeed everyone – the strictest orders not to fire unless the Tibetans fired first. A similar order, it appears, had been given by the Tibetan general to his troops. Furthermore, each Tibetan had been presented with a charm – a scrap of paper bearing the Dalai Lama's personal seal – which, they were promised by their priests, would make them bullet-proof.

Macdonald's plan proceeded like clockwork. By noon all his troops were in position. The Sikh sepoys had halted just in front of the stone breastwork. The British held their fire, and so did the Tibetans. A stalemate now ensued, for the Tibetans, although totally surrounded, showed no signs of surrendering. Perceval Landon, special correspondent of *The Times*, recalled afterwards: 'The main body of the Tibetans were bewildered but not subdued. The whole thing must have been incomprehensible to these poor men. No order had been given to them to retire. Gathered together in a body, their enormous superiority in numbers must have struck them. They had no idea, of course, of the advantage which we possessed, and there was a growing murmur as they discussed the matter excitedly behind the wall.'

Younghusband and Macdonald now looked around for the

Tibetan general. To their astonishment they spotted him on their own side of the defensive wall, sitting glumly on the ground among the legs of their own Sikh troops. O'Connor was sent over to demand his surrender and inform him that his troops would be disarmed. But the general merely ignored him and continued to sit there, muttering darkly. Macdonald now gave orders for the surrounded Tibetans to be disarmed, and the sepoys detailed for this began to wrest the matchlocks from their reluctant hands. What happened next left all those who saw it shocked and sickened, and sent a wave of revulsion through liberal consciences at home.

Views differ among the eyewitnesses over who was to blame for the tragedy. Edmund Candler, the greatly respected *Daily Mail* reporter, criticises Macdonald for the way he set about disarming so large a body of hostile Tibetans. 'To send two dozen sepoys into that sullen mob to take their arms away was to invite disaster', he wrote afterwards. But almost everyone agrees that the man who spilled the first blood was the Tibetan general himself. Fearful perhaps of the terrible fate which would await him in Lhasa were he to surrender and allow the invaders to advance towards the capital, he must have known he had little to lose. Rising from the ground and mounting his pony he began to call hysterically to his soldiers to resist. He then tried to force his pony towards the end of the wall and thus rejoin his men, but a sepoy seized his bridle. The general now drew a revolver from the folds of his coat and promptly blew the Indian's jaw off.

Within seconds the Tibetans lining the far side of the wall began to swarm across it, hurling themselves at the nearest sepoys. Simultaneously firing broke out as the Gurkhas and Sikhs on the flanks began to shoot into the mass of Tibetans still behind the wall. Candler, unarmed, found himself facing a huge Tibetan swordsman who brutally cut him down with a succession of blows. But for his thick sheepskin coat he would have been sliced to pieces. As it was one blow severed his hand – the hand which moments earlier had written a brief dispatch which was already on its way to London. Another Englishman, Major Dunlop, also received serious sword wounds. General Macdonald might have been the next casualty had his orderly not quick-wittedly thrust a shotgun into his hands which he fired point-blank from the hip at his assailants.

But meanwhile, on the far side of the wall, a terrible toll was being exacted on the Tibetans by the murderous Enfields and Maxims. 'It was an awful sight,' one subaltern wrote to his mother afterwards. 'I got so sick of the slaughter that I ceased fire, though the general's order was to make as big a bag as possible.' O'Connor, who took no part in the killing, wrote in his memoirs: 'It was sheer slaughter, but there was no stopping it. It had to be.'

In four terrible minutes nearly seven hundred ragged and ill-armed Tibetans lay dead or dying on the plain. The Lhasa general was among the first to be killed. As volley after volley of rifle and machine-gun fire tore into their ranks from either flank and from across the wall, the survivors turned to flee. But instead of running, the Tibetans walked slowly off the battle-field with heads bent. It was a horrifying but moving sight, a mediaeval army disintegrating before the merciless fire-power of twentieth-century weapons. Even while his wounds were being dressed, Candler watched the rout. 'They were bewildered,' he wrote. 'The impossible had happened. Prayers and charms and mantras, and the holiest of their holy men, had failed them. . . . They walked with bowed heads, as if they had been disillusioned in their gods.'

The shooting continued as the survivors streamed north-wards along the road towards the village of Guru, Macdonald's artillery now adding to the carnage. Finally the last straggler vanished from sight, leaving the plain strewn with dead and wounded. 'It was a terrible and ghastly business', wrote Young-husband. Like O'Connor, he had taken no part in the massacre. His revulsion, however, was shared by everyone, although General Macdonald's feelings are not recorded. The troops themselves, Younghusband tells us, had ceased firing 'instinctively and without direct orders'. The British soldiers' pity for the defeated Tibetans is echoed in a remark made by one of the machine-gunners, a private of the Norfolks. 'It's not likely them poor little slit-eyed bastards will stand up and fight again,' he was heard to say. He was soon to be proved wrong, however. Lieutenant Hadow, in command of the deadly Maxims, observed in a letter home: 'I hope I shall never have to shoot down men *walking* away again. . . .'

Why then did Macdonald not order a ceasefire once he saw the Tibetans turn and flee? Perhaps he did and no one heard above the clamour and the sound of shooting. But whatever the answer the British now set about trying to make amends by saving the lives of as many of the Tibetan wounded as possible. A field hospital was set up in a deserted hovel at Tuna, a cowshed serving as operating theatre. Here, amid the squalor and the vermin, Macdonald's doctors worked devotedly around the clock as the wounded Tibetans were brought in by yak and on foot. Extraordinary stoicism was shown by the wounded, some of them terribly mutilated by shell-fire, as they faced the scalpel of Lieutenant Davys of the Indian Medical Service. One man who had lost both legs joked with him: 'In my next battle I shall have to be a hero, as I cannot run away.' The Tibetans were quite unable to understand, Younghusband noted, 'why we should try to take their lives one day and try to save them the next.' Most of them, it seemed, had expected to be shot out of hand, humanity in victory not being something they were familiar with. Of the one hundred and sixty-eight wounded Tibetans brought to the hospital, only twenty died. Two of the wounded had been shot through the brain, and two others through the lungs, but even their lives were saved.

Candler, despite losing a hand, felt a great compassion for the Tibetans. 'They were consistently cheerful and always ready to appreciate a joke,' he wrote in *The Unveiling of Lhasa*. 'They never hesitated to undergo operations, did not flinch at pain, and took chloroform without fear.' He added: 'Everyone who visited the hospital at Tuna left it with an increased respect for the Tibetans.' The regard was mutual, and the doctors had difficulty in persuading those they had treated to return home, so intrigued were the Tibetans by their new-found friends with such magical healing powers. 'Morning after morning', wrote Landon of *The Times*, 'one or two dead figures would be found a few hundred yards away from our outposts – men who had been painfully trying to drag their broken bodies in to this miraculous healing, of which the fame had spread far and wide.'

Younghusband's advance on Gyantse, some sixty miles to the north, now resumed. If the tragic victory at Guru had achieved nothing else, then surely the bloody lesson learned there should prevent any more having to be shed. But very soon it became clear that the Tibetans had lost none of their stomach for the fight – or rather the fanatical lamas who sent these conscripted peasants against the invaders had not. At first the Tibetans fought a series of delaying actions, each time withdrawing at the last minute, and each time losing men. At Red Idol Gorge, twenty miles short of Gyantse, nearly two hundred had to be killed before Macdonald's force could pass safely through this spectacular defile with its rock-hewn Buddhas. British casualties were three wounded.

On April 11, 1904, they got their first sight of Gyantse, officially the mission's destination, lying seven miles away across the plain. Dominating the town, famous for its carpets, was a massive fortress, or *jong*, perched on a rocky mound several hundred feet above the plain. The question now arose of whether the Tibetans were planning to defend it. In *Lhasa*, his two-volume account of the expedition, Landon wrote: 'It was apparent, even at this distance, that it would be no light matter to drive an enemy, however weakly armed, from so strong a position.' They did not have to wait long for an answer. About two miles from the *jong* they were greeted by the *jongpen*, or garrison commander, who told them that were he to surrender the fortress his throat would be cut by the Dalai Lama (already all the property of the general killed at Guru had been seized). On the other hand, he added, as all his soldiers had run away he was in no position to defend it. The *jong* therefore fell to the British without a shot being fired. Because it had no water supply Macdonald decided not to occupy it (a decision he would later regret), but a Union Jack was left flying from its topmost rampart while the mission and escort moved into some buildings a mile or so away.

Younghusband now prepared for a long wait while Lhasa made up its mind whether or not to negotiate. Although life was much more comfortable in Gyantse than at Tuna, their supply lines were now greatly stretched and it was agreed that Macdonald would once again return to the Chumbi Valley with the bulk of the escort. Before departing, 'Retiring Mac' blew up the gates of the *jong* as a precaution against it being reoccupied by the Tibetans during his absence. At first the mission officers staved off boredom by shooting mountain hare, duck and the occasional gazelle, or by negotiating with the monks from the monastery behind the *jong* for carpets and even religious works of art. Captain Walton, the medical officer, opened a small outdoor dispensary for the Tibetans. His first patients were soldiers who had been wounded in the battle for Red Idol Gorge, but soon the dispensary was crowded each morning with sick of all kinds. But these peaceful days were destined not to last, for during the last week of April rumours began to reach them that, far from intending to negotiate with Younghusband, Lhasa was busy raising an army with which to drive him out.

A mounted patrol soon confirmed that a large Tibetan force was being formed on the lofty Karo Pass, some forty-seven miles ahead on the road to Lhasa. Colonel Brander, now in command of the escort at Gyantse, agreed with Younghusband that this must be broken up quickly before it became a threat to the mission's safety. Accordingly, and without consulting Macdonald, Brander set off with the bulk of his troops toward the Karo Pass, which stands at more than 16,000 feet. There he found some three thousand Tibetans lying in wait for him behind a six-foot-high stone wall stretching across the full width of the pass. A fierce battle now began as the Tibetans opened fire and the Maxims replied, filling the defile with thunder.

Brander ordered his Gurkhas to scale the towering heights to the left of the Tibetan position, while the Sikhs endeavoured to seize those on the right. Meanwhile, Captain Bethune and a second company of Sikhs tried to work their way along the bottom of the defile towards the defensive wall, preparatory to making a frontal attack. Here they ran into very heavy fire, and while leading a near-suicidal charge towards the wall Bethune was killed together with his bugler and a sepoy. Eventually the Tibetan position was overrun, but only after a courageous stand against greatly superior weapons and tactics. Some Tibetan troops positioned in *sangars*, or tiny stone-built block-houses, were driven out by the Gurkhas only to lose their footing and plunge to their deaths some five hundred feet below. After pursuing the fleeing Tibetans for several miles the chase was called off, and the British prepared to return to Gyantse. Brander had lost five men, Bethune included. Thirteen others were wounded. The Tibetans left behind them on the battlefield more than four hundred dead and wounded. The battle for the Karo Pass was to make military history. So far as is known, it was fought at a greater altitude than any other engagement before or since.

Carrying Bethune's body with them for burial at Gyantse, Brander and his troops returned through the teeth of a blizzard to discover that Younghusband himself had had a close shave during their absence. Without either machine-guns or artillery, he and his small force had successfully fought off a night attack by some eight hundred Tibetan troops. Without warning these had crept silently up to the wall surrounding the sleeping mission and suddenly opened fire at point-blank range through the loopholes with their matchlocks. But during the next quarter of an hour, as half-dressed Sikhs and Gurkhas grabbed their rifles and fired back, the attackers lost some hundred and forty men, while Younghusband's party suffered only four wounded. It was now discovered that the Tibetans had reoccupied the massive hill-top *jong* – from which Brander had neither the artillery nor men necessary to dislodge them. This would have to await the return of Macdonald and the main force.

Apart from news that Macdonald was furious with Brander for forcing the Karo Pass without first consulting him, the telegraph line from the south also brought welcome tidings. London had decided that if the Tibetans failed to negotiate with Younghusband at Gyantse within a month, the mission was to march on Lhasa. Younghusband was instructed to pass this on to the Chinese *amban* for him to communicate to the Tibetan authorities in the capital.

Tibetan resistance to the invaders had now become noticeably fiercer, partly because they were getting closer to the holy city, but also because the Tibetans were drafting troops from Kham, in eastern Tibet. These were known to be the best fighting stock in Tibet, and were led, moreover, by some of the most fanatical of Lhasa's priests. When still no word had come from the capital in reply to London's ultimatum, Younghusband was instructed to warn the Tibetans that if their negotiators had not arrived in Gyantse by June 25, then the march on the capital would begin. The day after the ultimatum's expiry Macdonald reached Gyantse with a greatly increased force sent from India, including a further stiffening of white troops. His small army now pitched its tents carefully out of range of the Tibetan *jingals*, or small-calibre cannon, which nonetheless kept up a sporadic fire from the lofty battlements of the *jong*.

Once or twice, at the last minute, it looked as though the Tibetans might be going to negotiate, but although the deadline was extended by several days this came to nothing. Finally, on July 5, Macdonald prepared to attack the *jong*. For this great fortress, with its large number of defenders, had first to be captured before any advance on Lhasa could safely begin.

The assault opened with a diversion intended to fool the Tibetans. Several companies of infantry stormed the low-lying outer defences of the north-west, demolishing these with explosives and driving the defenders up into the *jong* itself. That night Macdonald's troops lit camp fires there before withdrawing silently to their own lines. The object was to make it appear that the attack would come from the north-west the following morning. But instead, at four in the morning, the real assault was launched from the south-east corner of the fortress. First a breach was blown in the *jong* wall with artillery fire. The point selected lay immediately above the easiest route for an assault party to take to the top of the outcrop on which the *jong* stood. This shelling yielded a bonus, when a stray shell exploded a powder magazine inside the fortress, after which the defenders' fire, which had hitherto been intense, noticeably slackened.

Now the assault party, consisting of Gurkhas and Fusiliers who had been sheltering in houses immediately below the massive walls, crept forward and began their perilous climb. The swifter-footed Gurkhas, led by Lieutenant John Grant, soon outpaced the English troops and in ten minutes were crouching beneath the breach in the wall. The Tibetans above them were now frenziedly hurling large rocks down on the attackers. There was only room for one man at a time to clamber up to the breach. Revolver in hand, Grant began to crawl towards it. On his first attempt both he and the Gurkha havildar following him were knocked violently backwards by flying rocks. Both received injuries, but at once started to work their way towards the breached wall again, their men close behind them.

Captain O'Connor who, with Younghusband, was watching the assault from the mission roof through binoculars wrote afterwards: 'Every orifice and apparently every stone in the great building belched fire and smoke, and stones were being rolled down the slope on to the attackers. It appeared absolutely impossible that any human being could ever reach the top. But the little figures struggled on. Every now and then we could see one of them topple over and lie still, or go rolling down the slope, and gradually the leader reached the breach, then another man, and another.'

Leading his men through the gap, Grant shot down several of the defenders with his revolver. It was too much for the

Tibetans who were already demoralised by the heavy shelling. They turned and fled, some retreating into the warren of subterranean passages to hide, others escaping by rope over the far wall. By six o'clock that evening the entire fortress was in Macdonald's hands. His casualties were one officer and three other ranks killed, seven officers and twenty-three men wounded. The Tibetans had lost some three hundred killed or wounded. For his inspired leadership and gallantry, Lieutenant Grant was later awarded the Victoria Cross and his Gurkha havildar the much coveted Indian Order of Merit. It was, to quote Perceval Landon of *The Times*, 'one of the pluckiest pieces of work ever known on the Indian frontier.' Moreover, it was perhaps the only Victoria Cross ever to be won in full view of the press.

The surrender of the *jong* was to have a crushing effect on Tibetan morale. There was an ancient superstition that if ever the great fortress were to fall into the hands of an invader then further resistance would be pointless. After centuries of invasion by Chinese, Nepalese, Sikhs, Gurkhas and others this had now happened. For Francis Younghusband the road to Lhasa was at last open. Given a free hand, and an escort commander like Brander, he might have got there from start to finish in a matter of weeks. As it was it had taken him seven laborious months to reach Gyantse, still little more than half way. This snail's pace was partly due to indecisiveness in London, but also to the excessive caution of General Macdonald who, Younghusband complained to his father, always acted 'as if the Tibetans were commanded by a Napoleon'. But with Tibetan morale now virtually broken, the only obstacles remaining were the Karo Pass, which the defenders had reoccupied, and that formidable barrier, the mighty Tsangpo river. The pass was swiftly forced in an action almost identical to that fought there by Brander two months earlier, while the river was crossed in five days (with the loss of one officer and two Gurkhas drowned) using canvas boats. By the last day of July 1904, the mission and its escort were firmly established on the north bank of the

Tsangpo, ready to march on Lhasa, now only forty-five miles away.

The signal honour of being the first officer to set eyes on the celestial city, with its golden roofs and domes, was to fall to Major W. J. Ottley, commanding the mounted infantry. On August 1, when they were just twelve miles short of Lhasa, he had raced another officer to the top of a hill overlooking it. 'I must confess,' he wrote afterwards, 'I was so blown that I could not see twelve yards, much less twelve miles.' Younghusband himself, who was having to fend off a succession of emissaries from Lhasa begging him not to enter the capital, did not get his first glimpse of it until the following day. He was riding with O'Connor when suddenly it lay there before them. Turning in his saddle to his friend, he simply said: 'Well, O'Connor, there it is at last.'

Some fifteen years earlier, as a young subaltern, Francis Younghusband had dreamed of entering Lhasa alone, disguised as a Yarkandi trader. Now, in full diplomatic regalia and with a small armed escort, he rode into the holy city. The Tibetans, their morale broken, offered no resistance. The race at long last was over.

11. 'Golden Domes like Tongues of Fire'

The special correspondents now had a field day, with the outside world hanging on their every word. As both they and their readers were aware, they were about to enter the most mysterious city on earth. Its secrets would at last be known to all. 'Today is probably the first time in world history,' one newspaper reported, 'that the dateline Lhasa has been prefixed to a news despatch.' It was a claim difficult to refute. 'The Potala,' telegraphed Candler, 'surpassed the greatest expectations. The golden domes shone in the sun like tongues of fire, and they must strike with awe and veneration the hearts of pilgrims from the barren tablelands.' The building, wired Landon that same day, 'would dominate London, and Lhasa is almost eclipsed by it.' But once they had got over their professional euphoria and begun to look around them, the newspapermen found themselves wondering why so many brave men and women had risked – and some indeed lost – their lives to set foot in this remote and unprepossessing capital.

'Lhasa, like the Tibetans, is very dirty,' declared one, 'and there is little in it that will seem attractive to a native of the occident.' Even Candler, with his soft spot for the Tibetans, had to admit that Lhasa was something of a shock, reporting: 'We found the city squalid and filthy beyond description, undrained and unpaved. Not a single house looked clean or cared for. The streets after rain are nothing but pools of stagnant water frequented by pigs and dogs searching for refuse.'

Landon, while noting the 'black-scummed' pools, mangy dogs, and 'piggeries' of homes, nonetheless found much to fascinate him, especially the Ling-kor, or sacred way of the pilgrims, which circles the holy city. Even a non-believer, he wrote, would be spared the agonies of hell if he died while treading this Buddhist *via dolorosa* which attracted pilgrims from the most distant parts of Asia. Landon, who joined them on the five-mile walk, believed he was the first non-believer to make the circuit. He wrote: 'From dawn to dusk along this road moves a procession, men and women, monks and laymen. They shuffle along slowly, not unwillingly now and then to exchange a word with a companion overtaken . . . but, as a rule, with a vacant look of abstraction from all earthly things they swing their prayer-wheels and mutter ceaselessly beneath their breath the sacred formula which shuts from them the doors of their six hells.'

His circuit took him through some of the most squalid parts of Lhasa, including the quarter where the outcast *ragyapas*, or dismemberers of corpses, resided in appalling poverty. He reported with disgust: 'It is difficult to imagine a more repulsive occupation, a more brutalised type of humanity, and, above all, a more abominable and foul sort of hovel than those which are characteristic of these men. Filthy in appearance, half-naked, half-clothed in obscene rags, these nasty folk live in houses which a respectable pig would refuse to occupy.'

The one building which exceeded everyone's expectations, of course, was the massive, one-thousand-roomed Potala, nine-hundred feet long and rising sheer on its outcrop of rock against a backcloth of distant, snow-capped mountains. Landon hailed it as 'a new glory added to the known architecture of the world', while Candler called it 'not a palace on a hill, but a hill that is also a palace.' Later they hoped to explore its miles of darkened corridors, but now they had a more immediate problem. Where was the elusive Dalai Lama, with whom Younghusband had come so far to negotiate, and whom naturally they wanted to interview? The God-king, it was quickly learned, had fled. With him had vanished the equally mysterious Dorjief, whom everybody also wanted to interview. Where the two men had gone nobody would say, and it was three weeks before it was finally discovered that they had fled north to Urga, the Mongolian capital, lamaism's second holy city and today called Ulan Bator.

If the British had hoped to find damning evidence of Tsarist chicanery in Lhasa they were to be disappointed. There turned out to be no arsenals of Russian arms, as Kawaguchi had claimed, no advisers from St Petersburg, and no trace of evidence of a secret treaty of any kind. One rumoured arms factory turned out to be a ramshackle workshop making primitive native firearms which Younghusband did not even think worth destroying. So much for the intelligence reports of Tsarist intrigue behind Britain's back. So much for the Russian bogy.

But St Petersburg did not react with the fire and fury expected to this British trespass into Central Asia. For one thing they had nothing to hide there, and knew that London would be made to look silly when it found no Tsarists under Tibetan beds. But a more immediate and pressing reason for their silence was their own involvement in a desperate struggle with the Japanese, that aggressive new power in Asia. They needed now all the friends they could find, including the British, who anyway had given a pledge that the Tibet mission would be withdrawn the moment it had obtained whatever satisfaction it sought. Critics of Curzon's forward policy were even to suggest that he had deliberately chosen a moment when his rivals in St Petersburg were themselves in a tight spot in Asia to dispatch his force, although in the Foreign Office archives of the period there is no evidence of this. Chinese reaction to the invasion of what they considered to be their own sovereign territory was mixed. On the one hand they were in no position to drive the British out, which caused them considerable loss of face, even if the occupation was only temporary. On the other, provided Britain continued afterwards to recognise China's suzerainty – if not its full sovereignty – over Tibet, then this drubbing at the hands of a modern army might teach Lhasa a little respect, and serve to make its fanatic monks more manageable in future.

At risk of losing more face, the Chinese *amban* had come to see Younghusband when the British first pitched camp outside the town, instead of waiting for the latter to come to him to try to justify this outrage. He had greeted Younghusband warmly, moreover, warning him that he would find the barbarian Tibetans 'dark and cunning adepts at prevarication'. He had also provided the mission with a welcome larder of sheep and cattle, the bill for which, it later transpired, he doubled and then passed to Peking. But the real reason for his friendliness, Macdonald's officers reasoned, was relief that his own personal safety was now assured among a populace rapidly becoming more hostile towards the Manchus. Whatever the reason, though, this fraternising with the invaders was to cost him his job when Peking heard of it.

The unexpected flight of the Dalai Lama now presented Younghusband with a dilemma. Who was he to negotiate with? He even thought of giving chase, but found that no one would betray the God-king by revealing his escape route. 'We have spies and informers everywhere,' wrote Candler, 'and there are men in Lhasa who would do much to please the new conquerors of Tibet.' But even they, he added, drew the line at this. Before fleeing, the Dalai Lama had left his seal of office in the hands of the elderly Regent, a benign Tibetan who, Younghusband wrote afterwards, 'more nearly approached Kipling's lama in *Kim* than any other Tibetan I had met.' But mere possession of the great seal did not mean that he was constitutionally empowered to negotiate on behalf of the head of state. For the Dalai Lama had left no instructions on how the national crisis was to be handled in his absence. Nor had he given anyone the authority to speak for him.

This obstacle was unexpectedly removed, however, when the Chinese suddenly stripped him of all temporal powers for being absent in his people's hour of need. This move greatly incensed the Tibetans, and the edicts announcing it were torn down or splashed with mud. But apart from the sullen resentment of the more hostile monks (one of whom was hanged on Macdonald's orders for a murderous attack on two of his officers), the British found themselves well received by the people of Lhasa. Word had quickly spread of the merciful way they had behaved towards the wounded on the battlefield at Guru, as well as the respect they were showing for the holy places. Furthermore, to everyone's astonishment, they meticulously paid for everything they obtained from the populace, instead of simply seizing it as expected. The winning of Tibetan hearts and minds, Younghusband knew, was crucial to his task, even if for the time being the priestly hierarchy remained hostile.

Such then was the atmosphere in which Younghusband began the tortuous process of negotiating a treaty with the Tibetans. He had to work against a deadline imposed by the approach of winter which would make withdrawal a problem, and he was under continuous pressure from London – via the single telegraph line from Darjeeling – to get a settlement and depart. The Cabinet, after its hawkish decision to advance on the Tibetan capital, was now beginning to get cold feet. O'Connor (later Colonel Sir Frederick) wrote years afterwards: 'Its chief desire, once the treaty was signed, was to get out of the country as quickly as possible and try to assume an appearance of never having been there at all.'

As usual, Macdonald was no help whatever, demanding that they leave Lhasa by September 15 at the latest lest his soldiers begin dying of cold. The busy telegraph line was now carrying not only Younghusband's progress reports but also Cassandra-like warnings from Macdonald of the casualties from frostbite and pneumonia which could be expected if they delayed a moment longer. Inquisitive Tibetans who asked what this mysterious wire was for and where it led to were informed that it was there simply to enable the expedition to find its way back to India once negotiations were concluded. In this way they were deterred from severing this vital line of communication. In fact, more than thirty years later, when a party of British officials visited Lhasa, it was still intact.

While these delicate contacts were going on, those members of the expedition not involved busied themselves exploring every corner of the once-forbidden city, especially its monasteries and temples. 'We generally went in parties of four and five,' wrote Candler, 'and a company of Sikhs or Pathans was left in the courtyard in case of accidents.' The Tibetan faithful trudging the Ling-kor were, almost without exception, poor and ragged and frequently blind. 'It seems,' he noted, 'that the people of Lhasa do not begin to think of the next incarnation until they have nothing left in this.' Of the Potala he saw little beyond its soaring ramparts and golden roofs 'and thousand sightless windows that concealed the unknown'. But they were permitted to visit the Jokhang, the cathedral of Lhasa, and its holiest monument. Landon was deeply impressed by this famous shrine, with its great golden Buddha, describing it as 'the sacred heart and centre, not of Lhasa alone, but of Central Asia'. He and his two companions, he believed, were almost certainly the first infidels ever to enter it, for the descriptions of the pundits and others bore scant resemblance to what they themselves now saw by the flickering light of the butter-lamps.

With their revolvers in their pockets in case of trouble, and accompanied by the *amban's* secretary and an escort of Chinese soldiers, they entered this holiest of Buddhist holies. The next moment the great cathedral doors were closed behind them. Making their way through the gloom past a forest of pillars they found themselves in the heart of the building. Here they came upon chapel after chapel, dimly lit with butter-lamps, and each with its little altar and filled with images. The stench of rancid butter, Landon told readers of *The Times*, was abominable. 'Everything one touches drips with grease,' he wrote. 'The fumes of the burning butter have in the course of many generations filmed over the surfaces and clogged the carving of doors and walls alike.' The floor was like a skating rink.

The principal shrine of the Jokhang lay at the far end of the cathedral. Its central figure was the *Jo* itself, a twice life-sized gold sculpture of Buddha said to date from his lifetime and described by the enthusiastic Landon as 'beyond question the most famous idol in the world'. Lit by row upon row of butter-lamps of solid gold it cast its awesome spell over him and his companions. From its murky recess, Landon wrote, 'the great glowing mass of the Buddha softly looms out, ghostlike and shadowless'. Chanting monks added to a scene which could hardly have changed in centuries.

They left the cathedral in silence, only to find a hostile mob awaiting them. Its wrath, they quickly realised, was directed less against them than against their Chinese escort. But they need not have feared, for instantly a huge and powerfully-built lama began to advance towards the crowd wielding an eight-foot-long whip, metal tipped and made of what looked like rhinoceros hide. Striking out viciously to left and right, Landon relates, the monk inflicted 'appalling blows on the packed crowd'. Gratefully Landon and his colleagues chose this moment to slip away.

While the others were busy sightseeing, Younghusband had been locked in argument with the Tibetans who never wearied of telling him what problems they were having in restraining their army from wiping out the British force. However, using a judicious combination of carrot and stick, including a threat to turn Macdonald's artillery on the Potala itself if they continued to prevaricate, Younghusband eventually managed to persuade the Tibetans to sign an agreement which became known as the Anglo-Tibetan Convention. In view of the stubbornness of the Tibetans, and the short time available, it was a considerable personal triumph. It certainly bore out Curzon's assertion that Younghusband possessed a genius for handling Asiatics. Tri-lingual texts were now prepared – in Tibetan, English and Chinese – and to these the Regent solemnly affixed the Dalai Lama's seal and Younghusband his signature. The ceremony took place in the great Durbar Hall of the Potala palace on September 7, 1904. To give it the maximum of authority, Young-husband insisted that the treaty also bore the seals of the Council of the Regent, the three principal monasteries of Tibet and the National Assembly. The only missing seal was that of the Chinese *amban* who insisted that he was not empowered to sign it on behalf of his government.

Under its terms the Tibetans recognised the previously disputed (by them) Sikkim-Tibet frontier. They also agreed to the opening of two new trade marts, one at Gyantse and the other at Gartok in western Tibet, each with a resident British trade agent. They further agreed to raze all fortifications between Gyantse and the Indian frontier, and to keep open the roads leading to and from the new trade marts. Much more reluctantly they agreed to pay an indemnity of seventy-five lakhs of rupees (£562,000) in seventy-five annual instalments as part of the cost of the Younghusband expedition. At first the Regent had insisted that the British should pay *them* for the loss of life and damage which the expedition had caused. But finally, under the unpleasant threat of Macdonald's field guns (memories of what these had achieved at Gyantse were still fresh), they had capitulated. It was agreed, furthermore, that until the money had been paid in full the British would occupy the Chumbi Valley.

Another article prohibited the Tibetans from having any dealings with foreign powers (other than China) without British consent. This was aimed principally at Russia. There must be no more Dorjief missions to the Tsarist court or vice versa. A separate article in the treaty conceded the right of the newly appointed British trade agent at Gyantse (the first would be O'Connor himself) to visit Lhasa. In addition to all this, the Tibetans now released from their state dungeons three of their own countrymen who had been incarcerated – two for many years – for giving assistance to Sarat Chandra Das and to Ekai Kawaguchi. Candler describes the scene:

An old man and his son were brought into the hall looking utterly bowed and broken. The old man's chains had been removed from his limbs that morning for the first time in twenty years, and he came in blinking at the unaccustomed light like a blind man miraculously restored to sight. His offence was hospitality shown to Sarat Chandra Das in 1884. An old monk of Sera was released next. His offence had been that he had been the teacher of Kawaguchi, the Japanese traveller who visited Lhasa in the guise of a Chinese pilgrim. We who looked on these sad relics of humanity felt that their restitution to liberty was in itself sufficient to justify our advance to Lhasa.

The British finally rode away from Lhasa on September 23, 1904, just seven weeks after entering the Tibetan capital. They left amid noisy demonstrations of goodwill from their erstwhile foes and protestations of undying friendship from both sides. A cynic, of course, might have interpreted all this simply as the Tibetans celebrating the British departure. But to Young-husband and his officers it was evidence that after long years of misunderstanding and discord a truculent neighbour had finally been won over as a friend.

It is at this point in the story that we encounter a hitherto unsuspected side to Younghusband's character. On the evening before leaving Lhasa, this archetypal British hero had left his encampment and ridden off alone into the mountains to enjoy a moment to himself and to take a last look at the scenery. But something happened to him there which was to change the future course of his life. As he looked back at the holy city on that still autumn evening, he recalled later, 'I gave myself up to all the emotions of this eventful time.' But it was not just satisfaction at a difficult task accomplished. The emotions which Francis Younghusband experienced on that Tibetan mountainside bordered on a revelation. For behind the piercing blue eyes and the Kitchener moustache there lay a streak of religious mysticism.

In his book *India and Tibet* he describes the feelings which took possession of him that night: 'This exhilaration of the moment grew and grew till it thrilled through me with over-powering intensity. Never again could I think evil, or ever be at enmity with any man. All nature and all humanity were bathed in a rosy glowing radiancy . . . that single hour on leaving Lhasa was worth all the rest of a lifetime.'

But his rapture was soon to be shattered. Shortly after the new treaty had been signed, and the fact reported to London, telegrams began to arrive from the Government at home seeking to amend some of the terms. To suggest to the Tibetans at this late stage that changes should be made to an agreement which they had only just signed would, Younghusband felt, create the worst possible impression and keep the mission in Lhasa for months. He decided to ignore the instructions, telegraphing back that now the treaty had been signed and the mission was leaving the following day, it was impossible to start renegotiating it. With luck, by the time he reached home, it might all have been forgotten.

However, that was not to be. For behind the scenes in London and Calcutta a bitter struggle over the terms of the treaty was going on between the doves and the hawks, between a weak Cabinet anxious not to offend the Russians and the Russophobe Viceroy. The Cabinet were timorous of Curzon's aggressive forward policy in Central Asia and felt they had been forced by events beyond their control to authorise the advance on Lhasa. Furthermore, Younghusband had exceeded his brief over some of the concessions he had wrung from the Tibetans – even if these were very much to Curzon's taste – and now he was disobeying their instructions. Curzon, unfortunately for Younghusband, as well as being ill himself was on home leave with a desperately sick wife to think about. He was in no position to defend his own interests, let alone those of his protégé.

So it was that Francis Younghusband returned to London a popular hero, but at the same time to face Government censure. The row, which was to rumble on for many months, is largely beyond the scope of this narrative. Suffice it to say, several of the articles in Younghusband's treaty were considerably watered down. The indemnity was reduced to two-thirds of the original sum, and the period of occupation of the Chumbi Valley reduced to a mere three years. The latter modification was less out of consideration for the Tibetans than to forestall accusations from St Petersburg of annexation. Similarly, the right of the British trade agent in Gyantse to visit Lhasa was also withdrawn. For the original treaty, while denying access to Lhasa to all others (and clearly this was aimed at Russia), appeared to reserve this privilege exclusively for the British.

By the time the Cabinet had finished emasculating Younghusband's hard-won concessions, what remained of the treaty made it hardly worth the time, cost, effort and lives (the Tibetans had suffered some 2,700 casualties) that had been expended on it. Just what the bewildered Tibetans made of this astonishing climb-down by their erstwhile conquerors is not known, for only in the West does this most controversial of imperial adventures continue to exercise historians. To the Tibetans the whole affair long ago paled into insignificance with the arrival, in 1950, of an infinitely more ruthless invader.

Although Younghusband found himself made the scapegoat for the Cabinet's inept and vacillating policies (they had even sent him a congratulatory wire before beginning to have second thoughts) he was not short of allies. For a start there was the British public to whom he was a hero in the classic mould. Then there were the officers who had accompanied him, and any one of them (Macdonald probably excepted) would gladly have followed him over the edge of the world. They were unstinting in their praise of his leadership and uncanny way with Asiatics, whether their own British Indian troops or the Tibetans themselves. As serving officers, however, they were prevented from speaking up publicly for him. But the four special correspondents – particularly the influential Perceval Landon of *The Times* – were his to a man, and they were under no such restraints.

His most powerful ally, though, was the King, who personally overruled the Government's objections to his receiving any recognition at all in the mission honours list. After a brisk tussle behind the scenes between King and Cabinet, Younghusband was awarded a knighthood – albeit a KCIE, the lowest order of knighthood in the Indian Empire. Macdonald, originally destined for a KCB, found that this had been inexplicably withdrawn at the very last minute and a lesser KCIE substituted.

Some ten years were to pass, however, before Austin Chamberlain, then Secretary of State for India, after reading the papers relating to the affair, sent for Younghusband. Apologising to him for the grave injustice which he felt had been done him, Chamberlain immediately recommended him for a KCSI, the highest order of knighthood in the Indian Empire. So it was, somewhat belatedly, that Francis Younghusband was officially absolved from all blame and his reputation was restored. But by then he had had enough of soldiering and diplomacy. At the age of forty-seven, after four years as British Resident in Kashmir, he had retired from government service to devote his life to what had become his real love, religion. Had he remained in the Indian Political Service he would almost certainly have achieved the highest honours and position. But the streak of mysticism which had momentarily transfixed him on that Lhasa hillside could not be ignored. In 1936 he founded the World Congress of Faiths which aimed (and still does) to unite Christians, Buddhists, Moslems, Jews and Hindus. But it is as a man of action that Younghusband will be remembered. When he died in 1942, Sir Frederick O'Connor wrote in *The Times* of their months in Tibet together:

During all those months, which included cold, discomfort, fatigue and danger, I never knew him, even once, to show irritation or impatience. . . . He remained, in fact, quite impe. turbable through it all – like a rock. And as a rock we all came to admire and rely on him. But, besides this, those of us who knew him well loved him. Although an exceedingly shrewd judge of character and of human failings he was never betrayed into an ill-natured, angry, or even impatient word. Everyone in the little force, I think I may say, from the oldest to the youngest, European or Indian, admired and respected him. The success of the Mission (and it was not an easy task) was due to his personal character and influence more than anything else, as were also the friendly feelings which we left behind us at Lhasa and which have continued unimpaired to the present day.

*   *   *

Within months of the return of the expedition, books began to pour off the presses of eager publishers laying bare the long-hidden secrets of the holy city. To rush out his own account, Perceval Landon had left Lhasa a whole month ahead of anyone else. This was a risky move for a reporter, for the treaty was still being negotiated. However, his departure did not prevent *The Times* from obtaining a scoop. For the great Dr George Morrison, its resourceful Peking correspondent, published the terms of the treaty on September 17, well ahead of his rivals and correct in most details. Meanwhile, riding fast, Landon had covered the four hundred miles to Darjeeling, the nearest railhead, in eleven days, reaching London in thirty-five. His monumental, two-volume work, *Lhasa*, filled with remarkable photographs, was in the London bookshops just four months after his departure from Lhasa, an amazing tribute to both himself and his publisher. It was closely followed by three further accounts of the expedition – Edmund Candler's *The Unveiling of Lhasa*, Lt. Col. L. A. Waddell's *Lhasa and its Mysteries*, and a curious little volume, *To Lhassa at Last*, pseudonymously written by someone calling himself Powell Millington, who, so far as I know, has never been identified. The following year there appeared Captain (now Major) Ottley's *With Mounted Infantry in Tibet*. Finally, some four years later, John Murray brought out Younghusband's own modest account of the affair, *India and Tibet*. Meanwhile, determined to have its own say, the Government rushed out no fewer than three official Blue Books, followed later by a fourth.

These, their critics alleged, were aimed at justifying the Cabinet's inglorious behaviour, the documents and reports having been deliberately selected to suit its case. Captain O'Connor and the Reuter correspondent, Henry Newman, were also to publish accounts of the expedition, both strongly sympathetic to Younghusband.

After such massive exposure, Lhasa could no longer claim to be the most mysterious city on earth. To explorers and travellers the race for the Tibetan capital was over. Now every Tom, Dick and Harry in the Indian Army seemed to have been there. But if Lhasa had yielded up the last of its secrets to an inquisitive world, there were still vast tracts of this mysterious land, nearly half the size of Europe, to be explored and mapped. Not only were there giant mountains to be conquered, including the world's highest, but there were new plants and perhaps unknown animals to be discovered. For those interested in the occult or the paranormal, Tibet with its tales of men who could fly and perform other amazing feats, promised a rich hunting ground. And if that were not enough, there was always its gold.

But anyone who thought it was going to be any easier to get into Tibet now that its citadel had fallen was due to be disappointed. The British Government was determined that it should remain a forbidden land. Balfour's tottering Conservative Government had finally succumbed in December 1905 and had been replaced by a Liberal one under Sir Henry Campbell-Bannerman. He wanted no further trouble over Tibet. One way of ensuring this was not to let anyone in.

Among the first to fall foul of this ban was the formidable Swedish explorer Sven Hedin. One of the greatest of Central Asian travellers, Hedin had spent the best part of a decade filling in the blanks on the maps of Chinese Turkestan. More than once he had crossed into northern Tibet, and it was from there, as we have seen, that in 1901 he made an unsuccessful attempt to reach Lhasa disguised as a Buryat pilgrim. Now, in May 1906, he arrived in India from where he planned to cross into Tibet. He had long ago lost any interest in reaching Lhasa, his sole object being the systematic scientific exploration of southern Tibet. For this undertaking he had received, only a few months earlier, the personal approval and support of Lord Curzon, who greatly admired his work. The Viceroy had even arranged for three Indian surveyors to be specially trained at Dehra Dun to accompany him. But all that was before the fall of the Conservative Government and Curzon's own departure from India. Now, to Hedin's fury, the new Government gave orders that under no circumstances was he to be allowed to enter Tibet. If necessary he was to be restrained by force.

Lord Minto, Curzon's successor, who believed that Hedin's scientific work could prove valuable to the British Government, did his best to change London's mind. But apart from any political considerations, it was thought in Whitehall that Hedin, a trained geologist, was planning to prospect for gold. Minto therefore suggested that Captain Rawling, an experienced traveller who had served in the Younghusband expedition, might be sent with Hedin to keep an eye on him. But the new Secretary of State for India, Lord Morley, would have none of it. 'My God, how I hated Morley . . .' wrote Hedin afterwards, adding that 'the English were worse than the Tibetans.'

The Prime Minister, Campbell-Bannerman, now added his veto to that of Morley, personally telegraphing his decision to Hedin. Furious at what he regarded as this breaking of a promise made to him by the British, the Swede vowed to outmanoeuvre them and show them, as he put it, 'that I am more at home in Asia than you. . . .' Heading rapidly for Kashmir, he halted in Srinagar just long enough to assemble a caravan before making for Ladakh. From there, he announced, he would be returning to his old haunt of Chinese Turkestan, lying to the north. But once out of sight he planned instead to turn east and cross, behind Campbell-Bannerman's back, into Tibet. Whitehall, guessing what he might be playing at, gave orders that he was not to leave for Chinese Turkestan without a valid Chinese passport, which they knew he did not possess. Hedin, however, had friends in the Indian Government, and the telegram conveying this instruction was mysteriously delayed until he was beyond recall.

Having successfully outwitted the British Government, making it look distinctly foolish in the process, Hedin was to spend the next two years travelling freely across southern Tibet, mapping its rivers, mountains and sacred lakes, and eventually producing a massive scientific report on the area amounting to nine large volumes of text and a further three of maps. This has been described as 'one of the most comprehensive works on any region in any age'. The British Government appears to have been sufficiently impressed by the results of Hedin's work, and its value to British India, to award him an honorary knighthood, and conveniently forget the illicit nature of his journey. But Hedin found it less easy to forgive, and when geographers in Britain questioned some of his claims he reacted angrily. 'For a hundred and fifty years,' he told one Swedish newspaper, 'the English have owned India and yet done so little to explore Tibet that when a stranger comes and makes discoveries – in spite of their having done their utmost to keep him out – it is naturally exasperating for them.'

The fiery Swedish explorer, however, was far from being the sole critic of British policy towards Tibet. They existed in plenty even in the ranks of the administration in India, especially among the frontier officers. One such dissenter was Captain O'Connor, the British trade commissioner in Gyantse, and close friend of Francis Younghusband. It had been his disagreeable task to have to translate into Tibetan and transmit to Lhasa the greatly watered-down version of Younghusband's hard-won concessions. Officially there to see that the trade mart was run in accordance with the Lhasa agreement, or what still remained of it, his principal function appears to have been to collect political intelligence from his lonely listening post for his chiefs in India. Contemptuous of the soft frontier policies now emanating from Westminster and Whitehall, O'Connor pressed his chiefs, in the continued absence of the Dalai Lama from Lhasa, to transfer their support to the Panchen Lama. While rejecting his suggestion that the Panchen Lama should be supplied by Britain with modern rifles, they agreed that the pontiff should be presented with a motor-car by the Government of India.

So it was, in 1907, that the first motorised vehicle ever to enter Tibet – an eight horse-power Clement – was borne over the Himalayan passes and introduced to an astounded populace. Accompanying it, sometimes carried on poles and at other times hauled and pushed by sweating coolies, was O'Connor's own more modest Peugeot. 'Once across the Tang La,' he recalls in his memoirs, 'it was delightful to drive along, at the terrific speed of fifteen to twenty miles an hour – the utmost we could manage – over the great Tuna plain.' But as every drop of petrol had to be brought over the Himalayas from India, motoring in Tibet was an expensive pastime. The altitude, moreover, was to create special problems of its own, especially with the carburettors, and after a couple of years O'Connor's own car ended up ignominiously in a shed, where it may still be. What happened to the Panchen Lama's motor-car is not known.

Despite his popularity with the Tibetans, O'Connor's spell in Gyantse was far from easy. The Chinese, still smarting from their loss of face over the Younghusband expedition, were bent on making life as difficult as possible for this British official stationed in what they regarded as their own sovereign territory. They were quick to sense that he and the handful of British officers serving in Tibet with the small force temporarily occupying the Chumbi Valley had only the lukewarm backing of their home government. 'We made diplomatic protests, of course,' O'Connor recalls in his memoirs, *On the Frontier and Beyond*, 'but there was not much heavy metal behind them, and they produced little effect.'

The Chinese must have been every bit as mystified as the Tibetans as they watched the British conceding one by one the gains they had gone to such lengths to obtain in Lhasa. But they were not slow to see that, for whatever reason, the British

Government was anxious to wash its hands of the whole Tibetan adventure. As the British backed away, leaving a vacuum, the Chinese set about filling it. No one, it seems, gave a thought for the Tibetans. Yet the Anglo-Tibetan Convention signed by Younghusband in Lhasa had acknowledged the right of the Tibetans to negotiate on their own behalf, thus effectively revoking Britain's long-standing recognition of China's suzerainty over them. However, this was very quickly put right. Bent on reconciliation with Peking, and without even informing the Tibetans, the new Campbell-Bannerman Government signed a treaty with China in April 1906 which effectively restored Britain's recognition of the latter's suzerainty over Tibet. The following year a treaty was concluded with Russia – the Anglo-Russian Convention – in which both governments recognised China's 'suzerain rights' over Tibet, and agreed not to interfere in the country's internal affairs. Once again the Tibetans were neither consulted nor informed.

What happened next was something the British Government had failed to foresee. Although it could have given them no satisfaction, Great Game veterans like Younghusband and O'Connor must have felt vindicated. For, without any warning, the Chinese advanced into Tibet, leaving a trail of slaughtered monks and others behind them. The Dalai Lama, who had only just returned to his capital after five years in exile, appealed to the outside world for help, but in vain. In February 1910, two thousand Chinese troops seized Lhasa, firing on the crowd which had gathered to see them arrive, but just failing to catch the Dalai Lama and his ministers. When they discovered that he had fled, they at once put a price on his head and sent two hundred mounted troops in pursuit of him.

Riding day and night, and taking routes sometimes chosen by divination, the fugitives struck south towards British India. After numerous narrow escapes, they crossed exhausted into Sikkim. Late at night, and still fearing pursuit, they hammered on the door of the small frontier signal station at Gnatong, run by two British ex-sergeants named Luff and Humphreys.

Alerted by telegraph that the Dalai Lama was heading their way and must be given all the help and protection they were able to provide, the two men leaped from their beds. Opening the door to the royal party, they are said to have asked: 'Which of you blighters is the Dalai Lama?' Embarrassed by the modesty of their quarters, they suggested that the God-king might prefer to spend the night in the official government bungalow. However, the Dalai Lama said he would rather remain where he was, feeling safer perhaps in the company of these sturdy and cheerful representatives of the British Raj. After brewing tea for the royal party and offering them what food they had, the two Englishmen sat up on guard, their rifles at the ready, for the rest of the night while the weary Dalai Lama slept in Sergeant Luff's bed. The following morning, after cooking breakfast for the entire Tibetan government in exile, Luff and Humphreys bade farewell to their grateful guests, who rode on into British territory and safety.

Thus, in the Year of the Iron-Dog, the greatest of living Buddhas arrived in the small Himalayan market town of Kalimpong where the entire population – Hindu and Moslem, Christian and Buddhist – turned out to welcome him in his hour of sadness. Some bowed, others salaamed, while the Buddhists prostrated themselves in the dust. Among those who rode into town to see him that day were the three fair-haired daughters of a Scottish missionary. As the Dalai Lama dismounted outside the bungalow which had been hastily prepared for him, he spotted one of them. Never in his life had he seen such golden hair. Incredulously, he reached down to feel its texture. The little girl smiled back. It was a simple beginning to the friendship which was to blossom between the Dalai Lama and his former foes, the British, during his two years of exile in India. Throughout this period Britain's relations with the Tibetans were to grow closer than at any time before or since, largely due to the influence of one Englishman, Charles Bell. Bell, a Tibetan-speaking political officer, had been assigned to look after him during his exile, and a close personal friendship was to develop between the two men which later would bear valuable fruit for Britain.

Meanwhile, back in Lhasa, things were not going well for the Chinese. They could get no cooperation from the people, the Tibetan parliament was proving obstructive, while in parts of the country a resistance movement calling itself 'The Dawn' had begun to harrass them. When the Chinese invited the Panchen Lama to Lhasa, hoping to use his authority, angry Tibetans expressed their disapproval by dropping old socks and mud on his head as he and the Chinese *amban* rode through the streets together. Taxes soon began to find their way to Darjeeling, where the Dalai Lama was now living, instead of to Lhasa, and the Chinese had to search Tibetans leaving for India to prevent this. Finally the Chinese became so desperate that they were forced to approach the Dalai Lama and plead with him to return, but in vain.

By now time had all but run out for the Manchus in Tibet, as everywhere else. In October 1911 revolution erupted at home. This quickly spread to the Chinese garrison in Lhasa which, unpaid for months, mutinied. Several of its officers, including a colonel, defected, joining the Sera monastery as monks. Encouraged by rumours that the Dalai Lama was returning to lead them in a holy war against their oppressors, the Tibetans turned in fury on the Chinese. Armed only with primitive firearms and swords they suffered severe losses at first, but gradually the demoralised and homesick Chinese were driven from outlying garrisons into the capital.

Here a bizarre form of trench warfare developed, with the Chinese occupying the south of the town and the Tibetans the north. Dividing the two front lines was a barricaded street, the doors and windows of the houses on either side of which were blocked with sandbags. Both sides dug tunnels into each other's sectors and crawled along these to plant explosives beneath key enemy positions. To lessen the shock waves which travelled back along the tunnels, these were never dug in straight lines. Simple but ingenious devices were developed by both Chinese and Tibetans to detect tunnellers at work. It was all too reminiscent of a new type of warfare which was shortly to engulf Europe.

Much of Lhasa was reduced to ruins during this fighting, and before long the Chinese began to run desperately short of food. Eventually a ceasefire was agreed. In exchange for safe passage home via India, the Chinese surrendered their arms. On January 6, 1913, the last of their beleaguered garrison marched out of Lhasa for Kalimpong. The Tibetans had finally rid themselves of these latest uninvited guests, although this time it had taken them three bitter years. Only now did the Dalai Lama return to his capital to resume his twice-interrupted rule. The new Republican Government, anxious not to let go of Tibet entirely, telegraphed the God-king apologising for the excesses of the previous regime's rough soldiery, and informing him that they had decided to restore him to his former rank in the Chinese Empire. In a reply which to this day Tibetans consider as terminating centuries of Chinese colonial rule and marking the dawn of modern Tibetan independence, the Dalai Lama declined their offer and announced his intention of taking over full control of his country. Some thirty-seven years, and another divine reincarnation, were to pass before Peking was to challenge this.

The thirteenth Dalai Lama's friendship with Charles Bell was to continue uninterrupted after the former's return to Lhasa. To Bell, in whom he had absolute trust, he would often turn for advice on more sophisticated matters. It had been Bell's idea, in 1913, to send four Tibetan boys to an English public school. By familiarising them with western ways it was his hope that on their return they would help to steer Tibet out of the Middle Ages and into the twentieth century. The experiment, conducted at Rugby, was only partially successful. One British frontier officer recalled: 'They went away shy, uncouth children. They came back speaking perfect English and polished men of the world.' The only trouble was that they had forgotten almost every word of their Tibetan. But, more disappointingly, the very ideas they had been sent to England to assimilate were to prove unacceptable to too many of the priestly hierarchy. One boy even returned with a motor-bicycle, the first ever seen in Tibet, but after a high official had been thrown from his terrified mule the machine was confiscated, ending its days in a storeroom in the Potala. But another boy, trained as an electrical engineer after leaving Rugby, was eventually responsible for the electrification of parts of Lhasa.

A tribute to Bell's friendship with the Dalai Lama, whose biography he was later to write, was the Tibetan ruler's gesture to Britain on the outbreak of World War I. Not only were his prayers, and those of Tibet's monasteries, directed towards a British victory, but he also offered a thousand of his best troops to fight alongside British soldiers wherever they might be needed. Bell's influence at the Potala was also to give British mountaineers a head start over their rivals in the race after the war to climb Mount Everest. For it was entirely due to him that British climbers were the first to be allowed into Tibet to challenge the great mountain, whose allure was soon to eclipse even that of Lhasa.

In fact, unknown to either of them, while the Dalai Lama was in exile in Darjeeling a clandestine reconnaissance of the approaches to Everest had already taken place.

12. The Riddle of the Snows

It had long been the dream of Captain John Noel, a young Indian Army officer, to be the first white man to come face to face with Mount Everest. At the time he was preparing for his secret journey – in the spring of 1913 – no European had ever approached it. Although for sixty years it had been known to be the world's highest mountain, it lay tantalisingly out of reach astride the forbidden frontier between Tibet and Nepal, both closed lands. Its awesome height, some five and a half miles, had been calculated by the Survey of India as long before as 1852, using observations taken from the plains of India. The Survey's chief computer, Radhanath Sikhdar, is said to have rushed excitedly into the Surveyor General's office and gasped: 'Sir, I have discovered the highest mountain in the world.' The official histories, however, discount this as folklore and attribute the discovery of its height of 29,002 feet (a figure later slightly adjusted) to team work. Thirteen more years were to pass before Peak XV, as it was then called, acquired its present name – a tribute to Sir George Everest, 'father' of the modern Survey of India. This was only done after every attempt had been made to discover its native name.

Proposals for expeditions to Everest had twice been turned down by the government of the day. The first, in 1893, was put forward by Lieutenant Charles Bruce, a Herculean young Indian Army officer famous throughout the Himalayas as a traveller – and for once throwing three Gurkhas simultaneously in a wrestling match. The second, thirteen years later, had been turned down because the British Government was then in the process of negotiating the all-important Anglo-Russian

Convention of 1907, and was anxious that nothing remotely should be allowed to jeopardise it. But Everest could not remain unchallenged for ever. In April 1913, disguised as a native and without permission from either his own government or from Lhasa, Captain Noel entered Tibet from Sikkim determined to reconnoitre the approaches to Everest. An experienced Himalayan traveller who spoke the languages of the hill tribes, including some Tibetan, he had hired three well-tried and trusted native companions to accompany him before entering Tibet by a pass used by Sarat Chandra Das on his clandestine journeys.

With some trepidation Noel and his men had approached the frontier post, a small stone hut which in the pundit's day had been occupied by Tibetan border guards. To their relief they found it abandoned, a sign perhaps of the improved state of relations between the two neighbours. A little further on they came to the lonely Buddhist monastery of Chorten-Nyim which they discovered to be inhabited by seven Tibetan nuns. Three of them, somewhat to the relief of the disguised (but blue-eyed) Englishman, were totally blind. But Noel's journey cannot here be described in detail – he was to do that himself before the Royal Geographical Society after the War. Suffice to say, only forty miles short of his goal he was turned back by armed Tibetans after a scuffle and a brief exchange of fire. Fortunately this was not before he had obtained a clear view of the upper part of Everest from much closer than any other European so far.

Although he was forced to retreat before reaching the foothills of Everest, the route Noel reconnoitred was that subsequently taken by the early official British expeditions. It was the first of these, a reconnaissance, which thanks to the influence of Charles Bell was in 1920 to receive the blessing of the Dalai Lama. But it was Noel's account of his illicit journey delivered before the Royal Geographical Society the previous year which was principally responsible for this post-war revival of interest in Everest.

But it is unlikely that any of these expeditions would have taken place had not the Dalai Lama invited his friend Bell (now Sir Charles) to Lhasa, the first European ever to be so honoured. For the only alternative route to Everest involved crossing Nepal, a country still closed to European travellers at that time. The motive for his invitation was not one that the Dalai Lama made any attempt to conceal. He had for some time been having trouble with the Chinese on his eastern frontier, where his troops had been in action (with surprising success) against those of the new Republican Government. Anxious to obtain British support against this difficult neighbour, he hoped that Bell, although officially retired, might be able to prevail upon his own government to supply Tibet with much needed weapons and ammunition, as well as military training. The Cabinet, deciding that the Bolshevik Revolution had rendered nul and void Britain's commitment to the Anglo-Russian Convention (which prohibited such visits), pressed Bell to accept the invitation. In November 1920 he arrived in Lhasa, the entire population turning out to welcome him, and moved into the Potala where he was to stay for the best part of a year, regularly seeing the Dalai Lama and his ministers.

It was during this time that Bell raised the question of an Everest Expedition. While Everest was less sacred to Tibetans than some other mountains, notably Kailas in the south-west, it did possess a sanctity for those living in the region. 'An expedition of white men who did not believe in Tibetan spirits and stood outside the Buddhist brotherhood, would of necessity disturb the spirits of the place,' wrote Bell afterwards. But he was able to convince the Dalai Lama that, however eccentric, there was nothing sinister in Englishmen wanting to be the first to stand on the highest place on earth. Anxious to please his friend, as well as the British Government (he would in due course get his arms), the Dalai Lama agreed and a special passport bearing the Great Red Seal of the Holy Rulers of Tibet was presented to Bell. It read:

Be it known to Officers and Headman of Phari-jong, Khampa, Tin-ki and Shekar, that a party of Sahibs will come to the Sacred Mountain. . . . You shall render all help and safeguard them. . . . We have requested the Sahibs to keep the laws of the country when they visit the Sacred Mountain and not to kill Birds and Animals as the people will feel very sorry for this. . . . His Holiness the Dalai Lama is now on great friendly terms with the Government of India.

It was dated the seventeenth day of the eleventh month of the Iron-Bird Year. The way to Everest was now officially open, and in May 1921 a small reconnaissance party jointly mounted by the Royal Geographical Society and the Alpine Club crossed into Tibet from Sikkim. Accompanying it was a master from Charterhouse whose name, George Leigh-Mallory, would go down in the annals of heroic endeavour. As the finest climber of his day he was prepared, if the chance presented itself, to make a bold bid for the summit. However, as one Himalayan expert forecast at the time: 'They will have a big enough job to find the mountain, let alone doing anything else.' But find it they did, although worsening weather ruled out any question of Mallory making a dash for the top. Meanwhile, preparations for the main expedition were going ahead in London.

Such already was the charisma of Everest that Sir Francis Younghusband, now retired and chairman of the expedition committee, was inundated with letters from applicants all over the world begging to be allowed to come in any capacity. But there was no shortage of experienced and well-tried climbers at home to choose from. For a start, Mallory was again selected. Although too old at fifty-six to climb, Brigadier-General Charles Bruce was picked to lead the expedition. It was he who as a Gurkha subaltern nearly thirty years before had first put forward the idea for such a venture. With his lifetime's experience and encyclopaedic knowledge of the Himalayas, its languages and peoples, Bruce was the obvious choice. Captain John Noel was also included, his principal task being to film the climb.

No sooner had the encouraging reports from the reconnaissance party reached London than Younghusband's hand-picked team of climbers sailed for India. Late in March 1922, a small army of mountaineers and porters set out from Darjeeling on the long trail through Sikkim and Tibet to Rongbuk Monastery, some fifteen miles from the foot of Everest's northern face. There was little time to waste. The final attack on the summit had to be made before the monsoon broke early in June, turning the mountain into a nightmare of avalanches and melting glaciers. Although there had been some disagreement over the ethics of using oxygen, a supply of the gas was taken. No one had ever before climbed above 24,600 feet, and the effects of even greater altitudes on the human body and brain could only be guessed at. Not many mountaineers then believed, that even with the aid of oxygen, Everest would ever be conquered.

The four-hundred-mile trek to the remote Rongbuk monastery took a month. Standing alone in a valley at 16,000 feet, in full view of Everest, it is the highest in the world. Many of the monks lived as hermits, imprisoned in a rock-hewn cell for months or years at a time. One recluse, revered locally as a saint, had sat motionless in total darkness for fifteen years, only interrupting his meditation long enough to receive food – a daily cup of water and a handful of barley meal passed through a small aperture by monks he never saw or spoke to. The silent valley, untouched by the passing of time, ran wild with small creatures which showed no fear of man. Perhaps it was the climbers' accounts of this lost Tibetan valley and its monastery which inspired James Hilton's Shangri La in *Lost Horizon*. Today the monastery is no more, having been totally destroyed by Red Guards. But it was here, where the expedition established its base camp, that they first learned of the *yeti*, or snowman, which sometimes carried off women, it was said, or bit through the necks of yaks and drank their blood. Four at least were believed to live in the area. They were also warned of the protecting spirits of the mountain which assuredly would try to prevent them from climbing it.

The ascent, it had been decided, would be made by what was termed the 'Polar method', with the tough and cheerful Sherpa porters advancing as far up the mountain as possible and setting up depots or camps, each some two thousand vertical feet above the last. The climbers would then use these as a kind of ladder to carry them as near the summit as possible for the final assault of perhaps two thousand feet. The first attempt was led by Mallory. He and three other climbers, without oxygen and all suffering from mountain sickness, reached 25,000 feet – a world record – on May 20, 1922, moving even higher – to 26,985 feet – the following day. But to reach the summit would have meant setting up one more camp. This they were not in any position to do, being low in food, weakened through altitude sickness and having none of the necessary equipment. The weather, moreover, was deteriorating rapidly.

Now two more climbers, both using oxygen, were sent up by General Bruce to try to reach the top, passing Mallory on his way down. Despite the fact that their oxygen equipment developed alarming faults, they managed to climb to 27,235 feet, higher even than Mallory, before being driven back as the weather once again closed in on the mountain. But they had got to within half a mile of the highest spot on earth, and everyone was now convinced that it could be done. Although the weather was worsening with the approach of the monsoon, Bruce decided to launch one more assault, again led by Mallory, the wonder climber. Noel, with his cameras (which were proving too heavy for the Sherpas to keep transporting up and down the mountain), watched from below as the party set off. With a companion he observed the tiny black specks – climbers and Sherpas – moving slowly up the mountainside. Then, suddenly, he saw them vanish.

'Good God, they are gone!' he gasped. 'Avalanche,' his stunned companion replied. Using Noel's telescope they desperately searched the spot where the climbers had been only moments before. An entire cliff of solid ice and snow had broken away. There was no sign of anyone. Setting hurriedly off up the mountain, before long they saw ahead of them a cluster of motionless figures. They were sitting silently in the snow immediately above the spot where the mountainside had collapsed. Noel realised at once what had happened. 'They were squatting at the very edge of a sheer ice wall about eighty feet high,' he wrote afterwards in his book, *Through Tibet to Everest*. 'The avalanche had carried them to the edge, and they dared not move lest they should slip over.' This had been the fate of some of their luckless colleagues. The ropes joining them to those above had snapped like string, and eight Sherpas had been hurled into the crevasse. The three Europeans, being ahead, had survived. They now climbed back down to join Noel and his companion at the bottom of the shattered cliff. There, to their dismay, they found the bodies of five of the Sherpas, killed instantly as their bodies smashed against the solid ice. A severed climbing rope led to two more lying buried under the snow. One was dead, but miraculously the other was found to be alive although unconscious. He was to live and accompany the next expedition. A seventh dead Sherpa, still roped to him, was also located. But he was buried beneath tons of snow and ice, and the party had not the strength to try to recover his body.

There was now the nightmare task of rescuing those Sherpas still trapped precariously on the shelf above. One by one they were manouevred away from the edge by Mallory and another of the climbers. 'The men had completely lost their nerve and were crying and shaking like babies,' Noel recounts. 'It was pitiable to see their condition and their grief.' Several had lost brothers, and all of them friends, in this appalling ending to the expedition. Noel describes the scene: 'They went to the crushed bodies and took their amulets and other religious family tokens from their necks. We asked the men if they wanted us to bring the bodies back. But they did not wish it, and so we covered them with snow, and left them.'

This time the protecting spirits had won. But it would not be long before the Englishmen, wiser and more determined than ever, would return for another confrontation with Everest. It also was to end in tragedy but give to mountaineering perhaps its finest hour. There is not the space here to tell the story from the beginning, but the first week in June 1924 saw the climbers once more camped high on Everest. They had fought their way back there after being driven from the mountain by severe blizzards in which they had lost two Sherpas. By the morning of June 4, two of the party – Colonel Edward Norton and Dr Howard Somervell – had climbed to nearly 27,000 feet and were still ascending. At midday they had reached around 28,000 feet. But now Somervell felt too weak to go any further. He was having difficulty with his breathing and was close to collapse, his pulse racing at 120 to the minute. He urged his companion to try to reach the summit by himself. But Norton, too, was on his last legs, suffering from both exhaustion and the beginnings of agonising snow-blindness. Nonetheless he struggled painfully on, finally being forced back at 28,126 feet, just 876 feet from the top. Deeply disappointed, he made his way down to where he had left Somervell.

The monsoon was now imminent, so there was little time left. On the morning of June 6, Mallory and Irvine (at twenty-two the youngest Everest climber) set out to make one last desperate attempt to reach the summit. They had spent the night before with the dispirited Norton and Somervell, both of whom were in poor health. All that Norton, now temporarily sightless, could do that morning was to squeeze the hands of his two fellow climbers and wish them success. With eight Sherpas, Mallory and Irvine now set off for Camp V where they spent the night of June 6 after sending back four of the Sherpas. The next morning, in perfect weather, they moved on again, reaching 26,700 feet – and Camp VI – in safety. From here Mallory wrote a note to Noel, at Camp III, advising him that they hoped to reach the foot of the final pyramid by eight o'clock the next morning, so that his cameras could be ready. This was sent back with the four remaining Sherpas. One of them, named Lakpa, delivered the note to Noel that evening. Already that day he had climbed from 25,000 feet to 27,000 feet, carrying equipment for

Mallory and Irvine, then descended from 27,000 feet to 21,000 feet, an astonishing feat.

Mallory's scribbled message was the last that was ever to be heard from the two climbers. But it was not the last that anyone would see of them. Another climber, Noel Odell, had come up to Camp V in the meantime to give Mallory and Irvine any support they might need. On that fateful morning – June 8, 1924 – he had begun to follow in their trail, hoping to be the first to greet them on their return from the summit. Shortly after midday, when he had climbed to a point just over 26,000 feet, the clouds which had been covering the top of Everest suddenly parted. It was then that he saw them. Like two tiny flies on a whitewashed wall they stood out clearly against the snow. In a despatch to *The Times*, Odell described what he saw far above him. 'My eyes became fixed on one tiny black spot silhouetted on a small snow crest . . . and the black spot moved. Another black spot became apparent and moved up the snow to join the other on the crest. The first then approached the great rock step and shortly emerged at the top. The second did likewise.'

Moments later, clouds obscured his view. Mallory and Irvine were never seen again. But from what he had seen through his binoculars, at the time Odell had no reason to be particularly anxious about them. He was an extremely skilled and experienced climber himself and, in his own words: 'They seemed to be going strong.' However, they were running very late if they hoped to reach the summit and get back to Camp VI before nightfall. He now returned to Camp IV, leaving the single tiny bivouacs at the two higher camps to Mallory and Irvine. Camp VI was slightly hidden, and he reckoned that they might overshoot it and return to Camp V that night. The weather on Everest was now deteriorating rapidly, and the next morning, June 9, Odell anxiously scanned the two camps through his glasses. But he could see no sign of movement. Gravely worried now, he set off up the mountainside in bitterly cold crosswinds. There was no sign of the two at Camp V, and Odell spent that night there. Next morning, with his hopes of finding them still alive fading fast, Odell fought his way on through appalling weather towards Camp VI. But everything in the small tent was exactly as he had left it. He knew then that his two colleagues had died.

The loss of Mallory and Irvine in Tibet, like the death of Scott and his companions at the Pole, is one of the great epics of exploration. Ever since, mountaineers have debated what became of them. Did they reach the top before they died? Did they lose their way and plunge over one of the many precipices around the summit? It seems unlikely that the answer will ever be known, and anyway it lies beyond the scope of this book. But to the monks of Rongbuk Monastery, the warnings that they had given to the climbers had clearly been fulfilled, not once but twice. 'The mountain will destroy you,' they had insisted when first being told of the plan to scale it. Among the many religious paintings on the monastery walls climbers later found one showing the angered deity of the mountain surrounded by demons and hairy men. At his feet, pierced by spears, lay the naked body of the white man who dared to violate the Goddess Mother of the World, as the Tibetans locally call Everest.

News of the tragedy, carried first by runner and then by telegram, stunned a world that had been expecting victory. But those eleven lives – the nine Sherpas and now Mallory and Irvine – had not been entirely wasted. There was no longer any doubt that Everest could be climbed, although it was to take far longer than anyone could then have guessed. Perhaps Sir Francis Younghusband best summed up the feelings of other mountaineers about the loss of Mallory and Irvine. He wrote: 'Where and when they died we know not. But there in the arms of Mount Everest they lie for ever – lie 10,000 feet above where any man has lain in death before. Everest indeed conquered their bodies. But their spirit is undying. No man onward from now will ever climb a Himalayan peak and not think of Mallory and Irvine.'

*   *   *

But the Tibetan giant had not claimed its last victim. On April 23, 1933, banner headlines in the British press announced: THE MOST AMAZING AIR ADVENTURE EVER ATTEMPTED. . . . PLAN TO PUT UNION JACK ON EVEREST. The Sunday *Reynolds News*, now long deceased, reported: 'One of the most amazing air adventures ever planned, which has as its object the planting of the Union Jack on the summit of Mount Everest, will be attempted tomorrow when Mr Maurice Wilson, a member of the London Aero Club, will set off from Stag Lane Aerodrome, Hendon, to conquer the 29,000-foot giant of the Himalayas.'

His plan was to crash-land his Gypsy Moth halfway up Mount Everest, then climb to the summit which he would claim in the name of Britain with his Union Jack. As a subaltern in World War I, Wilson had won a Military Cross for single-handedly destroying a German machine-gun nest. But he had no experience of mountaineering, and little enough of flying, having flown solo for the first time only two months previously. That he was utterly determined to go through with it, however, none of those who knew him doubted. 'One fit, trained man can succeed where a larger group will fail,' he confidently assured reporters. His training, it seemed, consisted of progressive fasting, on the theory that if the stomach could be conditioned to need less and less food, then one could use this additional capacity to breathe from and thus greatly increase one's oxygen supply. To this was added a mystical dimension. Wilson was convinced that if a man went without food for three weeks or so he would reach a stage of semi-consciousness on the borderland between life and death. From this he would emerge washed of all bodily and spiritual ills – like a new-born child but with all the experience and knowledge of his previous life. If he succeeded in conquering Everest single-handed, as he once had done that German machine-gun nest, then it must win for his theories thousands of converts.

As the official files of the time show, it took the authorities in London and Delhi several days to react to newspaper reports.

At first, it appears, they had not taken his threat to gatecrash Tibetan air space very seriously. But before long the wires were buzzing between Whitehall and the airfields at which he planned to refuel on his way to Purnea, the nearest landing field in India to Everest. Every difficulty was put in his way – in Cairo, in Bahrain, in Karachi – but Wilson flew determinedly on. Finally, when it became clear that he seriously intended to infringe air traffic regulations by flying across Nepal and entering Tibet, his secondhand Gypsy Moth was seized by the authorities in India.

Realising that he would not be able to proceed with his original plan to crash-land on Everest, Wilson changed his tactics. But this time he kept quiet about it. Moving to Darjeeling, he secretly hired three Sherpas who had accompanied one of the previous expeditions to Everest. They agreed to smuggle him, disguised as one of themselves, through Sikkim into Tibet and guide him to Rongbuk Monastery. With money raised through the sale of his aircraft, he bought ponies and quietly set off on the four-hundred-mile trek to Rongbuk. It was some time before the authorities discovered that he was missing from his hotel in Darjeeling, and by then he and his three Sherpas were well inside Tibet.

To the very last Wilson kept a diary, and it is largely from this that the story of what followed was pieced together later by the mountaineer Eric Shipton who with a colleague found his body the following year, and with it the diary. Leaving the Sherpas at Rongbuk, where he told the abbot that he was a member of an earlier expedition, Wilson started up the mountain alone, convinced that he would reach the top in three or four days. He took with him a shaving mirror which he intended to use as a heliograph from the summit so that the Sherpas would know that he had got there. On his first attempt he only managed to get as far as Camp II before being driven back exhausted by the spring storms. After resting at the monastery for two weeks, he set out again, this time taking the Sherpas.

Although he knew nothing about cutting steps in ice, and

carried no ropes, they managed to reach Camp III, standing at 21,000 feet. Here the Sherpas showed him one of the food dumps, half a mile or so further up the mountain, which had been left by one of the earlier expeditions. This contained all sorts of luxuries, including chocolate, sardines, baked beans and biscuits. Pitching his own tent here, he sent the Sherpas back to Camp III. Shipton describes what then followed.

> Though he had an ice-axe, he did not know how to use it and could make little headway up the slopes. He camped alone on the rocks near the dump and set out day after day to renew his fruitless attempts to reach the Col. Though he had plenty of food, he was gradually weakened by the severe conditions. This was clear from the entries in his diary, which became shorter and less coherent towards the end. But he would not give up and still clung to his faith in divine inspiration.

Wilson's diary ran out on May 31, 1934. He died either that night or the day after in his tiny tent. By the time Shipton and his companion came upon it this had been ripped to pieces by storms. All that was left of it were the guy-ropes which Wilson had fastened to boulders. His frozen body was dressed in thin grey flannel trousers, underpants, a shirt and a light Fairisle pullover. His boots were off, revealing thin socks. He had clearly died, not of starvation, but of exposure. Shipton and his companion buried Wilson in a crevasse. (Years later his body was thrown up by the movement of the glacier, for in 1960 Chinese climbers came upon it again and reburied it.)

On their return to Darjeeling Wilson's three Sherpas reported what had happened. They were lucky to escape prosecution for illegally crossing the frontier, but the British Indian authorities decided, as official correspondence of the time shows, that it was best to let sleeping dogs lie and hope that the Tibetans never discovered that anything untoward had ever taken place. The three men swore they had waited a month for Wilson at Camp III before abandoning their vigil. 'This',

Shipton observes, 'is clearly untrue for they would certainly have visited the food-dump from time to time and would have found the body.' That night, after burying Wilson, Shipton sat up in his tent reading the diary which he and his companion had found in the dead man's pocket. In Shipton's official report he described its contents as 'mainly sensible' and 'distinctly moving'. Today it rests in the archives of the Alpine Club in London.

But let final judgement on this strange hero – and no one questioned his courage – be passed by another Everest climber who himself failed three times to do what Wilson too had set his heart on. In his book *The Spirit of the Hills* Frank Smythe, one of the greatest mountaineers of the pre-war era, wrote:

It was not mountaineering yet it was magnificent. Call it madness, call it anything you like, but is there not an element of grandeur in the thought of this young man actuated, perhaps by a flame of idealism, a desire to express something, to expand consciousness, to escape from fleshly shackles, to rise above all earthly considerations, setting out alone to scale the world's highest mountain. . . ?

13. Lhasa Lowers its Guard

Maurice Wilson, would-be conqueror of Everest, has a whole file to himself in the political and secret archives of the period. However, he was not the only traveller to gatecrash Tibet between the wars. Although Lhasa had lost much of its magnetism, a succession of trespassers – including mystics, plant-hunters, explorers and pure adventurers – now began to cross illegally into Tibet. While their country was still officially closed to all foreigners (except by the rare invitation of the Dalai Lama himself), the Tibetans had relaxed considerably their watch on the passes leading to British India, which they looked upon as friendly. Provided Lhasa was given a wide enough berth, to gatecrash Tibet in the 1920s was far less difficult or dangerous than at any time since it had turned its back on the rest of the world in the eighteenth century. Some of these intruders, as their files show, sought permission first. But when they were refused, they went nonetheless.

One particularly determined trespasser was Alexandra David-Neel. Despite her English-sounding name, this remarkable woman was French. Indeed, she had little time for the British. Renowned among orientalists as a scholar of Tibetan Buddhism, she is perhaps more widely known as the first white woman ever to enter Lhasa. Needless to say she did so illegally, disguised as a Tibetan beggar, a revolver concealed beneath her rags. But in 1972, three years after her death, a disparaging book – *A. David-Neel au Tibet* by Jeanne Denys – was published in France claiming that she had never been to Tibet, let alone to Lhasa. Written (from what motive is not clear) by a fellow French woman who had known her in her old age, its case, never very strong, has been effectively demolished by an American scholar. There would appear to be little reason to doubt that Alexandra David-Neel's own narrative, *My Journey to Lhasa*, is true, although some of her other claims, made elsewhere, certainly do stretch one's credulity.

When Alexandra David-Neel made her bold dash for Lhasa in October 1923, she was fifty-four and a seasoned Asiatic traveller. Having been received by the Dalai Lama during his exile in Darjeeling – the first western woman to be so honoured – she was fired with zeal to discover more about Tibetan Buddhism, and had crossed illegally into Tibet in 1914 to a monastery situated a few miles inside the frontier. The following year, after living for some months as a hermit in a cave in Sikkim, she had again entered Tibet, this time travelling as far as Shigatse. On returning to Sikkim she found that the British authorities had got wind of her illicit journeys and had ordered her deportation. The order was signed by Sir Charles Bell. Infuriated, she was to write many years later of the British: 'What right had they to erect barriers around a country which was not even lawfully theirs?' She was now more determined than ever to extend her travels in Tibet and, if humanly possible, to visit Lhasa. But to try to enter Tibet again from India would now be hopeless. The only possible way would be through China, thus outflanking the British. She was in no hurry, however. The longer she spent improving her Tibetan and enlarging her knowedge of the religion and customs of the country, the better her prospects of success.

Making her way eastwards, she travelled through Burma, Japan – where she met Ekai Kawaguchi – and Korea, staying in Buddhist monasteries and immersing herself in the oriental way of life. Accompanying her was a young Sikkimese monk named Yongden whom she had hired as a companion-servant when he was only fifteen (later she was to adopt him as her son). From Peking, which they reached in the winter of 1917, they made for the great monastery of Kumbum, travelling two thousand miles by mule across a China then torn by civil war and banditry. It was at Kumbum that nearly a quarter of a century earlier the unfortunate Rijnharts had sheltered before making their ill-fated attempt to reach Lhasa. Alexandra David-Neel and Yongden were to spend the best part of three years there, studying Tantric Buddhism and translating sacred texts. Eventually moving on again, they made a number of extended journeys through the Tibetan borderlands and, once, into neighbouring Mongolia.

At last, in 1923, Alexandra felt ready to attempt the forbidden journey to Lhasa. By now her Tibetan was perfect. This claim has been challenged by her recent detractor, but David Macdonald, the British trade agent at Gyantse, records in his memoirs that she spoke it 'like a native' – as he himself did. With her sketch maps and route notes concealed in her boots, she and Yongden turned westwards into Tibet. To avoid unwelcome attention from either officials or brigands, they travelled disguised as Tibetan beggars – mother and son – purportedly making a pilgrimage to the holy city. In addition to wearing ragged clothes, Alexandra had dyed her hair with Chinese ink and darkened her face.

During the next four months, in the teeth of the Tibetan winter, they struggled on towards Lhasa, spinning their prayer wheels and telling their beads. Although Alexandra had a small bag of gold concealed on her (together with a revolver for emergencies), to add conviction to their cover story Yongden told fortunes to earn them money and gifts of food. It was a time of great hardship for them both, but particularly for Alexandra, now in her fifty-fifth year. Sometimes they slept out in the forest, using a tiny tent they carried concealed in their baggage. At other times they shared the primitive hospitality of Tibetan hovels. All the time, Alexandra was listening and learning, gathering material for the book she would write if she survived the journey.

There were moments when she doubted whether they would live to see Lhasa. Apart from their inevitable brushes with bandits in this lawless region, there was the ever-present fear of detection, perhaps of being recognised by someone – another pilgrim maybe – who had known them before they adopted their present guise. One night, as they approached Lhasa, a strange lama walked in out of the darkness and sat down uninvited at their campfire. For a long while he did not speak, but merely stared fixedly at Alexandra. Then suddenly he made a remark about her appearance which told her that he knew her secret.

'My heart stopped beating,' she wrote afterwards. 'This man knew me!' But from where? Seeing her bewilderment, the lama added even more mysteriously: 'Do not try to remember. I have as many faces as I desire, and you have never seen this one.' They talked until late in the night about mysticism and the Tibetan religion, and soon Alexandra knew intuitively that this enigmatic traveller would never betray her. Then suddenly, without another word, he strode off into the night. 'He arose,' she recounts, 'and staff in hand vanished like a phantom, as he had come. His footsteps made no sound on the stony path. He entered the jungle and seemed to melt away in it.'

One night, after a nineteen-hour march over a particularly high pass, they halted just below the snowline and prepared, utterly exhausted, to pitch their tent. After gathering fuel for a fire, they discovered to their dismay that their flint and steel had become wet and would not ignite. It was still some hours before sunrise, and they knew that if they lay down to sleep in sodden clothes and without a fire they would freeze to death. But how were they to dry their flint and steel? Alexandra resolved to dry them by means of the Tibetan art of *thumo reskiang*, into whose secret she had been initiated years before when living as a hermit. This is a way, devised over the centuries by holy men in the Himalayas, of raising the body temperature and thus surviving the terrible cold of winter. She herself had seen:

Hermits seated night after night, motionless on the snow, entirely naked, sunk in meditation, while the terrible winter blizzard whirled and hissed around them. I saw under the bright full moon the test given to their disciples who, on the shore of a lake or river in the heart of winter, dried on their bodies, as on a stove, a number of sheets dipped in the icy water. And I learned the means of performing these feats. I had inured myself, during five months of the cold season, to wearing the single thin cotton garment of the students at a 13,000-foot level.

Sending Yongden off to gather as much dry cow dung and sticks as he could find, so keeping himself warm by exertion, Alexandra pressed the clammy flint and steel to her body beneath her rags and began the ritualistic process which calls for intense concentration. 'Soon I saw flames arising around me; they grew higher and higher; they enveloped me, curling their tongues above my head. I felt deliciously comfortable.'

She had fallen asleep, but a loud crash – the ice cracking on the nearby river – awoke her. The flames died down, and she opened her eyes. A bitter wind was blowing, but her body was glowing. Quickly she gathered together some dry grass and cattle dung, and struck the flint with the steel. This time, dried out by the heat of her body, it produced a shower of sparks and within seconds the grass was ablaze. This seemingly paranormal phenomenon which enables *sadhus*, or Himalayan holy men, to survive half naked in sub-zero temperatures has, it should be said, more than once been attested to by independent and sceptical European witnesses.

But if *thumo reskiang*, or self heating, is within the bounds of scientific credibility, the same perhaps cannot be said of *lung-gom*, or the art of flying, which Alexandra claims to have witnessed while previously travelling in Tibet. One day while crossing a deserted plain she recounts seeing a black spot in the distance advancing rapidly towards her. Quickly focusing her field-glasses on it, she observed that it was a man moving at high speed in a series of spectacular leaps. As he came nearer she could see that his upturned gaze was fixed on some invisible, apparently far-distant point in space. She describes what she saw: 'The man did not run. He seemed to lift himself from the ground, proceeding by leaps. It looked as if he had been endowed with the elasticity of a ball and rebounded each time his feet touched the ground. His steps had the regularity of a pendulum.'

Anyone daring to make such a claim today would, like someone reporting a flying saucer, expect to face ridicule. But when it was written, around half a century ago, the reading public was more receptive to such possibilities. This, after all, was the era of the Indian rope trick, and everyone knew someone who knew someone who had seen *that*. In secret and mysterious Tibet anything might be possible, even flying. Alexandra's books, best-sellers in their day, appeared at a time when interest in eastern mysticism and the occult was at a peak. This had its origins in the work of serious nineteenth-century scholars like Max Muller, as well as in the more questionable teachings of Madame Helen Blavatsky. Curiously, Alexandra's account of this extraordinary incident – for which she gives no precise date or location – is omitted from her two travel narratives, appearing only in another work, *With Mystics and Magicians in Tibet*, dealing largely with the paranormal. Why, one may ask, did she not attempt to speak to, or at least photograph, this apparition? Alexandra explains that she was prevailed upon not to by her Tibetan companions of that journey since, they insisted, this would result in the holy man's death.

But leaving the reader to believe what he will, we rejoin Alexandra and Yongden as they prepare to enter the holy city. By chance, their arrival coincided with the Tibetan New Year festivities, when Lhasa was thronged with pilgrims and revellers from out of town, and when one strange face was unlikely to attract undue attention. 'For two months,' Alexandra recounts, 'I was to wander freely in the lamaist Rome, with none to suspect that, for the first time in history, a foreign woman was beholding the Forbidden City.' In the busy streets, bazaars, tea houses and temples she exchanged wisecracks with other pilgrims and was usually taken by them for a Ladakhi. She noted the shoddy goods imported from India, Japan and Britain on the market stalls, especially the cheap crockery and hideous cotton prints. She noted, too, the khaki-clad soldiers headed by a band playing English tunes – 'not too badly'. Like the European rifles they carried (specially doctored by British holy men, she was told, so as not to harm westerners) this was part of the aid sent to the Dalai Lama following Sir Charles Bell's visit to Lhasa. But some Tibetans assured her quite seriously that Britain paid tribute to the Dalai Lama, explaining that Bell had come to Lhasa especially to receive their God-king's orders for the King of England.

She was also able to visit the Potala – opened to pilgrims during the New Year festival – and look down from its lofty heights on the city below. Although her detractor was later to claim that it was a fake – a montage – she was even photographed by Tibetan friends posing before the Potala. Inside this great building, part palace, part temple and part fortress, she saw 'sumptuous suites of apartments' in addition to the myriad temples, tombs and shrines. There were even shrines dedicated to the evil demons and deities of the ancient Bon faith, some so dangerous, she was told, that special precautions had to be taken to prevent their getting loose. Alexandra describes these dreaded monsters:

Even worse creatures are symbolically fed in special buildings, and the offerings placed there stand as a substitute for the more realistic and bloodier sacrifices of the pre-Buddhistic cult. It is only – so the Tibetans believe – strict attendance to their needs, and a due reverence, that keeps human beings and animals safe from their ferocity. Other dread Malevolent and Invisible Ones are chained by the power of magic charms, and a perpetual watch has to be kept in order that the spells and other occult devices, whose strength prevents the dangerous beings from escaping, shall be recited and performed at the right time.

After living undetected in Lhasa for two months, Alexandra and Yongden suddenly found themselves forced to leave town in a hurry. They had witnessed a furious domestic quarrel in the hovel where they lodged, and were due to give evidence in court. To be exposed to such scrutiny, Alexandra realised, could be fatal. They had no choice but to slip quickly away, heading south to Sikkim and British India. Some miles out of Lhasa Alexandra turned and looked back at the holy city for the last time. 'From that distance,' she wrote, 'the Potala alone could be seen . . . a tiny castle suspended, it seemed, in the air like a mirage.'

The two travellers reached Gyantse towards the end of August 1924. There, still disguised as a Tibetan, she introduced herself to the dumbfounded British trade agent, David Macdonald, as the troublesome French woman who some eight years earlier had been expelled by the British from Sikkim. It must have been a moment of some satisfaction for her. Not only had she succeeded where Annie Taylor, Mrs Littledale and Susie Rijnhart had all failed, but she had also outwitted the British Government.

'She must have undergone incredible hardships,' Macdonald wrote afterwards in his memoirs, adding that for a woman of her age and frail condition the journey was 'a wonderful feat' calling for amazing courage. But she would tell him very little about her journey, explaining that she wanted to keep it all for her book. However, the Tibetan-speaking Macdonald was clearly convinced that she had come from Lhasa, whatever her detractor might claim later, for he wrote her a note verifying this. And he, as a veteran of the Younghusband expedition, had spent some time in Lhasa himself.

Had he chosen to, Macdonald could have diminished Alexandra's moment of triumph. He could have broken it to her that although the first woman, she was not, after all, the first westerner to have entered Lhasa in disguise. For exactly a year before, Dr William Montgomery McGovern of the School of Oriental Studies, in London, disguised as a native caravan porter, had entered Tibet from India and successfully got to Lhasa. He had had to sleep in infested cowsheds with the other caravan men, live off dried raw meat, and at times struggle chest-deep through snowdrifts. But in Lhasa illness had forced him to drop his disguise and confess his presence to the authorities. While they were deciding on his fate, word got around that there was a trespasser in town. Soon a large crowd had gathered outside the house where he was lodging, shouting 'death to the foreigner' and hurling sticks and stones at the windows. Fortunately none of the mob knew what he looked like, so before they could force their way into the house he managed to escape, still disguised, through a side door. Making his way to the back of the crowd, he tells us in his book *To Lhasa in Disguise*, he joined it for a while. 'Not to be outdone by the others, I occasionally let out a yell myself, and to make things very realistic picked up a small stone and threw it at my own window.' By now the authorities had troops positioned to rescue him if the crowd broke into the house, but by evening the mob had drifted away and he was able to return home from the Tibetan official's house where he had found shelter. For the rest of his stay in Lhasa, during which he was visited by one of the ex-Rugby boys, guards were placed over the house to protect him.

McGovern was allowed to remain in the holy city under house arrest for the best part of a month while he recovered from dysentery and what appears to have been pneumonia. (It is surprising, perhaps, that Alexandra David-Neel heard nothing of all this while she was in Lhasa.) Finally, after an audience with the Dalai Lama, and being pardoned by the authorities, he left for India with an armed escort. One is left with the feeling that he owed the leniency with which the Tibetans treated him to Sir Charles Bell's longstanding friendship with the Dalai Lama. On his return to England, somewhat late for the start of the London University term, Dr McGovern's story was serialised in eight parts in the *Daily Telegraph*.

The kudos of having been to Lhasa, whether legally or

illegally, was now beginning to wear a bit thin. Besides Sir Charles Bell, two other British officials had been there by invitation, Macdonald himself and Colonel Eric Bailey, the Political Officer in Sikkim. Not only had Lhasa's mysteries been revealed to the outside world by a succession of visitors, invited or otherwise, but it had now virtually ceased to be a Forbidden City. But Alexandra David-Neel was not one to allow this to detract from her triumph at being the first white woman ever to enter the Tibetan capital. No one could rob her of that. And her compatriots saw to it that nobody did. On her return to France, after fourteen years away in Asia, Alexandra was lionised and showered with honours. Not only was she awarded the coveted Gold Medal of the Geographical Society of France, but she was also made a Chevalier of the Legion of Honour. The Royal Geographical Society of Belgium also awarded her their silver medal. But the Royal Geographical Society in London gave her nothing. After all, her contribution to the scientific exploration of Tibet had been nil. Her book, *My Journey to Lhasa*, did not contain a single map, as Sir Francis Younghusband pointed out in his review of it in the Society's journal. But he acknowledged generously her extraordinary fortitude and courage.

Surprisingly perhaps, Alexandra's health appears not to have suffered from her years of extreme hardship in Tibet and Central Asia. Her faithful companion Yongden, more than thirty years her junior, was to predecease her by some fourteen years. But the redoubtable Alexandra, by now a venerated figure, was to live on until 1969 when she died at the grand age of one hundred.

* * *

The worldwide publicity which Alexandra's secret journey to Lhasa attracted, and the charisma which immediately surrounded her, was to lead to other women trying to emulate her. One such traveller whose name appears more than once in the

Indian Government's 'unauthorised entries' file of that time was a Miss Gertrude Benham. The British frontier authorities, for reasons that are not spelt out, found this middle-aged English-woman particularly troublesome. She made her first un-authorised attempt to reach Lhasa soon after Alexandra David-Neel's triumphant return, apparently getting as far as Gyantse. An exasperated Colonel Bailey reported that Miss Benham 'made a thorough nuisance of herself', but failed to explain how or why. In 1929, some four years later, she was still trying to gatecrash Tibet. By now her confidential file bore the damning, if somewhat ungrammatical, verdict: 'She is a bad type of British traveller to be allowed to enter Tibet.' But just why, we shall never know.

Colonel Bailey has been dead now some sixteen years, and Miss Benham presumably longer, but very likely still alive, and living somewhere in Sweden, is a Miss Aina Cederblom. In 1937, as an engaging young woman of twenty-five, she turned up on the frontier determined to give the British the slip and make her way secretly to Lhasa. She entered Sikkim quite legally, but somehow managed to avoid signing the statutory declaration in which visitors undertook not to attempt to cross into Tibet.

Cross she did, disguised as a Tibetan. Raj officials quickly learned of this through their frontier intelligence system. Not merely had she entered Tibet illegally, but – horrors – she had also gone native, sleeping in the servants' quarters of the dak bungalows along the route. To throw off pursuers, and reduce the risk of detection, she chose to travel by night. The young Swedish traveller, reported one frontier officer, 'is of a rather headstrong and romantic turn of mind'. She had clearly entered Sikkim 'with the evil intention of going to Lhasa incognito'.

By chance, a doctor attached to the British trade mission at Yatung – Captain W. S. Morgan – was travelling in the neigh-bourhood at the time. He was instructed to round up Miss Cederblom immediately and escort her back across the fron-tier – preferably without letting the Tibetans discover that she had entered their country in the first place. But Miss Cederblom was not going to give in that easily, and set to work on the young doctor. As Captain Morgan reported: 'She offered to accompany me as a cook-companion to Gyantse and wherever my duties might take me – in fact her attitude throughout was perfectly charming. But after mature reflection I had to indicate my inability to fall in with such an accommodating suggestion.'

So it was that duty triumphed, and the delectable Miss Cederblom was escorted by the doctor back to Darjeeling. There, after one attempt at escape, she was fined fifty rupees for infringing frontier regulations. In addition a promise was obtained from her not to try again. This, it appears, she honoured, for at this point she vanishes from the files.

*   *   *

Although by this time much of Tibet had been explored and mapped, legally or otherwise, there were still large tracts where few, if any, white men had ever set foot. Between the wars a strange rumour began to circulate in mountaineering circles of a mysterious peak in the eastern borderlands of Tibet even higher than Mount Everest, and known locally as Amne Machin. The first western traveller to see it – admittedly from many miles away – had been General George Pereira, the British military attaché in Peking, while on a journey across China and Tibet to India in 1922. Towering above everything else, it looked to him 'well over 25,000 feet high'. He had intended taking a closer look at it on his return journey but died before being able to. Nor was this remote mountain everyone's idea of a picnic, for the extreme hostility of the tribes living in the neighbourhood meant that anyone approaching it took his life in his hands.

But one man prepared to do this was an American botanist, Joseph Rock, who spent many years plant-hunting and exploring in the Chinese-Tibetan borderlands between the wars. It was Dr Rock, more than anyone else, who was responsible for starting the legend that there was another mountain in Tibet possibly even higher than Everest. Determined to reach it, he set off in 1925 for Amne Machin at the head of a small but well-armed expedition. For months their approach to the mountain was held up by a holy war between fanatical Muslim and Tibetan tribesmen, waged with the barbaric cruelty for which the region had always been notorious. Rock describes how the fierce Tibetan horsemen charged the Muslims with their terrible thirty-foot lances, impaling them 'like men spearing frogs'. Captured Tibetans, in their turn, were hung up by their thumbs and disembowelled alive. Red hot coals were then heaped inside them. In one small township, one hundred and fifty Tibetan heads were strung up like a grisly garland of flowers, while the 'heads of young girls and children decorated posts in front of the barracks'. Such was the region's reputation that Chinese troops dared not venture there.

After months of delay, Rock and his party were able to proceed, passing over corpse-strewn battlefields and scenes of recent massacre. Eventually they came to the upper reaches of the Yellow River, in a bend of which lay Amne Machin. 'No other white man, since time began, ever stood here,' wrote Rock. In this back of beyond, where the great river flows at over 10,000 feet, he came upon a holy man 'printing' sacred images of the Buddha on the water with brass moulds attached to a wooden plank. By keeping up this strange ritual hour after hour, the monk believed he was acquiring religious merit.

At last they found themselves facing the towering, snow-capped Amne Machin range. 'I counted nine peaks,' Rock wrote, 'one a huge pyramid at least 28,000 feet in height. It may prove higher than any Himalayan peak, including Everest.' But not being equipped with a theodolite (a curious omission from such an expedition) he was unable to measure it with any degree of scientific accuracy. According to his biographer, Rock arrived at his figure of 'at least' 28,000 feet by the dubious combination of an aneroid barometer 'and inspiration'. In other words, it seems that he calculated his own height at 16,000 feet, then added a further 12,000 feet – the height that the summit *appeared* to be above him. He was sufficiently confident of this figure to publish it in the American *National Geographic Magazine* of February 1930.

Once started, the legend persisted, encouraging a whole generation of mountaineers and explorers to believe that there might be a mountain in this remote and dangerous corner of Tibet even higher than Everest – if only one could get there. The legend gained credence during World War II when pilots blown off course reported seeing a vast peak in the region. One pilot, who was later killed, claimed to have looked *up* while flying at 29,000 feet and seen the snow-capped summit towering above him. During the war, it seems, a superstition even grew among pilots that anyone who saw 'The Thing', as it became known, was doomed. As recently as 1948 an American pilot told reporters that he and his aircrew had calculated its height as a full 30,000 feet, and therefore higher than Everest. More than twenty years were to pass, however, before a true height – a deflating 24,982 feet – was finally established for Amne Machin.

But Rock, to be fair, was a botanist and not a surveyor – one of a small but distinguished company who hunted for rare and unknown plants in Tibet and its borderlands before, and even during, World War II. Most of them were gifted amateurs. The only other professional was Frank Kingdon-Ward, perhaps the foremost plant-hunter of modern times, and best remembered as the man who brought back the fabulous Blue Poppy of Tibet from the mountains east of Lhasa for cultivation in English gardens. The amateurs were for the most part British frontier officials who were able to enter Tibet legally in the course of their official duties. But one or two botanists, as the files of the period reveal, were gatecrashers, and at least one of Kingdon-Ward's early journeys into Tibet was made illegally. Between them, they brought back literally thousands of specimens, including new types of primulas, poppies, gentians, lilies, rhododendrons and other plant treasures. The names of several of these – including *Incarvillea younghusbandii* and *Gentiana przewalskii* – recall memories of men who left their mark on Tibetan history.

Some of the British officials who collected plants were able to operate in the botanically-rich Lhasa area during and after World War II when a small British Mission was established in the capital. This had come about through a process of gradual acceptance rather than any written agreement or treaty. Its exact status was somewhat vague. In the words of one of its incumbents, it was an example of 'the Central Asian tendency to avoid precise definitions'. Under the watered-down terms of the Younghusband agreement, British officials were entitled to travel no further than Gyantse, where the trade mart was situated. On the other hand, if the Dalai Lama wished, there was nothing to prevent him from inviting individual Raj officials to Lhasa. Sir Charles Bell, as we have seen, had thus visited the Tibetan capital in 1920. He was followed, in the summer of 1924, by Colonel Eric Bailey, then Political Officer in Sikkim. Bailey's successor in Sikkim, Colonel Leslie Weir, made a similar visit in 1930, accompanied by his wife. She thus became the first Englishwoman (and the second ever white woman) to enter Lhasa. The Weirs spent two months there, living in a house called Deyki Lingka, or 'Garden of Happiness', lent them by the Tibetan authorities. It was eventually to become the permanent home of the British Mission to Lhasa.

Two years later Colonel Weir was again invited to Lhasa by the Dalai Lama who was having problems with the Chinese, and sought British assistance. This time, in addition to his wife, he took his nineteen-year-old daughter Joan Mary. 'The Tibetans,' she recalls today, 'were a tonic to live among. However poor, ragged or toothless, they were always laughing, always singing and always fun. Their parties sometimes went on for days.'

If those days were idyllic for the Weirs, their successors, the Williamsons, were less lucky. For Harry Williamson, who twice visited Lhasa, was to die there. It was rumoured that this was because he had taken photographs of a particularly venerated deity, but the medical cause was rather more mundane. When he first became ill, Calcutta had wanted to send an aircraft up to Lhasa to fly him out, but the Tibetan authorities objected lest it antagonise the spirits. For no aircraft had ever landed there before. Williamson was buried in Gyantse, alongside British troops who died on the Younghusband expedition. His widow later travelled up from Calcutta with a tombstone for his lonely grave.

Williamson was in turn replaced as Political Officer in Sikkim by Mr (later Sir Basil) Gould who visited Lhasa at the Tibetans' invitation in 1937. Following the death of the thirteenth Dalai Lama, they were again having trouble with the Chinese, and wanted British advice. The Chinese, under the pretence of sending a special mission to convey their condolences, had established a small office in Lhasa which, long after the funeral was over, they showed no signs of closing. When finally the time came for Gould's departure, he left behind him in Lhasa a young Tibetan-speaking official, Hugh Richardson (whose knowledge of Tibet and its people would eventually eclipse even that of Sir Charles Bell). When they discovered this, the Chinese protested to the Tibetans who assured them that the moment they withdrew their own mission and shut down their radio transmitter, the same would be asked of the British. However, Peking was anxious to hold on to its newly-won toehold in the Tibetan capital – its first since 1913 when the Chinese garrison had been driven out of Tibet. So it was that the small British Mission in Lhasa now became more or less permanent, although still without any official diplomatic status.

The outbreak of World War II saw Tibet as a neutral power, with a five-year-old Dalai Lama – the fourteenth – on the throne. The British Mission, with its radio transmitter, remained there throughout the war. It was first headed by Frank Ludlow, a celebrated plant-hunter, then by his companion of many botanising expeditions in Central Asia, Captain George Sherriff. Sherriff was accompanied by his wife, who gradually transformed Deyki Lingka into a civilised home, with a dazzling garden which lived up to its Tibetan name. Betty Sherriff has described their first audience with the Dalai Lama, then just eight. Among the official gifts they had brought up from Calcutta for him were a toy train set and a clockwork speedboat. Although it was considered ill-mannered among Tibetans to show pleasure on receiving gifts, she could not fail to note that 'his eyes opened with surprise and delight at the sight of the Hornby train and speedboat', just like any other small boy.

During their two happy but isolated years in wartime Lhasa, the Sherriffs introduced table tennis and croquet to the Tibetans. The lamas, Mrs Sherriff observed with amusement, became adept at cheating, using their long robes to manoeuvre their croquet balls into better positions. The mission also had its own cinematograph projector, and the Tibetans never tired of watching Charlie Chaplin, while the Sherriffs spent the long evenings playing three-handed bridge with Reggie Fox, the British radio-operator.

But the war was not entirely to pass them by in this distant listening-post. For in 1943 they were to find themselves caught up in one of the most bizarre gatecrashings of all. It came, without warning, from the sky.

14. Jumping into the Land of God

One winter's night in 1943, a US Air Force cargo plane on the supply run between India and China found itself in a violent tropical storm somewhere over the mountains of northern Burma. For the crew of five, all in their twenties or younger, it was to mark the start of an extraordinary misadventure. The aircraft, a converted B–24 bomber, was commanded by a Texan, Lieutenant Robert Crozier, already an experienced pilot at the age of twenty-three. On that stormy November night, he and his crew were returning the four-engined plane empty from Kunming in south-west China to its base at Jorhat, five hundred miles away in northern India. Their route, which would carry them over the eastern Himalayas, was one which Crozier and his crew had often flown before. To the allied aircrews ferrying arms and other strategic supplies to Chiang Kai-shek it was known always as 'The Hump'.

Previously, supplies had been transported overland across Burma, but the swift Japanese advance had made this impossible. An alternative route was proposed further to the north which involved building a road across the south-eastern corner of Tibet. But despite pressure from Britain and threats from China – allies now in face of a common enemy – the Tibetans strongly resisted this idea, pointing out that they wished to remain neutral in a conflict which did not concern them. In World War I the Dalai Lama had prayed for a British victory and offered her the loan of Tibetan troops. But this time Lhasa remained determinedly neutral, prayers being merely offered for an end to the fighting between the Great Powers. Thus the India-China airlift became a vital strategic link between the two theatres of war.

The strange adventure in which Lieutenant Crozier and his young crew were about to find themselves caught up remains to this day one of the least-known stories of the war. Only by chance did I stumble across a copy of Crozier's own narrative, *Jump to the Land of God*, as related to a friend after the war. Published in Idaho, it appears in no modern Tibetan bibliography. Not that there is the least doubt about its authenticity, for Mrs Betty Sherriff, now dead, refers briefly to the incident in her memoir of life in wartime Lhasa.

Crozier and his crew first ran into trouble at 23,000 feet and some four hundred miles short of Jorhat where they were due to land. Only minutes earlier the Asian night had been peaceful, with a faint moon shining. Now, as the angry storm enveloped them, the aircraft began to buck violently. Thick black clouds quickly blotted out everything, even the aircraft's wing-tip lights. Though they did not realise it, the plane was fighting its way through a 120-mile-an-hour gale which was gradually forcing them off course. When they failed to arrive over Jorhat at the estimated time, it began to dawn on them that something was wrong, and before very long they realised that they were hopelessly lost somewhere over Central Asia. Their nightmare had begun.

Attempts to call up Jorhat by radio were met by silence, and very soon they found that both their radios were dead. By now fuel was beginning to run perilously low. Unless by some miracle they were able to spot the lights of a town below, soon they would have no choice but to bale out into the stormy night. Then, all of a sudden, a huge white cone loomed out of the clouds very close to the aircraft. In a split-second they realised that it was a giant Himalayan peak. As others began to appear, Crozier hastily swung the plane away from this new and unexpected peril. The B–24, describing a complete U-turn, was thus saved from flying straight into a mountain together with its crew.

The gauges now showed that they had only enough fuel left to remain airborne for a further fifteen minutes. Crozier ordered everyone to buckle on his parachute and prepare to jump at a moment's notice. It was then that a sudden miracle occurred – or what seemed like one to the frightened crew. Through a brief gap in the storm clouds they were astonished to see, twinkling faintly below them, the lights of a town. Acting instinctively, Crozier thrust the aircraft's nose sharply downwards while the lights were still visible. He noticed that instead of being some 23,000 feet below them, this mysterious town appeared to be very much closer. Unless his altimeter was faulty, this could only mean that it lay at some 12,000 feet above sea level. Descending as low as he dared, Crozier swung the aircraft in a wide arc around the lights in the valley, desperately hoping to see some sign of an airport or landing strip. But no welcoming runway lights were switched on for them. Clearly it was a town without an airport. Their last hope had now gone. There was nothing for it but to bale out as quickly as possible. Minutes later one of the four engines spluttered and then cut out, followed almost at once by another. As the aircraft began to lose height they kicked open the rear hatch and leaped out, one after another, into the icy darkness. Shortly afterwards, in the distance, there was a dull explosion as the plane hit the foot of a mountain.

Meanwhile, in the town which they had just circled, the roar of the aircraft had brought people running in near panic from their homes. This town without an airport was Lhasa. Its inhabitants had long before been assured by their priests that any aircraft daring to fly over the holy city and look down upon the Dalai Lama would automatically be doomed. This was the first ever to do so. And now the entire population had heard the explosion which followed. Clearly the priests had been right.

But none of this, not even the name of the country they were in, was known to Crozier and his crew as, one by one, all five touched down safely on a mountainside some fifty miles south-east of Lhasa. The outside temperature was well below zero, and to keep alive that night they wrapped themselves in their parachutes, not daring to move far in the darkness for fear of plunging over a precipice. Having just left a pressurised air-craft, they also found themselves struggling for breath in the oxygen-thin atmosphere.

Their hurried descent that squally night left the five airmen separated, but two nights later all but one of them were reunited beneath the roof of a friendly Tibetan family. The following day the villagers brought in on a makeshift toboggan the fifth member of the crew. He was suffering from mildly frost-bitten feet and so unable to walk. By now his colleagues had worked out that this grim, treeless landscape with its distant snow-capped mountain ranges could only be Tibet. Just how they were going to find their way home across the Himalayas to India was something they could not even begin to contemplate.

Within hours of word getting around of their amazing des-cent from the angry skies they had become the object of incredulous but friendly curiosity, with people arriving from far and wide just to look at them. With the aid of a few words of pidgin Hindustani, which one of the villagers spoke, they managed to establish some sort of communication with their hosts. A messenger was dispatched on horseback to Lhasa, three days off, to seek official instructions on what was to be done with these foreign invaders.

Meanwhile, among those who had arrived at the village to look at them was a Buddhist pilgrim from one of the small Himalayan states to the south. He spoke a little English, and Crozier questioned him as to how they could get back to India. But the man warned him that to attempt this alone and unarmed would be nothing short of suicide. Not only would they almost certainly be murdered by bandits, but without animal transport and thick clothing they would die of exposure in the high Himalayan passes. He shook his head too at Crozier's sugges-tion that they might try floating down the Tsangpo, which flowed close to the village, and reach India that way. 'Some have tried it,' he warned Crozier, 'but have never been heard of since.' Their only hope of getting back alive, he insisted, would be by travelling to Lhasa and surrendering to the authorities who would then arrange for them to be escorted out of the country through Sikkim.

This decision was soon made for them, for an official now arrived from the capital with orders to escort the aircrew there. By this time warm friendships had developed between the young Americans and the Tibetans, and their departure was to be marked by emotional scenes. The villagers gave each of them a locally-made fur coat, a pair of fur-lined boots and blankets for the cold, mid-winter journey ahead which included scaling a 20,000-foot pass. Crozier and his crew were embarrassed to have nothing to give in return except for their gratitude. They were only too aware that had the villagers not offered them the shelter of their homes and the warmth of their yak-dung hearths they would almost certainly have perished. By now they had learned that the village was called Tsetang, and its entire population came down to the banks of the Tsangpo to see them off. They sang farewell songs to their strange guests and stuck out their tongues in salute. Desperate for something to sing in reply, all the airmen could think of was 'God Bless America', a performance which nonetheless was greeted by the villagers with rapture. And so, somewhat tearfully, they rode away to the sound of cheering Tibetans, and to become, no doubt, part of the region's folklore as the men who fell from the skies. But in Lhasa, as they would soon discover, they were to get a very different reception.

They had not been travelling long before they came upon a grim reminder of what would have been their fate had they remained a moment longer in their doomed aircraft. It lay beside the Tsangpo, smoke-blackened and shattered, like some huge dead bird. For several days, they learned, no one had dared approach it. Now, like columns of ants, hundreds of Tibetans could be seen moving up the mountainside carrying away bits of it to their villages. Others crawled over the wreckage prising off what salvageable pieces remained. One villager, finding one of the B–24's radios too heavy to drag away, was busy chopping it in half with an axe.

The journey to Lhasa included a gruelling and often hair-raising ascent of the ice-covered Gokar Pass. They and their Tibetan escort rode in single file along narrow ledges, a fearsome drop on one side, their ponies frequently stumbling on the very edge, sending rocks crashing into the abyss and the Americans' hearts into their mouths. They had also to beware of frost-bite, dismounting every so often and walking, to maintain the circulation in their limbs, while the oxygen-thin air gave them – and even their ponies – trouble with their breathing. But eventually, after spending two nights in villages on the way, they found themselves looking down on Lhasa, still ten miles off, lying in the middle of a wide valley. To the exhausted Americans it must have seemed like Shangri La. The party halted while the five airmen gazed in awe at the thirteen-storey Potala. Told by their escort that it contained a thousand rooms, one of the Americans joked that he would not like the job of washing its windows.

As they approached the town they found that Chinese officials, whose wartime allies they were, had erected a tent just outside. Here a welcoming celebration had been prepared. They were seated on cushions and made to drink large quantities of brandy to the accompaniment of numerous toasts. They drank first to their hosts; then to Tibet, China and America; then to the Dalai Lama, Chiang Kai-shek and President Roosevelt, and finally to New York and their own home states. The Chinese now informed them that they would be proceeding into the holy city where a banquet was awaiting them at the Chinese Mission. While their future was being decided, they would be staying at the only western home in the capital – the British Mission – as the guests of Captain and Mrs Sherriff. A brief note from Sherriff, welcoming them to Lhasa, was handed to Crozier. It ended with the words: 'I'm sure your troubles are now almost over.' This reassurance proved to be premature.

The Chinese Mission lay in the heart of the old town and to reach it they had to ride, still glowing from the effects of the brandy, through a labyrinth of muddy, refuse-strewn streets and alleys thronged with people, yaks and ponies. None of the houses, they noted, had glass in the windows. It was all infinitely more primitive than anything they had ever seen in India or China. At the Chinese Mission they dismounted and were led into a small banqueting hall. There, seated around a table, they were served with a succession of Chinese dishes by their smiling hosts. It was when they were about half-way through these that they first became aware of trouble in the square outside.

This began as little more than a murmur. But as the meal progressed it grew steadily louder. Eventually Crozier turned to one of the hosts and asked him what was going on. 'A great crowd has gathered,' he was told. But Crozier, assuming that their presence in Lhasa must have aroused much curiosity and excitement, thought no more about it. Anyway, the effects of the brandy were such that at that moment neither he nor his companions felt that they had a trouble in the world. It was only when they rose to thank their Chinese hosts and prepared to make their way to the British Mission that they discovered the truth. A large and angry crowd of Tibetans was waiting for them outside.

Before they had time to ponder why, the first missile struck the building with a heavy thud. It was followed by shouts of rage and a general quickening of the clamour outside. Their Chinese hosts now disappeared, although it transpired merely to bring their ponies to the front entrance. The five Americans, their hosts told them, were going to have to make a dash for it. Still no explanation of what was going on was offered them. More Chinese had now appeared, and the airmen were led to the entrance which opened onto the square. There, Crozier estimates, some ten thousand Tibetans confronted them, their faces filled with hatred.

On seeing the Americans the crowd began to surge forward. A stone struck one of the airmen, fortunately not injuring him. At this the Chinese, who had mounted their horses, rode straight into the mob, laying about them mercilessly with their whips. They were immediately joined by a group of Tibetans, apparently policemen or soldiers. With staves and whips they too hit out at anyone within reach. Among them was a robed official of some kind armed with a unique but devastating weapon. This was a heavy metal key attached to his wrist by a leather thong which he swung at head level, cracking skulls to left and right. Together they forced the mob back far enough to allow the Americans to mount their ponies and make their way through it. Eventually, thanks to the ruthlessness of their escort, they managed to reach the far edge of the mob un-harmed. More stones began to fly but the Americans spurred their ponies out of range and were quickly joined by their escort and hosts. But it was not until they reached the safety of the British Mission, some two miles away, that they learned from Captain Sherriff the reason for the mob's fury.

There, in the ordered calm of Deyki Lingka, with drinks in their hands and surrounded by old copies of *The Times*, he explained to them how, unintentionally, they had committed an act of blasphemy against the Dalai Lama. 'I suppose you know,' he pointed out, 'that you are the first people ever to fly over Lhasa.' In doing this they had done something which no Tibetan, let alone a foreigner, had ever been allowed to do. They had looked down on the Dalai Lama. 'You were above him, you know,' Sherriff explained. 'There is resentment among the population. You saw a demonstration of it when the mob stoned you.' In order to calm the population the author-ities had spread the belief that their aircraft had been snatched from the sky by way of punishment. 'But more to the point,' Sherriff added, 'the Government want you to get out as quickly as possible.' A caravan, with a small escort of Tibetan soldiers, was being organised at that moment. Until it was ready they would have to remain in the mission compound. After what had happened there could be no tours of the holy city. The Amer-icans were glad to rest, however, before embarking on the long and gruelling journey home across the snow-filled passes to the south. But they listened, fascinated, to the Sherriffs' tales of this strange, mediaeval land. They met, too, the only other westerner living in Lhasa, Reginald Fox, the British radio-operator, who had settled down with a Tibetan wife. They promised him that if they got safely back to India they would call him up on their radio and exchange news, if ever they were flying near Tibet.

At last, on December 19, 1943 – at midday, so that everyone could see them go – the five Americans and their escort rode out of Lhasa. It is almost the last that we hear of them. We know from Crozier that his young flight engineer did not survive the war. We know also that he and his crew were put back on 'The Hump' and that they kept their promise to Fox – or attempted to. For although they tried many times to call up station AC4YN, they never once succeeded in raising an answer. And so, except for their memories, they lost all contact with Tibet.

*   *   *

Just as Switzerland was to provide a haven for allied servicemen who escaped from prisoner-of-war camps in occupied Europe, so too did a neutral Tibet become a refuge for two Austrians who managed to escape from British India through the Himalayas. The story of Heinrich Harrer and Peter Aufschnaiter who, starving, ragged and with bleeding feet, eventually reached Lhasa in January 1946, is probably too well known to need repeating here. The two men, both pre-war mountaineers of distinction, were given asylum in Lhasa until forced to flee the Chinese invasion of 1950. Harrer, moreover, was to become tutor and confidant to the young Dalai Lama, introducing him to modern science and history.

But another epic tale of escape into wartime Tibet – *The Long Walk*, by Slavomir Rawicz – is perhaps less well remembered, although at the time of its publication it was to engender considerable controversy among Central Asian experts. It told the harrowing story of how, with seven companions, the Polish-born author escaped from a Stalinist slave camp in Siberia and fled across Tibet to safety in India. While most reviewers hailed the book – published more than ten years after the events it described – as a masterpiece of travel literature, others with a closer knowledge of the area began to question its bona fides. Foremost among the doubters was Peter Fleming, who had travelled widely in Central Asia before the war. Writing in *The Spectator* shortly after the book's publication, he challenged the author on a number of points.

For a start, he asked, how could Rawicz cross the main wartime highway between Lanchou and Urumchi, in Chinese Turkestan, without apparently recalling it? But more puzzling, how had he reached the Tibetan plateau without appearing to notice the 20,000-foot mountain bastion he would first have had to scale. Fleming also wondered why, in view of the widespread publicity the book had attracted, neither the author's three surviving travelling companions, nor any member of the staff of the Calcutta hospital in which he recovered from his ordeal, had come forward.

'The doctors and nurses who looked after him, the officers who interrogated him or studied the reports of his interrogation have remained silent. Both the then Director of Military Intelligence in India and his principal subordinate in Calcutta have no recollection of an incident which might have been expected, even after fourteen years, to leave some impression on their minds.'

Fleming concluded: 'One is regretfully forced to the conclusion that the whole of this excellent book is moonshine . . . he did not do the journey at all.' But Rawicz, who today lives quietly outside Nottingham, did not take this challenge lying down. In a letter to *The Spectator* in which he insisted that every word of his book, by then a best-seller, was true, he added: 'I would remind everyone that we were not an expedition of exploration: we were starved fugitives fleeing from a terror that only those who have suffered under Communism can understand. I do not remember what roads or mountains we crossed – we never knew the names of most of them and had no maps or previous knowledge.'

And there the matter rested, as it does to this day. But one book about Tibet over which there is no such uncertainty is *The Third Eye*. Published the same year as *The Long Walk* it, too, became a best-seller. Beginning with the words 'I am a Tibetan. One of the few who have reached this strange Western world', it purported to be by a lama named Lobsang Rampa. He took his entranced readers into the secret world of the lamasery where, he claimed, he was singled out at the age of seven to undergo an operation to open his 'third eye'. A splinter of wood was inserted in his forehead, stimulating a gland which intensified his powers of clairvoyance. He described graphically how (to quote his publisher) 'in the volcano caves underneath the Potala he submitted to the astonishing mystical experience known as the "living death"'.

An avid public drank in his every word – even after the rather more prosaic truth became known. Lobsang Rampa, it transpired, was none other than Cyril Henry Hoskins, a plumber from Cornwall with a taste for the occult. So far as anyone could discover, the shaven-headed Hoskins had never been outside England. He had certainly never been to Tibet. But public exposure (by a private detective hired by a suspicious oriental scholar) failed to discomfit him. His life in a Tibetan monastery, he explained to reporters, had been in the course of a previous incarnation. Unrepentant to the end, he wrote some nineteen books about his experiences as a Tibetan lama. When he died at the age of seventy he had sold more than four million copies of these. But although Hoskins was a fraud, as a best-seller writer he had proved one thing. The public appetite for everything to do with Tibet was as insatiable in the mid-twentieth century as ever it was in the nineteenth.

But literary trespassers were one thing. Armed invaders were quite another. We come now to the darkest period of Tibet's history. For gathering in strength on its eastern border were the Chinese, the last of the gatecrashers. And this time they were determined to stay.

15. Red Guards in Lhasa

The Chinese invaded Tibet on the twenty-third day of the ninth month of the Year of the Iron Tiger – or, by our own calendar, on November 7, 1950. Ever since their Manchu predecessors had been driven so humiliatingly from Lhasa thirty-seven years before, the Chinese had been waiting for this moment. Among the first to learn that they had crossed the frontier was an Englishman named Robert Ford. Employed by the Tibetan Government as a radio operator, he was stationed in the remote town of Chamdo, some five hundred miles east of Lhasa and less than one hundred from the Chinese border. Because of the extreme isolation of his post, the former RAF sergeant-instructor was known to the newspapers at home as 'the loneliest Briton in the world'. His solitude was soon to become absolute. For the Chinese, crushing all Tibetan resistance, attacked from the east. Within days Chamdo – and with it Robert Ford – was in their hands. But not before the Englishman had managed to flash warning of the invasion to Lhasa. Had he chosen to, he could even then have fled westwards in time to save his own skin. Instead, he worked around the clock at his transmitter, reporting regularly to Lhasa on the progress of the Chinese thrust into eastern Tibet. When finally he did abandon his radio and head for safety with the retreating Tibetan troops it was too late. The captured Tibetans were merely disarmed and sent home. Ford was taken prisoner. His devotion to duty cost him the next four years of his life which he spent enduring relentless interrogation and brainwashing in a Communist prison.

The invasion had not come entirely without warning. Earlier

that year, shortly after coming to power, the Chinese Communists had publicly announced that they considered Tibet to be part of sovereign China, warning that they proposed shortly to liberate it from British and American imperialism and restore it to the great motherland once and for all. From his remote listening post, Ford had himself heard the Tibetan-language news-reader of Peking Radio declare this to be one of the tasks of the People's Liberation Army for 1950. He had passed this on to Lhasa, together with the other news he regularly monitored from Chinese radio, in the uneasy knowledge that he was just the sort of example of such imperialism that the Chinese would be looking for.

For months the authorities in Lhasa had been watching Communist China, with its atheistic creed and rapidly growing military power, with increasing apprehension. Now, as Peking's intentions towards Tibet suddenly became clear, the National Assembly sent urgent appeals for help to the outside world. Telegrams were sent to Britain, the United States, India and Nepal. The Dalai Lama, then only sixteen, recalls in his memoirs:

The replies to these telegrams were terribly disheartening. The British Government expressed their deepest sympathy for the people of Tibet and regretted that owing to Tibet's geographical position, since India had been granted independence, they could not offer help. The Government of the United States also replied in the same sense, and declined to receive our delegation. The Indian Government also made it clear that they would not give us military help, and advised us not to offer any armed resistance, but to open negotiations for a peaceful settlement. . .

Once again, in their hour of need, the Tibetans discovered that they were on their own. Just as in 1910 when the Manchus invaded Tibet, their appeal fell on deaf ears. It was by Britain in particular, whom they had long regarded as their friend and protector against the Chinese, that they felt especially betrayed. Worse, the British Government appeared to have given *de facto* recognition to the new régime in Peking. 'Does this mean,' Ford was asked by Tibetan officials, 'that the British have made friends with the Communists?' All he had been able to do, in his inadequate Tibetan, was to try to explain the meaning of *de facto*. It did not mean that the British Government liked the Communists. 'It doesn't,' he assured them. 'But it cannot see any gain in pretending they do not exist.'

Following their seizure of much of eastern Tibet and part of the west, the invaders now halted. They were no doubt waiting to see the world's reaction to their incursion, and also hoping perhaps that the Tibetans would realise the futility of offering any further resistance, thus allowing the occupation to proceed peacefully. In Lhasa, the Cabinet were anxiously consulting the state oracles about what they should do next. As a result, although he had not yet reached his majority, in an unprecedented move the young Dalai Lama was invited to take over the leadership of the country. After much soul-searching, for the teenage God-king was only too conscious of his inexperience in worldly matters, he agreed.

It was around this time that the already disillusioned Tibetans received another shock. On the day of the Chinese invasion they had appealed to the United Nations for help. Now they learned that the General Assembly had decided not even to consider their case. This was largely due, moreover, to British arguments that the precise legal status of Tibet was uncertain. Considering that for more than thirty years Britain had been treating with Tibet as a country enjoying *de facto* independence, Tibetans found this inexplicable, if not downright hypocritical. And so the awkward question of Tibet was shelved by the civilised world, only being resurrected nine years later when the Tibetans were to try painfully to throw off the Maoist yoke. Further pleas by Tibet to the United Nations about the Chinese occupation of their territory failed to elicit so much as an acknowledgement.

Now, in a despairing attempt to reach a settlement with the Chinese before they thrust further into Tibet, the youthful Dalai Lama dispatched a four-man delegation to Peking. Here the overawed and inexperienced Tibetans were treated as virtual prisoners and subjected to abuse and humiliation. They were coerced, under threats of further military action being taken against Tibet, and without being allowed to consult Lhasa, to sign an 'agreement' prepared by the Chinese. This, called the 'Sino-Tibetan Agreement for the Peaceful Liberation of Tibet', effectively transferred Tibet's sovereignty to China. When the Tibetan delegates protested that they did not have the official seals with them to validate the document, the Chinese had some hurriedly made in Peking, which were then ceremoniously affixed to it.

Armed with this *laissez-passer*, a Chinese general arrived shortly afterwards in Lhasa accompanied by several thousand armed troops. In his memoir, *My Land and People*, the Dalai Lama describes peering through the window to get a glimpse of him. 'I do not know exactly what I expected. What I saw was three men in grey suits and peaked caps who looked extremely drab and insignificant among the splendid figures of my officials in their red and golden robes. Had I but known it, the drabness was the state to which China was to reduce us all before the end, and the insignificance was certainly an illusion.'

The Chinese demanded that the Tibetans supply their troops with food and other necessities, explaining that lack of roads and airfields prevented these from being supplied from China. Prices – and with them Tibetan resentment – at once began to soar. One must be wary of refugee stories, but in view of what Peking has since admitted about the 'grave errors' it had made in Tibet, there seems no reason to doubt that the presence of several thousand Chinese troops (some put the figure as high as 20,000) in the Lhasa area alone stretched the country's frail economy to the point of collapse. 'For the first time in history the people of Lhasa were on the verge of famine,' Tsepon Shakabpa, Tibet's Finance Minister at that time, wrote afterwards. When, faced by mounting protests from their own people, the Tibetan authorities asked the Chinese to cut down drastically on the size of their garrison in Lhasa they were told that the soldiers were there for the Tibetans' own protection. In any case, they were asked, had not their own representatives signed the document agreeing to the troops being stationed there in the first place?

Initially the Chinese behaved well, the troops having strict instructions not to alienate the Tibetans. But if they had expected to be welcomed as liberators, or as members of the same family, they were to be rudely shaken. The children threw stones at them, adults spat at them and sang rude songs about them which they could not understand, while some of the bolder monks tied knots in their shawls and hit them as they rode by. At first the Chinese turned the other cheek to all this. But as conditions turned from bad to worse, and resentment continued to grow, the Chinese gradually began to abandon their initial benevolence. Their own morale, moreover, was far from high in this benighted land, not merely among the soldiers but also among the civilian workers drafted there to help bring about the new reforms. To the comfort-loving Chinese, Tibet has always been a hardship posting. And now, not only were they made to feel unwelcome by these barbaric people whom they had been told they were there to help, but the reforms themselves met with obstruction at every turn.

By the mid-1950s, the Chinese mask had finally been removed. Conciliation, they discovered, had got nowhere. Marxism must henceforth be made to replace Buddhism in the lives of Tibetans. Anti-religious propaganda was stepped up. Buddha himself was denounced as a reactionary by the puppet press. The one thing the Tibetans most feared – the destruction of their religion and way of life – was coming about. It was this ancient fear, amounting almost to a national phobia, which had driven them to turn their backs on the rest of the world and for so long to close their frontiers to all foreigners. Ironically, it was the Chinese who had encouraged that fear in the first place, warning them that the British and Russians would one day come and destroy their religion, replacing it with an alien one. The British had come, but had respected their religion. Now the Chinese were proposing to do the very thing they had accused the British of conspiring to do. Hostility turned to hatred.

Armed resistance was now beginning to spread, particularly in eastern Tibet, a traditionally lawless region inhabited by the fiercely independent and warlike Khamba tribesmen. Supply columns were attacked, roads and bridges destroyed. The Chinese hit back, demolishing by shellfire and bombing entire monasteries known to be the focal point of resistance. Sacred buildings and monuments were desecrated. In an effort to undermine their influence, monks were made to work on road-building and other construction projects, and also subjected to public humiliation. Some were dragged from their cells and challenged to prove publicly that they possessed supernatural powers. The result was that more and more Tibetans joined the guerrillas. At first resistance was mainly confined to the east, but gradually it spread to other provinces of Tibet. Chinese attempts to crush the movement by means of harsh sentences, executions, deportations and other forms of reprisal were unsuccessful. But little of all this reached the outside world. Occasional rumours filtered through to India, but as these were impossible to check they were largely discounted in the West. It was Nehru's policy at that time, moreover, to placate his powerful Communist neighbour by discouraging such unfriendly stories. One British journalist living in Kalimpong was threatened with expulsion if he continued to write them. But then, in the autumn of 1958, reports began to reach India that a full-scale anti-Communist revolt was in progress in Tibet. The truth could no longer be denied.

Its climax – bloody, tragic and dramatic – came, as the world now knows, in March of the following year. The battlefield was the very heart of Lhasa. Accounts of what happened vary greatly. Until the uprising, resistance in the holy city had been largely passive, confined to poster campaigns calling on the Chinese to 'go home'. But news of the guerrillas' successes, as they crept closer and closer to Lhasa, spread through the bazaars and streets of the capital. One major victory, towards the end of 1958, had been the annihilation of the Chinese garrison at Tsetang, where Lieutenant Crozier and his aircrew had been so warmly received some fifteen years earlier. Morale in Lhasa was riding high, while anti-Chinese feeling had reached flashpoint. It was in this heady atmosphere that the mid-March uprising broke out

It was a rumour which ignited it. The Chinese, it was whispered, were planning to kidnap the Dalai Lama and carry him off to China. He had been invited to attend a theatrical show at the Chinese army barracks the following evening, but had been asked to come without his bodyguard or his ministers. The reason for this, whether innocent or otherwise, will probably never be known, but to the people of Lhasa it could mean only one thing. The Chinese were planning to kidnap their God-king. It was widely known that on four previous occasions high lamas in eastern Tibet had been lured to functions in similar circumstances and never seen again. The people were both angry and frightened, and that night Tibetans began to converge on the summer palace where he was residing, begging him not to go.

'The following day,' the Dalai Lama recalled afterwards, 'was destined to be the most momentous Lhasa had ever seen.' In fact, it was merely the first of twelve momentous days which were to leave the streets of the holy city sodden with Tibetan blood. From early that morning people headed in hundreds, and later in thousands, to the summer palace. Forming a cordon around it and shouting anti-Chinese slogans, they declared that they would use force, if necessary, to prevent the Dalai Lama from leaving the palace to keep his rendezvous that night with the Chinese. Some of them, notably the Khambas, were armed. All were angry. The young Dalai Lama now found himself torn. A devout believer in non-violence who for nine years had maintained an uneasy coexistence with the invaders, he now realised that a showdown was inevitable whatever he did. In the event, he sent a message to the Chinese general who was to have been his host declining his invitation, pointing out that he was prevented from leaving his palace by the crowds. At the same time the huge throng outside – estimated at some 30,000 – was informed that he would not be going. But this only partially removed their fears. For what was there to prevent the Chinese from coming to the palace and removing him by force? To forestall any such move, defensive positions were prepared at all the exits, while patrols guarded the walls.

By now, word of what was happening had reached Tibetan army units stationed in and around the capital, and they too joined the crowds surrounding the palace. They brought with them extra weapons which, with others that had lain hidden for years in monasteries and homes, were distributed among those who knew how to use them. A committee had in the meantime been set up to organise anti-Chinese rallies and demonstrations in the town. At these it was proclaimed that Tibet no longer recognised Chinese authority and was once more independent. Furthermore it was demanded that the Chinese withdraw their troops from the country immediately. The Dalai Lama, still hoping to prevent bloodshed, sent a message to the rebel leaders pleading with them not to aggravate an already explosive situation. His moderate stance at this crucial time has been criticised by some Tibetans and others as being too conciliatory when forceful leadership was called for. Letters he sent to the Chinese have been cited by his critics as evidence of this, for in these he disowns the rebels and professes friendliness towards the Chinese. Embarrassed by the subsequent publication of these by the Chinese, the Dalai Lama has since argued that they were a desperate expedient aimed at defusing a very dangerous situation and buying time. They appear to have achieved the latter, for a tense stalement followed, lasting for several days. Just what the Chinese were up to during this period is not certain, but most likely they were awaiting instructions from

Peking. Meanwhile the anger of the rebels and the crowd around the palace had shown no signs of abating. One unfortunate Tibetan official, regarded by the crowd as a collaborator, was seized and lynched when he tried to enter the palace. Another was attacked and badly injured when he was mistaken for a Chinese coming to take the Dalai Lama away.

The stalemate continued uneasily until March 16, when word reached the palace that during the night the Chinese had brought up artillery and positioned it within point-blank range of the city, and particularly of the summer palace. That same day Chinese soldiers were seen observing the latter through instruments of some kind. It was assumed by the Tibetans, who knew little of modern gunnery, that they were taking range-readings for the artillery. There were rumours, too, of Chinese reinforcements arriving by air. The Tibetans around the palace now prepared to defend their God-king with their lives.

The first shots of the battle which was shortly to tear the city apart came at four o'clock the following afternoon. Two mortar bombs landed in the grounds of the summer palace. They did no damage but caused much alarm. Although they turned out to be isolated shots, fired for no obvious reason, to the Tibetans it seemed that a bombardment of the palace had begun. Pressed by his ministers and closest advisers, the Dalai Lama agreed to escape from Lhasa that night under cover of darkness.

The saga of his thirteen-day flight to asylum in India is now part of history, and certainly of Tibetan folklore. Clutching a rifle, and dressed as a Khamba guerrilla, he slipped through one of the palace gates without being recognised. Ahead of him, also disguised as Khamba soldiers, were his mother, sister and young brother. Their immediate destination was the rebel stronghold of Loka, beyond the Tsangpo, where for the moment he would be safe from pursuit. For at that time most of Tibet south of the river was firmly in Khamba hands. The only way the Chinese could now injure or kill him, presupposing they could find him, was from the air. As the Dalai Lama hurried south, with an armed escort of Khambas and Tibetan regulars, he still clung to the hope of remaining somewhere in southern Tibet from where he would continue to lead his people and endeavour to negotiate with the Chinese. But this hope was quickly dashed when a horseman caught them up with appalling news of what had happened in the capital after their departure.

Some hours before the Chinese discovered that the Dalai Lama had escaped, they had begun to shell the summer palace, believing him, presumably, to be still inside. It should be said in fairness that they had already warned the Tibetans, through loud-hailers, that unless they surrendered, Lhasa would be shelled. This 'threat', as she considered it, was remembered clearly by Rinchen Dolma Taring, an educated Tibetan woman who followed the Dalai Lama into exile in India. But those defending the palace were in no mood to be threatened or warned, let alone to surrender. In order to give the Dalai Lama's party time to get beyond reach of any Chinese pursuit, it appears that the crowds around the palace had not been told that he was no longer there. They believed, tragically, that they were still protecting their God-king from the Chinese.

The bombardment began in the dark early hours of March 20 – some say one o'clock, others two – more than forty-eight hours after the Dalai Lama had escaped. It was heard with dismay from ten miles away by the fleeing Rinchen Taring who, fearing arrest and disguised as a nun, spent that night on the floor of a dairy. It was the sound that they had all been dreading – 'first one shell, then more, followed by too many to count.' In her memoir, *Daughter of Tibet*, she recalls praying to Dolma, her *karma* deity, for her friends and family and for all those left behind in Lhasa to face the Chinese gunners. The bombardment continued until first light, when it ceased for a while, recommencing at eight o'clock.

In and around the summer palace the shelling caused heavy loss of life among the defenders, for few of them were properly dug in, and all refused either to flee or to surrender. Just how many died will probably never be known, but the Dalai Lama refers in his autobiography to 'thousands of bodies' being seen afterwards strewn about the palace grounds and walls. But ill-armed and untrained as the Tibetans were, resistance flared fiercely all over the town. In many places, as the enraged populace attacked Chinese positions, ferocious hand-to-hand fighting took place, with the fanatical Khambas usually in the forefront. But the Chinese, although not a fighting race like the Khambas, had long experience of such warfare which they had acquired in their struggle against both the Nationalists and Japanese. In fire-power and numbers alone, moreover, the two sides were totally unmatched, many of the Tibetans being merely armed with sticks and stones. From all accounts, the Tibetan women fought as bravely as their men. But the Tibetan uprising of 1959 was all too reminiscent of the desperate but equally hopeless Hungarian revolt against Soviet armour just three years earlier. Having silenced the defenders of the summer palace, the Chinese now switched their artillery and mortars to other targets, including the hilltop medical school, which was fiercely defended, and the great Sera Monastery, a focal-point of anti-Chinese feeling, four miles out of Lhasa.

But the insurrection, largely Khamba inspired and led, was clearly doomed from the beginning. What chance had the Tibetans of expelling the Chinese this time? With their tanks and artillery and superior tactics, the Chinese gradually gained the upper hand. By March 23 the last of the fighting was over. The Tibetan uprising had been bloodily crushed. It was what the Dalai Lama had feared from the start. He had seen the insurrection as a certain path to self-destruction but had found himself powerless to prevent it.

Why then had so many ordinary Tibetans decided to join in this futile confrontation with the Chinese? Was it simply due to national fury over the assaults made by these heathen invaders on their religion and way of life, culminating in the fear that their God-king himself was to be abducted? Or could, as some allege, the ubiquitous hand of the Central Intelligence Agency be discerned somewhere in the background? Whatever the truth about that, it is possible that many Tibetans were stirred by their own history into believing that, as once before, their gods would ensure them victory.

One respected Tibetan scholar now in the West, Dr Dawa Norbu, sees it essentially as a religious uprising. 'The simple-minded Tibetans,' he wrote in a recent issue of *The China Quarterly*, 'saw their [previous] easy expulsion of the Chinese troops from Tibet, which was really made possible by the 1911 Revolution, following the speedy departure of the Younghus-band Expedition in 1904, as simply the work of their faith.'

Just how much loss of life there was during the three days of bitter fighting which followed the attack on the summer palace is hard to say. Following India's independence, the British Mission had been withdrawn, and there were no longer any westerners living in the capital. However, had his lips not been sealed by an anxious Nehru, a valuable eye-witness would have been the Indian Consul General, a former army officer. It had been his official dispatches to Delhi, transmitted by radio, which had given the first substantiated reports of the Lhasa uprising to the world. But they were primarily concerned with the safety of the consulate general and its staff who found themselves uncomfortably close to the fighting. One is there-fore left entirely in the hands of witnesses deeply committed to one side or the other. The Tibetans themselves, in a semi-official history written by one of the Dalai Lama's former ministers, put the death toll at a staggering twelve thousand. Anna Louise Strong, a life-long sympathiser with Communist China, claims on the other hand that Tibetan casualties totalled only some six hundred, a figure she was told by Chinese officers when an official guest in Lhasa. She, somewhat predictably, saw it as an uprising by Tibet's 'serf-owning rulers'. But most other commentators believe that some three thousand dead is a more likely figure. To this must be added many Tibetans who were summarily executed by the Chinese immediately after-wards.

There now followed for the Tibetans a long and unhappy

period of religious and political repression. The uprising, which day after day had dominated the world's headlines, caused the Chinese enormous embarrassment internationally, and lasting damage in the Third World. They now set about, once and for all, destroying the power of the church and the land-owning families. With an almost Cromwellian fury they demolished, sacked or closed down monasteries across the country, confiscating their lands and wealth. Monks were forced to abandon their calling and forced to marry and settle on the land, or starve. Temples and shrines were stripped of their sacred images and Buddhist scriptures burned. Thousands of Tibetans were arrested and many others deported, often to China, to reduce the risk of further armed resistance. Large numbers of Chinese settlers were moved into Tibet. There were executions, beatings, public denunciations – and suicides. Identity cards were introduced for all and freedom of movement severely curtailed. Political indoctrination, at compulsory daily meetings, became part of the Tibetans' new way of life, and every means of coercion was used to try to force them to abandon their old faith and embrace that of Marx and Mao.

But many thousands of Tibetans reacted against these repressive measures in the only way still open to them. They voted with their feet, trudging hundreds of miles southwards through the Himalayas into exile in India. Only a small percentage were from the noble, former land-owning families. In all, some eighty thousand reached safety, but many others are known to have perished while fleeing, either dying from cold and starvation in the passes or being shot down by Chinese border guards. Many of the refugees brought with them treasured works of religious art and sacred texts to protect these from destruction or confiscation by the heathen Chinese. Meanwhile, in the more remote parts of Tibet the guerrillas continued to harass the Chinese troops who had been strongly reinforced by a Peking determined to crush any remaining resistance. But it was a losing battle, and the hard-pressed guerrillas eventually withdrew across the frontier into Nepal where, for a while, they established a base of operations in the small mediaeval kingdom of Mustang.

The Chinese, naturally, see all these events in a very different light. To them Tibet was simply an anachronism, a pocket of intolerable backwardness in a China which had seen the Marxist light. They had tried using peaceful persuasion, only to be obstructed at every turn by reactionary elements. These now had to be ruthlessly purged if Tibetans were to enjoy the benefits of modern civilisation. Eggs had to be broken in order to make the omelette.

None of this painful process was witnessed by observers with any claim to impartiality – except for one, as will be seen. For Tibet was now even more of a forbidden land than ever, and it would remain so for nearly twenty years. The only westerners who were allowed in were one or two 'friends' of China, like the late Anna Louise Strong, who could be trusted to suspend their critical faculties. (The final chapter of Miss Strong's book on Tibet – *When Serfs Stood Up in Tibet* – is called 'Building Paradise'.) None of these 'friends' spoke any Tibetan, and even *their* movements were carefully controlled.

But there is one important eye-witness to all this, Prem Nath Kaul, who shortly after the Dalai Lama's flight was posted to Lhasa as the new Indian Consul General. On his retirement from Indian Government service, this former wartime officer in the British army produced a modest book of memoirs entitled *Frontier Callings*. Published in Delhi in 1976, and unnoticed outside India, it is written with the careful circumspection one would expect from a former senior diplomat still bound, presumably, by his country's secrecy laws. Even so it is clear from what he writes that, during those two years, he was living in a repressive police state rather than the paradise depicted by Miss Strong. He tells how Tibetans were forced by the Chinese to inform on their neighbours. He writes of the 'indiscriminate arrests' which followed the uprising, and of the 'many' who were still languishing in Lhasa's jails awaiting trial.

Kaul also tells how the Chinese tipped confiscated Buddhist

works of art into the river and city sewers until it suddenly occurred to them that they were throwing away precious foreign currency. Impounded tréasures from then on were taken back to China to be sold in Hong Kong for 'enormous prices'. But even in retirement, Kaul was obviously not free to tell the whole story. However, the International Commission of Jurists, based in Geneva, was under no such restraint. After taking evidence from the Dalai Lama and other Tibetan refugees, the committee of enquiry appointed by the Commission, which comprised eminent lawyers from Asia, Europe and Africa, concluded that the Chinese were guilty of genocide 'by the widespread killing of Buddhist monks and lamas'. They also accused the Chinese of violating most of the articles of the UN Declaration of Human Rights, including the use of torture, 'cruel and degrading treatment', forced labour, denial of religious freedom and enforced marriage between unwilling partners. There was only one problem, however. China was not a member of the United Nations, and in no mood to bow to world opinion.

Six years later, in 1965, the Jurists were to publish another report which maintained that the situation in Tibet had not changed. But the Tibetans had still to suffer yet another twist of the Chinese sword with the arrival of the dreaded Red Guards bearing the message of the Cultural Revolution in January 1967. These storm-troopers of Maoism gone mad rampaged through the towns and villages of Tibet spreading fear and destruction, as elsewhere in China. Buddhism and the old Tibetan way of life became their principal targets. Monasteries and other sacred buildings (of which Tibet had once possessed thousands) which had somehow escaped desecration or destruction hitherto, now came under attack. One villager from western Tibet who fled to India said that the first they knew of the Red Guards and the Cultural Revolution was when the Chinese began to form special groups in the villages and towns which they recruited from the poorest sections of the community. At their head were placed Tibetan collaborators who worked in the offices of the occupying administration. All wore red arm bands, carried *The Thoughts of Chairman Mao*, and were given the title Genlog Rukach – Red Guard.

Villagers who had previously been allowed to worship still were now forbidden to do so. They were forced to burn their sacred books – and show the ashes to the Red Guards as proof that they had done so. Some, however, managed to save important texts by burying them. Another Tibetan, a seventy-year-old lama, related how in his village the Red Guards held a meeting at which they were told that all old ideas were going to be swept forcibly away. Everyone was given a copy of Chairman Mao's *Thoughts* in Tibetan. He recounted: 'A little while after this the Red Guards came and destroyed my monastery and burnt the scriptures. They asked me what I was going to do now. I told them that I would read Chairman Mao's thoughts. They went away and that night I threw Mao's thoughts away and left the village with other people who brought me here.'

But if many thousands of Tibetans viewed China's occupation of their country as intolerable oppression (more than 80,000, it will be recalled, had fled the country), the half-Chinese writer Han Suyin was to see nothing but its virtues. Following her visit there as guest of the Chinese in October 1975, she was to claim that for Tibetans their reforms had proved 'eminently satisfactory and extremely popular'. Chairman Mao, she tells us in her book *Lhasa, the Open City* (it was anything but that at the time), had a particularly soft spot for China's impoverished national minorities, including the Tibetans. He had decreed, she writes, 'that they must have everything, and perhaps even more, than what was being done for the Han people.' But this had not been the experience of Prem Kaul, the Indian Consul General, who had witnessed the behaviour of the Han Chinese towards the Tibetans in Lhasa. He recalls how during the severe food shortages which marked his two-year stay those supplies which did reach the capital were intercepted and 'utilised for the needs of the Chinese P.L.A. and cadres [party functionaries]'.

But following Mao Tse-tung's death and the overthrow of the

Gang of Four, Peking was forced to admit that Tibet was not
quite the paradise that the world, including Miss Suyin, had
been led to believe. Indeed, less than five years after her own
officially-sponsored visit to Tibet, senior officials there admitted to visiting correspondents that they had made a mess of
things. The hardline general who for ten years had been in
charge of implementing Peking's policies there was ignominiously brought home and sent into retirement, disgrace – or
both. Two senior party officials who had been sent to Tibet after
the fall of the Gang of Four to find out just what was going on
there had been horrified at what they had uncovered. As a
result, not only had the general been sacked, but a new
policy – known as 'regulation 31' – was immediately introduced as the new 'correct' line. Religious persecution was
outlawed and Tibetans' traditional methods of agriculture and
husbandry restored.

How lasting all this will prove to be, it is still too early to say.
As the Dalai Lama recently observed: 'It is difficult to believe or
trust the Chinese. Once bitten by a snake, and you feel suspicious even when you see a piece of rope.' But under Peking's
new and relaxed policies, a growing number of Tibetan refugees
are being allowed back into the country to visit their families
after twenty years or more of separation. Also the children, by
now grown up, of refugee parents who were forced to leave
them behind in 1959 have been permitted to leave Tibet and be
reunited with their families.

Following secret contacts made over many months, three
official delegations representing the Dalai Lama – whose confidence the Chinese hope to win back – have visited Tibet. All
reported extremely unfavourably, however, on what they saw
during several months of travelling. Almost all the country's
monasteries and temples, they claimed, had been destroyed. A
few had been rebuilt or repaired as showpieces for foreign
visitors. Figures they were given to show how much progress
Tibet had made under Chinese tutelage were, they alleged,
largely bogus. This applied particularly to the building of

schools. Most of these, the Tibetans discovered, just did not exist.

The first of the delegations was mobbed by crowds so emotional, it is said, that even the Chinese interpreters were moved to tears. The arrival of the second, in July 1980, led to even more disorderly and rapturous demonstrations of support and affection for the Dalai Lama. As a result, they had to be hustled out of Tibet by the embarrassed Chinese, their tour cut short. They were even accused by their hosts of deliberate incitement. Peking's mortification was made worse by the fact that this was all witnessed by a group of western reporters who also happened to be visiting Tibet. One of them, David Bonavia of *The Times*, a seasoned China-watcher, reported 'an upsurge of piety and religious fervour which is by no means confined to the older generation'.

The gospel of Karl Marx, even after thirty years, has proved no more acceptable to the Tibetans than that other alien gospel which the fearless Annie Taylor and her tragic successors, the Rijnharts, had risked everything to try to bring to them. Today, for a while anyway, the old faith has triumphed over scientific atheism, although the Tibetans are still – at the time of writing – without their God-king in the Potala. But long-secreted rosaries and prayer wheels have been rescued from their hiding places, and prayer flags flutter defiantly from those wayside chortens which survived the Red Guards. Buddhist pilgrims, ragged and begrimed, once more trek to Lhasa to prostrate themselves before the holy places.

But after all they have suffered, and all they have learned, life for the Tibetans can never again be the same. Few probably would wish it so. No one today, not even the Dalai Lama himself, pretends that the old Tibet was a feudal paradise. Nor does anyone claim that, in three decades, the Chinese have done nothing at all to improve the lot of ordinary Tibetans. It is merely tragic that so much Tibetan blood had to be spilled to achieve so little. 'Given time,' one writer on contemporary Tibet has observed, 'there is no reason why they should not work together to give Tibet the happiness and prosperity which has so far eluded it.' It is a hope that anyone who has followed the long and painful saga of Tibet's encounters with the outside world must surely echo.

But already they face a new form of intrusion. This time it is the ubiquitous package tourist. For it is not the Tibetans who invited these latter-day Landors and Littledales into their homeland, but the Chinese. Just how they feel when they see coachloads of inquisitive foreigners peering into the Dalai Lama's private quarters in the Potala it is impossible to say. Perhaps, after more than a century of foreign intrusion, they have finally resigned themselves to this seemingly endless stream of uninvited guests. Even so, it is hard not to feel some sympathy for this gentle, cheerful and long-suffering people who only ever asked one thing of the outside world. And that was to be left alone.

That was written twenty years ago, when it looked as though some sort of a rapprochement between the Chinese and the Tibetans was still possible. Alas, any such hopes have long since been dashed, as Beijing has remorselessly and mercilessly tightened its grip on Tibet, insisting that it is an integral and permanent part of China. It has swamped the country with Chinese settlers and systematically set out to eradicate Tibet's ancient culture and religion. This, in turn, has provoked angry anti-Chinese demonstrations—blamed by the authorities on outside agitators—which have been brutally and bloodily suppressed. Somewhat feeble protests by Western governments at this blatant disregard for human rights have been furiously rebuffed by the Chinese, who argue that the affairs of Tibet are a strictly internal matter for themselves. Meanwhile, gallingly, the Tibetans have seen their Muslim near-neighbours in Central Asia, once part of the Soviet Empire, win seats at the United Nations, following the collapse of Russian communism. Yet, for the Tibetans, any dreams of independence must seem as far away as ever.

Bibliography of Principal Sources

This narrative has been pieced together from numerous sources, published and unpublished, written and unwritten. The following list of titles, although far from exhaustive, includes those works which I found especially valuable in researching and writing this book. Obituaries and articles in contemporary journals have, for the sake of brevity, largely been excluded. Except where otherwise indicated, all titles are, or were, published in London.

Anon. *Tibet*. Historical Section, Foreign Office, 1920.
Anon. British Government Blue Books. *Papers relating to Tibet*, 1904. *Further Papers.* . . 1904, 1905, 1910.
Bailey, Colonel F. M. *No Passport to Tibet*. 1957.
Barber, Noel. *From the Land of Lost Content*. 1969.
Bell, Sir Charles. *Tibet, Past and Present*. Oxford, 1924.
— *The People of Tibet*. Oxford, 1928.
— *The Religion of Tibet*. Oxford, 1931.
— *Portrait of the Dalai Lama*. 1946.
Bonvalot, Gabriel. *Across Tibet*. 1891.
Bower, Captain Hamilton. *A Diary of a Journey Across Tibet*. 1894.
Brereton, John. 'Mission to Tibet'. *Blackwoods Magazine*. May/June, 1977.
Cammann, Schuyler. *Trade through the Himalayas*. Princeton, 1951.
Candler, Edmund. *The Unveiling of Lhasa*. 1905.
Carey, William. *Travel and Adventure in Tibet. Including the Diary of Miss Annie R. Taylor's Remarkable Journey*. 1902.
Dalai Lama. *My Land and my People*. 1962.
Das, Sarat Chandra. *Journey to Lhasa and Central Tibet*. 1902.
David-Neel, Alexandra. *My Journey to Lhasa*. 1927.
— *With Magicians and Mystics in Tibet*. 1931.
Denys, Jeanne. *A. David-Neel au Tibet*. Paris, 1972.
Fleming, Peter. *Bayonets to Lhasa*. 1961.
Fletcher, Dr Harold. *A Quest of Flowers*. Edinburgh, 1976.
Ford, Robert. *Captured in Tibet*. 1957.
Galwan, Ghulam. *Servant of Sahibs*. Cambridge, 1923.
Gould, Sir Basil. *The Jewel in the Lotus*. 1957.
Grenard, Fernand. *Tibet: the Country and its Inhabitants*. 1904.
Hedin, Sven. *Trans-Himalaya*. 1909–13.
— *A Conquest of Tibet*. 1935.

Holdich, Sir Thomas. *Tibet, the Mysterious*. 1906.

Hooker, Sir Joseph. *Himalayan Journals*. 1854.

Huc, Abbé Evariste. *Recollections of a Journey through Tartary, Tibet and China*. 1852.

Hyer, Paul. 'Narita Yasuteru: First Japanese to enter Tibet'. *The Tibet Journal*. Autumn 1979.

International Commission of Jurists. *Tibet and the People's Republic of China*. Geneva, 1960.

Kawaguchi, Ekai. *Three Years in Tibet*. Benares, 1909.

Kipling, Rudyard. *Kim*. 1901.

Lamb, Alastair. *Britain and Chinese Central Asia*. 1960.

Landon, Perceval. *Lhasa*. 1905.

Lansdell, Rev. Henry. *Chinese Central Asia*. 1893.

Littledale, St George. 'A Journey across Tibet from North to South'. *Geographical Journal*, Vol. 7. 1896.

Macauley, Colman. *Report of a Mission to Sikkim and the Tibetan Frontier – 1884*. Calcutta, 1885.

Macdonald, David. *The Land of the Lama*. 1929.

— *Twenty Years in Tibet*. 1932.

MacGregor, John. *Tibet. A Chronicle of Exploration*. 1970.

Mariani, Fosco. *Secret Tibet*. 1954.

Marshall, Julie G. *Britain and Tibet 1765–1947*. A Select Annotated Bibliography of Printed Material in European Languages. Latrobe University, 1977.

Mason, Kenneth. *Abode of Snow*. 1955.

McGovern, William. *To Lhasa in Disguise*. 1924.

Middleton, Dorothy. *Victorian Lady Travellers*. 1965.

Mill, Hugh. *The Record of the Royal Geographical Society. 1830–1930*. 1930.

Miller, Luree. *On Top of the World*. 1976.

Montgomerie, Captain T. G. 'On the Geographical Position of Yarkund, and Some other Places in Central Asia'. *Journal of the Royal Geographical Society*, Vol. 36, 1867.

Moraes, Frank. *The Revolt in Tibet*. New York, 1960.

Mullin, Chris. *The Tibetans*. Report No. 49 of the Minority Rights Group, 1981.

Murray, W. H. *The Story of Everest*. 1953.

Newman, Henry. *A Roving Commission*. 1937.

Noel, Captain J. B. L. *Through Tibet to Everest*. 1927.

Norbu, Dawa. 'The 1959 Tibetan Rebellion: An Interpretation'. *The China Quarterly*. March, 1979.

Norwick, Braham. 'Alexandra David-Neel's Adventures in Tibet. Fact or Fiction?' *The Tibet Journal*. Autumn 1979.

O'Connor, Sir Frederick. *On the Frontier and Beyond*. 1931.

Ottley, Major W. J. *With Mounted Infantry in Tibet*. 1906.

Peissel, Michael. *Cavaliers of Kham. The Secret War in Tibet*. 1972.

Pereira, Brigadier-General George. *Peking to Lhasa*. (Compiled from his diaries by Sir Francis Younghusband) 1925.

Petech, Luciano. 'China and the European Travellers to Tibet, 1860–1880'. *T'oung Pao*, Vol. LXII, 4–5.

Peter, Prince of Greece. *Physical Anthropological Observations on 5,000 Tibetans*. Third Danish Expedition to Central Asia. Copenhagen, 1966.

Prejevalsky, Nikolai. *Mongolia, the Tangut Country and the Solitudes of Northern Tibet*. 1876.

Rampa, Lobsang. *The Third Eye*. 1956.

Rawat, Indra Singh. *Indian Explorers of the 19th century*. Delhi, 1973.

Rawicz, Slavomir. *The Long Walk*. 1956.

Rayfield, Donald. *The Dream of Lhasa. Life of Nikolay Przhevalsky*. 1976.

Richardson, Hugh. *Tibet and its History*. 1962.

Rijnhart, Dr Susie. *With the Tibetans in Tent and Temple*. 1901.

Robson, Isabel S. *Two Lady Missionaries in Tibet*. c 1911.

Rockhill, William Woodville. *The Land of the Lamas*. 1891.

— *Diary of a Journey through Mongolia and Tibet*. Washington, 1894.

Sandberg, Rev. Graham. *The Exploration of Tibet*. Calcutta, 1904.

Savage Landor, A. Henry. *In the Forbidden Land*. 1898.

— *Everywhere: the memoirs of an explorer*. 1924.

Seaver, George. *Francis Younghusband: Explorer and Mystic*. 1952.

Shakabpa, Tsepon W. D. *Tibet, a Political History*. Yale, 1967.

Sinclair, Lt-Col. William B. *Jump to the Land of God*. Caldwell, Idaho, 1965.

Snellgrove, David and Richardson, Hugh. *A Cultural History of Tibet*. 1968.

Strong, Anna Louise. *When Serfs Stood up in Tibet*. Peking, 1960.

Survey of India Department. *Exploration in Tibet and Neighbouring Regions*. Part 1: 1865–1879. Part 2: 1879–1892. 2 vols. Dehra Dun, 1915.

Sutton, Stephanne. *In China's Border Provinces. The Turbulent Career of Joseph Rock*. New York, 1974.

Suyin, Han. *Lhasa, the Open City*. 1977.

Taring, Rinchen Dolma. *Daughter of Tibet*. 1970.

Taylor, Annie. *Pioneering in Tibet*. c 1895.

Ullman, James Ramsey. *Kingdom of Adventure: Everest*. 1948.

Waddell, Col. Austine. *Lhasa and its Mysteries*. 1905.

Walker, General J. T. 'Four Years' Journeying through Great Tibet by one of the Trans-Himalayan Explorers of the Survey of India'. *Proceedings of the Royal Geographical Society*. February, 1885.

White, Sir Claude. *Sikkim and Bhutan*. 1909.

Winnington, Alan. *Tibet. Record of a Journey*. 1957.

Woodcock, George. *Into Tibet*. 1971.

Younghusband, Sir Francis. *India and Tibet*. 1910.

— *The Epic of Mount Everest*. 1926.

Index